Income distribution
and economic development

Income distribution and economic development

An analytical survey

Jacques Lecaillon
Felix Paukert
Christian Morrisson
Dimitri Germidis

International Labour Office   Geneva

ISBN 92-2-103366-X (limp cover)
ISBN 92-2-103559-X (hard cover)

First published 1984
Second impression 1986

Originally published in French under the title *Répartition du revenu et développement économique: Un essai de synthèse* (ISBN 92-2-203366-3)

Printed in Switzerland

IDE

CONTENTS

Tables

Note. The current designation of the country referred to in this volume as "Iran" is "the Islamic Republic of Iran".

INTRODUCTION

The main theme of this book is the distribution of income. Although other questions, too, form part of the book's subject-matter, including especially questions of employment and of economic development, this volume is primarily concerned with the distribution of income between the poor and the rich, or, in other words, with the distribution of income by size.

Two hundred years ago, when Adam Smith tried to systematise his ideas on economic development, he chose the title *The wealth of nations*. Today, as Cairncross has remarked,[1] if Adam Smith were expounding the same theme, he would be more likely to include in the title a reference to poverty as well as wealth. Since Adam Smith's time a fundamental change has taken place in the intellectual approach to economic development.[2] Poverty is a concept with which economists—and not only economists—are now more concerned than they are with wealth. In other words, thinking in terms of wealth and poverty, rich and poor—in terms of economic equality—is more prevalent than two centuries ago. Even so, poverty is nowhere as oppressive today as it was then, and the gap separating a rich man from a poor one, though still very wide, has become much narrower than it was in Adam Smith's time.[3]

It is the change in intellectual approach that has been mainly responsible for the growing concern with problems of economic inequality in the course of the present century, and especially since the Second World War. Inequality is no longer accepted as the immutable condition of mankind, and wide differences in standards of living are no longer held to be inevitable. The extension of social security schemes to cover all classes of the population is both a consequence of this changed intellectual approach and a reflection—at any rate in the developed countries—of the much greater possibilities that now exist for maintaining the real incomes of every member of society above a certain minimum.

An economic policy aiming to provide a minimum standard of living calls for the collection of the information, statistical data and reports needed for its formulation and for monitoring the progress made in its application. At the same time the flow of statistics and reports on poverty and economic inequality itself has the effect of focusing public attention on those questions, thereby further fostering the change in the intellectual approach to them.

The concern with economic inequality in industrialised countries is paralleled in the developing countries, where, however, the concern is intensified by more acute poverty calling more urgently for action. There has likewise developed some parallel between the concern over inequalities within countries and the concern over inequalities between countries.

As a result of the change that has taken place in the intellectual climate since the Second World War, both development economics and the economics of income distribution have come into the forefront of attention. They are in fact logically linked. However great may have been the growth of a country's gross national product, that country cannot be said to have made progress if the bulk of the population has remained at the same level of income. Conversely, little can be done to improve the situation of the poor unless there is some economic growth to release new resources and to facilitate changes in income distribution. While economic development and income distribution are thus inter-related, there is also another factor that interacts with both. That third factor is employment. Income from employment, be it wage employment or self-employment, accounts for the vast bulk of personal income in both developed and developing countries; and changes in the level and structure of employment are reflected in changes in the distribution of income. At the same time, the course of economic development is reflected in changes in employment, shifts in industrial structure and employment status being particularly telling indicators of the level and nature of development.

The concern with employment and income distribution as inseparable elements of the development process gained widespread acceptance during the 1960s. While the strategy of the First United Nations Development Decade (1961–70) was concerned primarily with economic growth, that of the Second Development Decade (1971–80) already reflected the trend towards associating employment and income distribution with economic growth as development targets. That trend is being further accentuated in the strategy of the Third Development Decade. Thus in the course of the 1960s the earlier concern with growth was superseded by a new approach to development in which employment and income distribution were also taken into account; and that approach was further developed in the course of the 1970s with a new emphasis on the satisfaction of basic needs.

In the process of establishing a new approach to development, a role

2

of particular importance was played by the World Employment Programme (WEP) which the International Labour Organisation launched in 1969. The central purpose of that Programme is to assist member States in drawing up specific guidelines enabling national political decision-makers and planners to reduce unemployment and underemployment by accelerating the creation of productive income-earning opportunities. The WEP was, however, conceived in much broader terms, and ranges over the whole field of development economics, even stretching beyond that field to problems of developed countries. Among the problems receiving particularly close attention under the WEP are those of population, rural development, appropriate technology, income distribution, migration and the international division of labour. All these problems are approached by a variety of means, including comprehensive country missions on the subject of employment and the establishment of employment teams for particular regions and countries, as well as research.

Research on income distribution and employment has occupied a central place in the World Employment Programme. That research had three main objectives:

(a) to show how income distribution has behaved in certain countries in the course of development and to specify the conditions under which the income distribution could be improved;

(b) to identify the major measurable factors associated with income inequality and the major characteristics of the poor; and

(c) to identify and assess the impact of the instruments at the command of governments to improve income distribution.

At first, research was focused mainly on the relationship between income distribution and employment; subsequently attention shifted to the elimination of poverty, to the role of fiscal policy and to public services.

Over 100 studies, on a very wide range of subjects, have been undertaken by the ILO in the course of its research into income distribution and employment.[4] It therefore seemed desirable to undertake a synthesis of the results, and such a synthesis is the purpose of this book. However, the scope of the book goes further. At the same time as the ILO carried out its own research, work on income distribution was also continued elsewhere, under the auspices of the World Bank and other international organisations and in national institutions and universities. There has been interaction between work done by the ILO and work carried out outside. Hence a meaningful synthesis cannot be confined to the ILO's own work: it must also take other developments into account. Within the ILO itself, some other research work that has a bearing on questions of income distribution has also been carried out and has been drawn upon in preparing the synthesis. Furthermore, the attempt made to review comprehensively the multiplicity of issues which the question of income distribution raises brought to light some hitherto unexplored territory. Original research was therefore undertaken for incorporation in this book, so that the scope of the book extends, in a number of directions, beyond the findings of work already published.

The book starts with a summary of views on the relationship between income inequality and economic development. The hypothesis of such a relationship was formulated by Simon Kuznets, according to whom income inequality at first increases during the process of development, and then diminishes once a certain level has been reached. The considerable body of material on the Kuznets curve that has accumulated over the past 25 years is surveyed in this book. Notwithstanding some dissenting voices, the relationship is confirmed by the available data, however imperfect. The Kuznets curve, however, represents a typical tendency of changes in income distribution in the course of development, and does not imply any historical determinism. The curve is understandable when sectoral dualism and the differences in productivity between the traditional and modern sectors of the economy are considered.

After noting in Chapter 1 the grave deficiencies of the statistics on which studies of the relationship between income distribution and economic development have been based, the book turns in Chapter 2 to a systematic treatment of income distribution statistics. A particular pitfall encountered in the existing data lies in the heterogeneous income recipient units used (households, families, individuals, income earners), each of which yields a different picture of income distribution even within the same country and for the same year. New estimates of income distribution have therefore been prepared for about 40 different countries of Africa, Asia and Latin America, for only two kinds of income recipient units, namely households and economically active persons. On this basis we have tested the Kuznets hypothesis by comparing distribution for the same income recipient unit in different countries. This more reliable comparison with more homogeneous units confirmed the Kuznets hypothesis that inequality first increases and later diminishes in the course of economic development. In the second part of Chapter 2, for the more specific purpose of comparing income inequality between developed and developing countries, we introduced further refinements taking into account the distribution of income over the life cycle, regional differences in the cost of living within countries and the problem of undistributed company income. This new approach to comparisons of degrees of income inequality has brought us to the conclusion that the actual difference in inequality between developed and developing countries is somewhat greater than previous studies would have led us to believe.

In Chapter 3 we take the first step towards explaining the forces which shape the changes in income distribution during the process of economic development. The underlying cause lies in the structure of the economy, and in particular in the relationship between the rural and the urban sectors of developing countries: the characteristic feature of that relationship is the great difference in average income between the two sectors. That difference is further accentuated in the course of economic development by growing inequality within both the urban and the rural sectors.

From that structural analysis, the book passes on in Chapter 4 to an examination of the factors causing income inequality. On the labour supply side, the obvious factors are such personal characteristics as sex and age, ethnic origin and nationality, together with state of health and level and type of education. Another factor is the influence of people's occupation and of their occupational status, i.e. whether they are employed for a wage or salary or work on some other basis, as employers, as workers on their own account or as unpaid family helps. Thirdly, the role played by unemployment and underemployment is examined, especially from the angle of their reciprocal relationship with the distribution of income, whereby the level of employment, as well as its structure, exercises an influence on income distribution while changes in the distribution of income affect the level and structure of employment.

The last two chapters of the book are devoted to a discussion of redistribution possibilities. Chapter 5 summarises a number of studies undertaken by the ILO on the effect of taxation and public expenditure on household incomes in a number of developing countries. It is shown that redistributive policies have resulted in some diminution of income inequality in all cases, though to an extent varying widely with the country.

Chapter 6 deals with the question of redistribution as a whole. In the first part of the chapter there is a novel approach to the decomposition and measurement of the redistributive effect of different fiscal measures, while in the second part there is a systematic examination of various proposals for increasing that redistributive effect by increasing either the progressivity or the intensity of the measures in question. That leads up to a discussion of the limits to the implementation of such proposals. A third part of the chapter is devoted to an examination of price and wage policies in relation to employment and income distribution. The book closes with some broad conclusions concerning the most effective combination of means available for the improvement of income distribution.

Notes

Bibliographical references have been kept to a minimum; fuller bibliographical data are given in the list of bibliographical references at the end of the volume.

[1] Cairncross: *Factors in economic development* (1962), p. 13.

[2] Hirschman: "The changing tolerance for income inequality in the course of economic development" (1973).

[3] There is a higher degree of income equality today than there was two centuries ago in most, if not all, of the developed countries, as well as in a number of developing countries, such as India; on the other hand it would appear that the dualistic form of development in many African countries has resulted in a higher degree of inequality, albeit at a much higher level of average income, than there was in Adam Smith's time.

[4] This research has produced some 20 books, over 100 working papers and numerous articles in academic journals. For the most recent report and bibliography on ILO research on income distribution and employment see ILO: *World Employment Programme: Ninth progress report on income distribution and employment* (1981).

INEQUALITY AND DEVELOPMENT: A SURVEY OF STUDIES

1

STATISTICAL STUDIES OF CHANGES IN INEQUALITY

The supply of statistical information on the distribution of income in developing countries is of relatively recent date. At the beginning of the 1960s the available documentary information referred mainly to a few countries in Europe and in North America, and in most cases that information extended no further back than the First World War. Much more abundant information is now available, and covers a large number of countries having reached very different levels of development. Since that information refers, however, to a recent past, the study of the relationship between income distribution and economic development cannot always be made on the basis of time series that are sufficiently long and of unquestionably good quality. Cross-country comparisons are then made between countries at different levels of development. Such comparisons may refer to data that are not always based on the same definitions of income and of its recipient; they involve an assumption that the distribution of income changes comparably in all countries and, consequently, that those changes can be expressed by collating observations for countries at different levels of development. Despite imperfections, the similarity of the results of most of the studies based on such comparisons is sufficient to reveal some general trends. The focal point of the research work that has been carried out is the "Kuznets hypothesis" that inequality of income first increases and then decreases during the process of economic development.

The Kuznets hypothesis

It was in 1954 that Simon Kuznets first expressed the view that income inequality tends to increase during the first stages of economic growth, then levels off and finally diminishes during the later stages.[1] He showed also that the distribution of personal income is more unequal in the less developed than in the developed countries.[2] That demonstration supported the observation that, in the developed countries, inequality is less pronounced than it was 50 or 100 years ago. Kuznets also observed that the share of the higher income groups was larger in the developing than in the industrialised countries: the top 5 per cent of families having the largest incomes were receiving more than 30 per cent of the aggregate income in the developing countries but only from 20 to 25 per cent in the developed countries. Although the share of the lower income groups was smaller in some developing countries, the difference was not a significant one, so that the share of the intermediate groups was relatively smaller in those countries than in the developed countries.

Kuznets' observations led him, in particular, to stress that the long-term trend towards a diminution of inequality once a certain level of economic development had been reached was somewhat puzzling: there were indeed at least two factors pointing rather to an accentuation of the inequality of incomes before tax.[3]

The first of these factors was the concentration of savings in the hands of the highest income groups. Among the reasons that could limit the effects of that factor, Kuznets gave political decisions (for example, inheritance taxes), the difference in demographic behaviour between the rich and the poor resulting in a progressive diminution in the size of the richest group, the social mobility resulting from the operations of free, market-oriented economies and, lastly, the weight of earnings from work in so far as individual ability is not inherited.

The second factor accentuating inequality of income lies in the structure of employment. Marked as it is by a process of industrialisation and urbanisation, economic development is invariably accompanied by some abandonment of agriculture. In the simplest model, the general distribution of income may be regarded as a combination of the distribution of urban incomes with that of rural incomes. Now the average income of the rural population is generally smaller than that of the urban population and there is no evidence that the disparity tends to diminish in the course of economic growth. Moreover, the inequality of distribution of income is generally greater in the case of urban than of rural incomes. In these circumstances the relative increase of the urban population should be reflected in a general increase of inequality; otherwise some countervailing forces must intervene, the principal one being, seemingly, a reduction of intrasectoral inequality, especially in the urban sector. Once the first disorderly stages of industrialisation and urbanisation had been passed, the diminution in the dispersion of urban incomes would be reflected mainly in an improvement of the relative position of the lowest income groups.

On the whole, Kuznets' intuitive perceptions were to be confirmed by later investigations.

In 1960 the hypothesis that inequality is more pronounced in the less developed countries was put forward again by Irving Kravis.[4] He discerned a positive, albeit complex, correlation between the degree of inequality and the level of real income per head. Like Kuznets, he reached the conclusion that in the underdeveloped countries, as compared with the industrialised countries, income dispersion was less pronounced in the lower part of the distribution scale and greater in the upper part. It was thus in that upper part of the distribution scale that the source of the greater inequality observed in the underdeveloped countries had to be sought.

According to Kravis, the international differences in degrees of inequality may be attributed to differences in the distribution of people's characteristics affecting their performance in the economic field; to legislative or customary obstacles to social mobility; to structural factors accounting for highly differentiated and unequally remunerated types of work; and to socio-political organisation.

In a general way, the developed countries are more egalitarian than the undeveloped because all classes of the population are better integrated into economic and social life, whereas in the less developed countries the obstacles to equality in education and the many forms of discrimination prevent certain groups from competing equitably with the others. Whereas the structural upheavals that occur at the outset of economic development may increase differences and inequalities, the subsequent course of economic growth, accompanied by the spread of education, the extension of social security, the diffusion of ownership of the capital of large undertakings and the increase of income from work relatively to income from property, contributes to a reduction of the general inequality of income distribution.

Harry Oshima[5] later stressed the fact that inequality is not necessarily more pronounced in the comparatively less developed countries: everything depended on their stage of development; that is, on whether they were undeveloped or underdeveloped or semi-developed or fully developed, the principal criterion of degree of development being the weight of the rural sector in the economy as a whole. In the initial stages of development, income inequality was indeed generally slight. The expansion of trade, industrialisation and urbanisation led to an accentuation of the general dispersion of incomes for as long as no palpable change took place in the rural areas. Once the economy reached the stage of semi-development, the tendency for the dispersion of capital per head to increase in the urban sector was counterbalanced by an increase in average income from agriculture and by a flight from the land; inequality then ceased to grow and subsequently decreased while at the same time there was a spreading of education.

All these indications are consistent with Kuznets' original hypothesis of increasing, then decreasing, inequality. That hypothesis was to become the subject of subsequent studies in depth carried out by a later generation.

Testing of the hypothesis

The principal studies undertaken in the form of statistical investigations have been carried out over a very short period of time since 1973. Only the more important of those studies will be considered here.[6]

The first systematic study was carried out by Felix Paukert within the framework of the International Labour Organisation's World Employment Programme.[7] Making use of, in particular, data compiled by Irma Adelman and Cynthia Taft Morris[8] but correcting and supplementing them, Paukert gave estimates relating to 56 countries, including over 40 developing countries. His estimated distributions refer to the incomes of households before tax.

Paukert's analysis shows that the degree of inequality, as measured by the Gini ratio or by the maximum equalisation percentage, is linked to the level of the gross domestic product per head (expressed in 1965 United States dollars). There is a sharp increase in inequality as one moves upwards from the group of countries with a GDP of under 100 dollars per head to the 101–200 dollars group of countries. Inequality increases further though less sharply in the 201–300 dollars group of countries. The countries in that group and in the next one (301–500 dollars) are those in which the differences in income are the most pronounced. Further up the income scale and especially in the group of countries with a GDP above 2,000 dollars per head there is a clear reduction of inequality. These findings are consistent with Kuznets' original hypothesis.

Paukert also found that the share of total income accruing to the top 5 per cent of recipients was highest in the countries in the 201–300 and 301–500 dollar groups, indicating that these are the countries with the greatest inequality of income. The picture is the same when we consider the share of total income accruing to the top 20 per cent of recipients. The share of total income accruing to the poorest classes—the bottom 20 per cent in the scale of incomes—falls to a minimum in the countries where the level of a GDP per head lies between 301 and 500 dollars. That finding tallies with the conclusions of Kuznets and of Kravis in so far as it indicates that the share of the poorest classes is larger in the least developed than in the other countries although it cannot be inferred that the share of those classes is larger in the developing than in the developed countries. When the range is widened to cover the poorest 40 per cent or even the poorest 60 per cent of the population, the same general pattern predominates, with the corresponding shares diminishing down to the level of a GDP of 500 dollars per head and then rising. In general, the dispersion of the lower incomes is much slighter in the developing countries than in the developed; the greater degree of inequality prevailing in the developing countries is due primarily to the large share of total income accruing to the rich top 5 per cent of the population.

In 1974 the World Bank took up an examination of the question on the basis of data relating to 66 countries classified by degree of income inequality and by income per head. The study carried out by Montek Ahluwalia[9] confirms that relative inequality is markedly greater in most of the underdeveloped countries than in the developed countries. Ahluwalia questions, however, the idea expressed by Kuznets in 1963 that that greater general dispersion is due mainly to greater inequality between the high-income group and the middle-income group: it appears from the larger sample of countries investigated that, in many underdeveloped countries, there is a high degree of inequality due to the small share of income accruing both to the middle-income group and to the lowest-income group.

Dividing the population into three groups—the richest 20 per cent, the poorest 40 per cent and the middle 40 per cent—the author examines, by the method of multivariate regression, the influence of certain variables: structural variables (income per head and share of agriculture in the GDP) and variables that may be influenced by socio-economic policy (growth of the economy, primary and secondary school enrolment, population growth); these variables "explain" about 50 per cent of the cross-country variation in income shares.

The Kuznets hypothesis is at first confirmed once again. The share of income accruing to the poorest group decreases sharply down to an income level of 400 dollars per head and then increases steadily. The movement is reversed in the case of the richest group. As for the share of the middle group, it does not appear to be significantly linked to the level of income. Education and the degree of income equality expressed as shares of income accruing to the poorest group and to the middle group show the same variations. The rate of population growth shows the same variation as income inequality as measured by the income share of the poorest group. Its influence is significant: a positive difference of 1 per cent in the rate of population growth is correlated with a negative difference of 1.6 per cent in the income share of the poorest group. There is no confirmation of the opinion that a high rate of economic growth is a source of income inequality. On the contrary, that rate is correlated positively, though, it is true, in a non-significant way, with the poorest group's share of income—a circumstance that makes it possible to argue that growth and equity are not necessarily inconsistent aims.

One of Ahluwalia's most important conclusions is that the distribution of incomes depends partly on variables on which socio-economic policy can exercise an influence—for example, the level of education and the rate of population growth. According to his estimates,[10] an increase from 250 to 500 dollars in income per head gives rise to a reduction from 12 to 10 per cent in the share of total income accruing to the poorest 40 per cent; it would be possible, however, to take countervailing measures to augment that share, which, for example, increases by 3.4 percentage points when the literacy rate is increased from 40 to 100 per cent; by 1.7 percentage points when the annual rate of population growth is reduced from 3 to 1.5 per cent; and by 1.1 percentage points when the urban proportion of the population is increased from 30 to 50 per cent through the development of employment in the modern sector; making a total of 6.2 percentage points.

In 1977 Harold Lydall examined, under the World Employment Programme, data for 71 countries that had been assembled by the World Bank.[11] He estimated that the turning-point of inequality, as measured by the Gini coefficient, that is, the maximum value of that coefficient, was reached when GDP per head amounted to 243 United States dollars (at 1971 prices). The share of income accruing to the richest 5 per cent reaches its maximum a little sooner—at the level of 200 dollars per head; on the other hand, the share of the 20 per cent continues to decline until GDP per head reaches the level of about 500 dollars. Income distribution is less unequal among households than among individual persons and still less than among economically active persons. Moreover, the dispersion is less pronounced in rural areas than in towns.

The share of income accruing to the richest 5 per cent varies in the same direction as the Gini coefficient, whereas the other shares vary in the opposite direction, except the share of the group situated between the eightieth and ninety-fifth centiles, whose behaviour is unpredictable. As for the share of the bottom 20 per cent, it begins by diminishing but then increases when GDP per head exceeds 500 dollars, its variation being very low: an average of 5.5 per cent when GDP per head is at the level of 200 dollars, 5.3 per cent when GDP per head reaches 500 dollars and 5.6 per cent when it reaches 3,000 dollars. This means that, even when that share decreases, the absolute level of the poorest group's average income rises significantly throughout the process of economic development. That conclusion, which is also Ahluwalia's, is at variance with that of Adelman and Morris, according to which economic growth is accompanied by an absolute fall in the income of the poor in the early stages of development.[12] In general, Lydall's findings are entirely consistent with those of Kuznets and of Paukert.

Reference may be made also to a study by Jerry Cromwell based on data relating to 67 countries.[13] While concurring with the Kuznets hypothesis, Cromwell finds a tendency for the income share of the poorest 20 per cent group to decline in the course of economic development: on the average, that group receives 9.1 per cent of total income when GDP per head amounts to 50 dollars, 5.2 per cent when it amounts to 120 dollars, 5.3 per cent when it amounts to 400 dollars and 4.3 per cent when it amounts to 1,950 dollars. The increase in the share of income accruing to the middle class would thus be at the expense of both the poorest and the richest. The influence exercised by the increase in income per head on a reduction of inequality would thus be, in the end, very slight.

Cromwell considers that inequality is inherent in the development of a capitalist system of production. Assessing the role of the capitalist sector in terms of the size of the share of wages in the national income, he establishes the existence of a non-linear relationship between that share and the Gini coefficient, according to which the turning-point of the inequality curve occurs when the modern capitalist sector employs 40 per cent of the labour force. At that stage, the dualism between the traditional sector and the capitalist sector generates a maximum inequality. In advanced capitalist societies, that dualism lessens and inequality becomes less pronounced.

Although the majority of writers confirm the existence of the Kuznets curve, some different opinions have nevertheless been expressed. Thus Gustav Papanek has not been able to establish any significant relationship between income inequality and the level of economic development.[14] William Cline, in his critical examination of the studies dealing with that question,[15] accepts what he calls the "modest proposal" that, in the course of economic development, "inequality is likely to increase after the very earliest subsistence stage once a surplus arises for some group to appropriate". In his opinion, "it seems more reasonable to postulate that particular policies, combined with the inherited social structure, make income highly unequal in some less developed countries while alternative policies and structure make it more even in others, but that there is no inexorable theoretical basis justifying a worsening of the distribution of income in the course of development". Yet, although none of the authors quoted above asserts that inequality necessarily increases in the course of economic development, the fact nevertheless remains that nearly all the studies, while approaching the question from different angles and making use of different data, do establish the existence of the Kuznets curve; and that empirical observation still has to be explained.

The last word in the debate belongs to James Guest,[16] who examined the previous studies and made his own calculations based mainly on the income shares of the groups with the lowest incomes (the 40 per cent at the bottom of the scale), the groups with the median incomes (the 40 per cent at the middle of the scale) and the group with high incomes (the 20 per cent at the top of the scale), making use of data for 43 countries (30 developing countries and 13 developed countries). Guest found that the share of the richest group increased rapidly in the least developed countries. The share of the group with the lowest incomes diminished at medium levels of development and increased only in the developed countries. Guest's conclusions relating to the behaviour of the incomes of the poorest groups and of the richest group thus likewise tally with the Kuznets hypothesis and with the facts established by Paukert, Ahluwalia and Lydall.

IMPLICATIONS

The Kuznets hypothesis is generally presented as a non-linear relationship in which income per head is taken as the principal independent variable and a measure of the inequality of the distribution of incomes as a dependent variable; it may be represented by an inverse-U shaped curve, known as the Kuznets curve. The identification of such a relationship raises certain problems concerning, in particular, the statistical methodology employed. The predictive value of the relationship also needs to be discussed.

Problems of statistical methodology

Two main problems regarding the statistical methodology employed have come under discussion. The first one concerns the general representativeness of the Kuznets curve.[17] The curve is obtained by making a quadratic adjustment on the basis of a sample of very unequally developed countries, including some countries in which income per head greatly exceeds the turning-point of 400 to 500 dollars a positive correlation between income per head and degree of inequality below that level changes to a negative correlation above it. In these circumstances it may be that the relatively high coefficients of correlation that can be obtained ($R^2 = 0.5-0.6$) are due to the high negative correlations found in the developed countries, for which the statistical data are the most reliable. Thus, when only the less developed countries which are situated below the turning-point of the curve are considered, it is found that whatever measurement of inequality is used, the positive correlations, while remaining significant, are much less high ($R^2 = 0.2-0.3$). A question that arises is whether these low positive correlations between level of income and degree of inequality may not be the result of statistical biases due to the poor quality of the data used. This in turn raises a question of interpretation: it will be referred to again below.

The second statistical question concerns the stability of the Kuznets curve. The focal point of the research work is, clearly, the behaviour of the share of income accruing, in the course of economic development, to the poorest groups in the less developed countries. As was noted above, the turning-point of the curve occurs more and more tardily with each step down the scale of incomes, some authors going so far as to deny its existence in the case of the group of the poorest 20 per cent. For the group of 40 per cent at the bottom of the scale, it is found that the turning-point varies markedly with the size of the sample of countries: it appears at the income level of 468 dollars per head with a sample of 60 countries or of 371 dollars if only the 40 developing countries are considered (according to Ahluwalia[10]) and at the income level of about 800 dollars per head with a sample of 30 countries (according to Bacha).[6] Sometimes the inclusion or modification of data concerning certain countries will even cause the turning-point to vanish or will be enough to deprive the results of significance. There is thus some instability in the Kuznets curve (analogous to that of the Phillips curve), at any rate so far as changes in the share of income accruing to the poorest group are concerned—an instability which, of course, limits the value of the curve for purposes of prediction.

Predictive value of the Kuznets curve

The use of a set of data concerning many unequally developed countries for the purpose of explaining particular historical changes is always bound to be fraught with difficulties. The Kuznets hypothesis was originally propounded in the light of the historical experience of the United States, the United Kingdom and Germany, where a trend towards a reduction of inequality was observed after the First World War. There is, however, no reason why the present situation of the industrialised countries should foreshadow the future situation of the less developed countries: on the contrary, there are a number of—partly divergent—reasons for ruling out that possibility.

In the first place, it has often been stressed that in the countries situated on the periphery of the industrial centre of the world economy industrialisation brings with it more inequality than it did in the course of the eighteenth and nineteenth centuries in the countries which are now developed.[18] Whereas the structural transformations inherent in the process of development have taken place at an even pace and progressively in the now industrialised countries, in the developing countries the industrial revolution is today much more rapid, and is not preceded by the modernisation of agriculture. Furthermore, technological innovations are imported from outside instead of issuing from the endogenous transformations of the units of production. As a result there are much greater disparities of productivity, incomes and levels of consumption. In general, the gains are more concentrated in the countries where intersectoral differences of productivity are more pronounced and increase more rapidly.

It has been pointed out, however, that there is no determinism in the process of economic growth and that the Kuznets model is not inevitable. A reduction of inequality of income distribution in a rapidly growing economy remains possible even under the conditions of industrialisation in the latter part of the twentieth century. It presupposes the adoption of an appropriate economic policy including in particular, the modernisation of agriculture, the development of rural industries and the application of labour-intensive techniques to urban activities.

While the Kuznets curve reflects an average trend in the changes in income distribution taking place in the course of economic development, what has to be stressed is the extent of the dispersion around the average, that is, the great diversity of particular situations, for there are indeed very many factors and numerous combinations of factors that may explain income disparities. Those factors will be analysed in later chapters. In the meanwhile, some general interpretations of the Kuznets curve will be given.

GENERAL INTERPRETATIONS OF THE KUZNETS CURVE

Since the problem under consideration is that of the relationship between income inequality and economic development, that is, a problem of historical changes, it has to be postulated that the findings based on a sample of unequally developed countries constitute an acceptable approximation of the historical evolution of each country. In other words, it has to be assumed that most countries follow more or less the same growth path. That being so, the general interpretations of the Kuznets curve lay stress especially on the structural modifications that take place in the course of development and on the relationships between the traditional sector and the modern sector.

Sectoral dualism

The first attempt at an explanation of the changes in the distribution of incomes that take place in the course of development was made by Kuznets himself.[19] His model is based on the division of the national economy into two sectors: the agricultural sector (A) and the non-agricultural sector (B). Development entails a transfer of population and of the labour force from sector A to sector B. If the average income in sector A is lower than that in sector B and if the degrees of inequality in each sector are the same, the transfer of population starts by giving rise to an increase of general inequality and subsequently reduces it. If, as Kuznets postulated, inequality is greater in sector B than in sector A, the shift of population generates an increase of inequality that is not automatically followed by a tendency for inequality to contract. The results of the model depend on the relative incomes of the two sectors, the degrees of inequality within each sector and the proportion of the population employed in each sector.

Kuznets formulated several hypotheses, some of which are summed up in table 1. It is assumed that income per head in sector A is half of that

Table 1. Percentage shares of the first and fifth quintiles in income distribution under varying assumptions, according to Kuznets

Items	Relative size of population of sector A (total population = 1)						
	0.8	0.7	0.6	0.5	0.4	0.3	0.2
Income per head of the total population (income per head in sector A = 50, in sector B = 100)	*60*	*65*	*70*	*75*	*80*	*85*	*90*
Distribution E for both sectors:							
Share of first quintile	10.5	9.9	9.6	9.4	9.3	9.8	10.2
Share of fifth quintile	34.2	35.8	35.7	34.7	33.2	31.9	30.4
Range	23.7	25.9	26.1	25.3	23.9	22.1	20.2
Distribution U for both sectors:							
Share of first quintile	3.8	3.8	3.7	3.7	3.8	3.8	3.9
Share of fifth quintile	40.7	41.9	42.9	42.7	41.5	40.2	38.7
Range	36.8	38.1	39.1	39.0	37.8	36.4	34.8
Distribution E for sector A, U for sector B:							
Share of first quintile	9.3	8.3	7.4	6.7	6.0	5.4	4.9
Share of fifth quintile	37.7	41.0	42.9	42.7	41.5	40.2	38.7
Range	28.3	32.7	35.4	36.0	35.5	34.8	33.8

Key: E: moderately unequal; U: very unequal (see the text).
Source: Kuznets: "Economic growth and income inequality" (1955), p. 13.

of sector B, or 50 units as against 100. For each sector, two distributions are possible: one of them is moderately unequal, the shares starting at 5.5 per cent for the lowest 10 per cent income group and increasing by 1 percentage point for each decile, reaching 14.5 per cent for the highest 10 per cent income group; the other distribution is much more unequal, the shares starting at 1 per cent for the lowest 10 per cent income group and increasing by 2 percentage points for each decile, reaching 19 per cent for the highest 10 per cent income group. Lastly, the proportion of the population of sector A relatively to total population ranges from 0.8 to 0.2. The table shows the changes that take place in the shares of the lower and upper groups of 20 per cent (first and fifth quintiles) when the population of sector A diminishes in relation to that of sector B, the inequality of income distribution never being greater in sector A than in sector B.

Within the limits set by the selected hypotheses, Kuznets draws a series of general conclusions.

If the difference in income per head increases to the advantage of sector B or if the distribution of income is more unequal in sector B than in sector A, an increase in the relative size of the population of sector B brings about a very marked increase of inequality of distribution at the national level.

If the degree of inequality of distribution is the same in both sectors and if the increase of inequality at the national level is due only to an increasing income differential per head in favour of sector B, the increase is greater when the degree of inequality in each sector is moderate.

If the difference in income per head between the two sectors is constant and if the distribution is more unequal in sector B than in sector A, the increase in inequality at the national level is all the greater when the difference in income per head is small.

If the difference in income per head between the two sectors increases and if the distribution of income is more unequal in sector B than in sector A, then with the shift of population from sector A to sector B the share of the lowest 20 per cent income group diminishes more than that of the top 20 per cent income group increases.

Even if the difference in income per head is constant and if the income distributions are the same in the two sectors, a mere shift of the population between sectors brings about significant changes in the distribution of income at the national level. In general, when the proportion of the population in sector A diminishes, the difference in incomes first widens and then diminishes.

The share of the highest income group diminishes at a very early stage, well before any increase in the share of the lowest income group: with industrialisation, the expansion of sector B brings about a rise in the average national income even when income per head and income distribution within each sector remain constant, so that the shares of the upper income groups could rise only if there were a sharper rise in income per head in sector B or if the inequality of income distribution in that sector became more pronounced.

Under certain hypotheses, the share of the lowest income group diminishes continuously instead of increasing. If empirical observations do not confirm that trend, it is, Kuznets suggests, no doubt because the inequality of distribution in sector B had to diminish sufficiently to enable the shares of the poorer groups to increase.

Intersectoral differences in productivity

The Kuznets model lays stress on the fact that, if there is a significant intersectoral difference of income, the transfer of population from one sector to the other exercises an influence on the general degree of inequality. For Lydall,[11] the question that immediately arises is: why should there be an intersectoral income differential? The answer lies in differences of productivity, which themselves result from the adoption of more efficient production techniques in the course of economic development, one of whose crucial elements is the transfer of labour to more advanced techniques. From that point of view, the relevant distinction is

Table 2. Changes in inequality as the proportion of the population in the modern sector (B) increases, with constant intersectoral and intrasectoral inequality, according to Lydall

Percentage of the population in sector B	Gini coefficient	Percentage income share of—		
		Bottom 20%	Top 20%	Top 5%
0	0.35	6.8	42.4	16.0
10	0.37	6.4	44.2	17.4
20	0.39	6.1	45.3	18.0
30	0.40	5.9	45.8	18.2
40	0.40	5.8	45.9	18.1
50	0.40	5.7	45.7	17.9
60	0.39	5.7	45.3	17.6
70	0.39	5.8	44.7	17.2
80	0.38	6.1	44.0	16.8
90	0.37	6.4	43.2	16.4
100	0.35	6.8	42.4	16.0

Source: Lydall: *Income distribution during the process of development* (1977), p. 15.

that between the modern sector and the traditional sector. If there is a shift of population from agriculture to the other sectors and from rural to urban areas, it is because modern techniques can be more easily introduced into industry than into agriculture. In that sense, it is better to identify Kuznets' sector A with the traditional sector and his sector B with the modern sector. It follows that, if economic growth is primarily a process of adopting more efficient techniques, if the proportion of the labour force using the new techniques increases and if incomes are determined by productivity, there will almost certainly be some tendency for the general inequality of incomes to increase and then to decline.

For purposes of illustration, a starting-point could be a very simple model allowing both for some dispersion of income within each sector and for inequality between the two sectors A and B. Lydall assumes that the mean income in sector B is twice as large as the mean income in sector A, that the distribution of income within each sector is lognormal and that the degree of relative inequality within each sector is the same and remains constant throughout, with a standard deviation of the logarithms of income in each sector of 0.65.

Table 2 shows how the indicators of inequality change when the proportion of the population in sector B increases. As may be seen from the table, the share of the high-income group—the 20 per cent at the top of the scale—increases and then diminishes while that of the low-income group—the 20 per cent at the bottom of the scale—changes in the opposite direction, the turning-point of the former occurring sooner than that of the latter, which is consistent with the empirical observations.

Still assuming equal and constant intrasectoral distributions, it is of interest to consider the effects of changes in intersectoral inequality resulting from a modification of production techniques. On the basis of a sample of 30 countries with very different incomes per head Lydall finds statistical relationships between value added per person engaged in different industries (V_i/L_i) and value added per person engaged in the whole economy (V/L). For the textile industry, for example, his estimated regression equation is—

$$\log V_i/L_i = 3.86 + 0.55 \log V/L$$
$$(0.352) \quad (0.05) \qquad\qquad (R^2 = 0.81)$$

The most significant facts flowing from these estimates are: that, in the poor countries, value added per person employed (or productivity) in the industry is much higher than the average productivity of the whole economy and that, when that average productivity increases, the productivity of the industry also increases, though less rapidly.

In order to study the effects of this type of relationship on the general distribution of incomes, certain further hypotheses have to be formulated. Lydall assumes that the foregoing equation represents the behaviour of productivity in sector B as average productivity in the whole economy increases; in other words, as the economy as a whole becomes more productive, there is some kind of "external" effect on productivity within the modern sector B. In the case of the traditional sector A, an assumption would be either that productivity in that sector is frozen and that the incomes of the workers in that sector never change, whatever may be the general level of productivity in the economy, or that productivity in sector A increases as productivity in the whole economy rises. An examination of these two assumptions shows that the second alternative is the more realistic one. After applying different tests, Lydall found that the assumption that gave results most consistent with the empirical estimates was the following:

$$\log V_1/L_1 = 1.59 + 0.70 \log V/L$$

where V_1/L_1 is productivity in sector A and V/L is productivity in the whole economy.

As before, it has been assumed that the distribution of incomes is the same in both sectors and that it remains constant throughout the process of economic development. The distribution of income within each sector is lognormal with a standard deviation of the logarithm of income of 0.65. Changes in the general distribution of incomes thus result solely from changes in the intersectoral difference in average incomes due to intersectoral changes of productivity and to population shifts from sector A to sector B. If consistently with the facts empirically observed, the hypothesis of constancy of productivity in sector A is rejected, it appears

Table 3. Changes in inequality as the proportion of the population in the modern sector (B) increases, with constant intrasectoral inequality but diminishing intersectoral inequality, according to Lydall

Productivity in—			% of population in sector B	Gini coefficient	Percentage income share of—		
Whole economy	Sector A	Sector B			Bottom 20%	Top 20%	Top 5%
200	200	875	0	0.35	6.8	42.4	16.0
400	325	1 281	7.9	0.43	5.7	49.5	22.6
600	432	1 601	14.4	0.46	5.2	52.0	23.6
800	528	1 875	20.2	0.47	4.9	52.8	23.3
1 000	617	2 120	25.5	0.47	4.7	52.9	22.8
1 500	820	2 650	37.2	0.47	4.5	51.8	21.4
2 000	1 002	3 104	47.5	0.45	4.4	50.2	20.2
2 500	1 172	3 510	56.8	0.44	4.5	48.8	19.3
3 000	1 331	3 880	65.5	0.43	4.7	47.4	18.5
4 000	1 628	4 545	81.3	0.39	5.4	44.9	17.2
5 000	1 904	5 138	95.7	0.36	6.4	42.9	16.2

Source: Lydall: *Income distribution during the process of development* (1977), p. 22.

from the two regression equations considered that intersectoral inequality diminishes in the course of economic development.

The results of a simulation of that model are shown in table 3. The productivities calculated for each sector reflect the changes that take place in income per head. The share of the top 5 per cent income group very quickly reaches its maximum (23.6 per cent) when the population of sector B represents only 14.4 per cent of the total population. The share of the top 20 per cent peaks at 52.9 per cent when the population of sector B reaches one-quarter of the total population. The turning-point of the bottom 20 per cent is reached much later: it shrinks to its minimum (4.4 per cent) when the population of sector B represents nearly one-half of the total population. The mean value of the Gini coefficient does not exceed 0.47.

These results do not, of course, necessarily describe the path along which each country has developed over time. It seems likely that in the countries which were the first to develop, the initial productivity differential between the two sectors was smaller than it has been in the countries which have begun to modernise more recently. Moreover, the results do not take into account the inequality of distribution within each sector, which seemingly depends primarily on the degree of relative scarcity of the various types of factor services and of the institutional environment in which those services are supplied.

Notes

[1] Kuznets: "Economic growth and income inequality" (1955).

[2] idem: "Quantitative aspects of the economic growth of nations: VIII. Distribution of income by size" (1963).

[3] idem: "Economic growth and income inequality", op. cit., pp. 7–18.

[4] Kravis: "International differences in the distribution of income" (1960).

[5] Oshima: "The international comparison of size distribution of family incomes with special reference to Asia" (1962).

[6] There is a fuller treatment by Bacha: *The Kuznets curve and beyond* (1977).

[7] Paukert: "Income distribution at different levels of development" (1973).

[8] Adelman and Morris: *An anatomy of patterns of income distribution in developing countries* (1971). See also idem: *Economic growth and social equity in developing countries* (1973).

[9] Ahluwalia: "Income inequality" (1974). See also idem: "Inequality, poverty and development" (1976), and "Income distribution and development" (1976).

[10] idem: "Inequality, poverty and development", op. cit.

[11] Lydall: *Income distribution during the process of development* (1977).

[12] Adelman and Morris: *Economic growth and social equity in developing countries* (1973) pp. 178 et seq. The position adopted by the authors is discussed by Cline: "Distribution and development: A survey of literature" (1975); Lal: "Distribution and development: A review article" (1976); and Little's bibliographical note on the works of Adelman and Morris: *Economic growth and social equity in developing countries*, op. cit., and of Chenery et al.: *Redistribution with growth*, published in *Journal of Development Economics* (1976).

[13] Cromwell: "The size distribution of income" (1977).

[14] Papanek: "Economic growth, income distribution and the political process in less developed countries" (1978).

[15] Cline: "Distribution and development: A survey of literature" (1975).

[16] Guest: *Income distribution, employment and economic growth* (1979).

[17] Beckerman: "Some reflections on redistribution with growth" (1977); Felix: *Trickling down in Mexico and the debate over the long term growth-equity relationship in LDCs* (1974).

[18] See for example Furtado: "The concept of external dependence in the study of underdevelopment" (1973); and Pinto and Di Filipo: "Notes on income distribution and redistribution strategy in Latin America" (1976).

[19] See Kuznets: "Economic growth and income inequality" (1955), pp. 12 et seq.; reprinted in his *Economic growth and structure*, pp. 269 et seq.

MEASUREMENT OF INCOME INEQUALITY 2

The statistics of income distribution used in the studies surveyed in Chapter 1 for interpretations of the Kuznets hypothesis have several shortcomings. First, income distribution by economically active persons in some countries is compared indiscriminately with distribution by households in other countries or with distribution per head, although within the same country and for the same year a different distribution is obtained according to the income-receiving unit chosen. Next, some of the distributions that are compared depend on estimates that are so unreliable that they must be either ignored altogether or at least corrected on the basis of an examination of all the sources available for each particular country. There is no study which examines the biases that make comparisons between developing and developed countries misleading. (As between one category of countries and another, changes in income during the life cycle, regional differences in prices and the savings of companies can modify in very different ways the estimation of real inequalities of income.)

The first purpose of the present chapter will be to put forward new, comparable and relatively reliable estimates of the distribution of incomes, thereby providing more trustworthy statistical information with which to test the Kuznets hypothesis.

A NEW SET OF ESTIMATES

Notwithstanding the many studies that have been carried out since 1972, there are several reasons warranting the preparation of a new set of estimates. Some collections of estimates, like that of Adelman and Morris, are already rather old. Much useful research work has since been carried out. The studies undertaken under the International Labour Organisation's World Employment Programme have provided new estimates for several countries or territories (Hong Kong, Iran, Malaysia, Swaziland, Turkey, Zambia) which had not yet been included in any series. As already mentioned, it has been usual hitherto in the compilations of estimates to include in them, though without even pointing out the fact, statistics relating to different income-receiving units: economically active persons, households, individual persons. Yet, as will be shown, a distribution by economically active persons differs markedly from a distribution by households, and it is not possible to compare distributions referring to different income-receiving units. It is advisable, too, to examine critically the different sources and to choose those in which the same principles are applied to each country. The World Bank has had the merit of bringing together most of the data available for a series of countries[1] but the commentary does not facilitate the user's choice. When examined critically, many estimates have to be rejected as wholly devoid of reliability or significance at the national level. It is, for example, out of the question to base, as Adelman and Morris do, an estimate of distribution in Nigeria on statistics of direct taxation inasmuch as only 3 per cent of households are liable to that taxation, or an estimate of distribution in the Sudan on a survey carried out only in one township.[2] There are questionable estimates also in Ahluwalia:[3] for Burma, the Dominican Republic and the Libyan Arab Jamahiriya, there are estimates from household budget surveys carried out in the capital city; for Uganda, where the majority of economically active persons are not wage earners, the estimates are based on statistics relating only to wage earners, excluding foreigners; for Guyana, the results of a budget survey that did not take into account the self-employed with high incomes have been accepted without corrections; lastly, for Iran, it is an urban family budget survey that has been used for estimating the distribution of incomes at the national level.

What makes it all the more necessary to approach critically any compilation of statistics on income distribution is that the data are then used to test certain relationships and to estimate the incidence of various factors (schooling, population growth, gross domestic product per head) on the distribution of incomes. It is better to consider a limited number of countries for which the estimates are sufficiently reliable than to accept, for the sake of covering a larger number of countries, estimates that are meaningless. Account will be taken here, therefore, only of 39 countries in respect of which relatively reliable estimates are available in various sources (direct results of national household budget surveys, estimates based on a large number of data: household budget surveys, wage statistics, national accounts, censuses, etc.). All estimates derived from incomplete sources, such as urban household budget surveys, have been rejected. Survey results have been corrected by reference to the national accounts and other available sources. Where an adjustment could not be made, the concentration revealed by the survey has been increased slightly by 0.03 (the Gini coefficient), since that kind of survey usually results in a relative underestimation of high incomes and, hence, of the rate of concentration. Moreover, the results of the surveys have been adjusted wherever there might be a bias due, for example, to over-representation or under-representation of a particular category of households or to the exclusion of a particular income group. Furthermore, the consistency of estimates made at different dates has been checked, so far as possible, by reference to the causes of the differences between the estimates (for example, agrarian reform or development of education in cases of falls in the rate of concentration). The results are given in tables 4, 5 and 6. Table 4 shows the distribution by quintiles for the first four of them and then the shares of the ninth decile and of the last two five-percentile groups. This breakdown is the most appropriate one because, much of the information on the distribution of low incomes being either somewhat condensed or of poor quality, it was better to indicate the shares of the first four quintiles than to give a more detailed breakdown. In any case, the estimates of the rate of concentration are not affected by broader aggregation at the low-income level, whereas they would be greatly affected by aggregation at the high-income level. Two measures of inequality have been used throughout: the Gini coefficient because it is used in the studies quoted in Chapter 1 and has properties that are useful for analyses of the redistribution of incomes (see Chapter 6), and the Theil index because it is one of the few indicators that can be decomposed at the level of the distribution itself.[4]

Choice of income recipient unit

Before commenting on the tables, an explanation of the way in which the income recipient unit was chosen is required. Depending on the sources, there are estimates of income distribution by households or by economically active persons or by individuals. For the purpose of international comparisons there must be homogeneous estimates all referring to the same unit.

It is clear that the most desirable situation—indeed, the only satisfactory one – would be to have income distributions available for the same country and for the same year by economically active persons, by households and by individuals. That would be the only way of allowing an accurate analysis of the effect of the structures and of the working of the economy on real inequalities of income and of the standard of living. The effects on incomes concern economically active persons, while for inequalities in the standard of living we are concerned with individuals. Income differentials between economically active persons depend on the market mechanisms in the field of production (factor endowments of the agents of production; supply of, and demand for, those factors), while

Table 4. Distribution of income among income groups and indicators of inequality in Africa, Asia and Latin America

Continent Country (or territory)	Year	Incomes recipient unit	Percentiles of recipients					D_{10}		Gini coefficient	Theil index
			Q_1 0–20%	Q_2 21–40%	Q_3 41–60%	Q_4 61–80%	D_9 81–90%	91–95%	96–100%		
Africa											
Benin (Dahomey)	1959	Individual	8.0	10.0	12.0	20.5	10.5	8.0	31.0	0.414	0.409
Chad	1958	Individual	8.0	11.6	15.4	22.0	13.0	7.0	23.0	0.347	0.253
Congo	1958	Individual	7.0	10.0	13.0	16.0	10.5	7.5	36.0	0.447	0.512
Gabon	1968	Economically active person	3.3	5.5	7.9	15.8	13.0	9.4	45.0	0.614	0.841
Kenya	1969	Economically active person	3.8	6.2	8.5	13.5	11.7	12.0	44.3	0.604	0.828
Ivory Coast	1970	Economically active person	4.0	6.4	11.8	20.6	16.1	11.4	29.7	0.517	0.506
Malawi	1969	Individual	5.8	9.1	13.3	18.6	14.0	10.0	29.2	0.452	0.420
Senegal	1970	Economically active person	5.8	7.2	9.4	13.2	11.0	12.5	40.9	0.549	0.713
	1970	Household	5.5	7.8	10.5	15.3	15.5	12.7	32.7	0.513	0.547
	1970	Individual	5.7	8.1	11.4	16.8	14.9	12.6	30.5	0.490	0.489
South Africa	1965	Individual	1.9	4.3	10.1	25.7	18.6	11.8	27.6	0.563	0.573
Swaziland	1974	Individual	2.8	4.2	7.1	17.7	13.7	12.3	42.2	0.637	0.844
Tanzania	1968	Household	5.5	8.0	10.5	15.0	16.0	15.0	30.0	0.509	0.522
	1968	Individual	5.0	8.5	11.5	15.0	15.0	11.0	34.0	0.508	0.550
	1968	Economically active person	5.0	8.0	11.0	15.0	13.0	12.5	35.5	0.523	0.593
Togo	1957	Individual	8.0	12.0	16.5	23.0	10.0	7.5	23.0	0.338	0.247
Tunisia	1970	Economically active person	4.1	7.7	12.0	21.6	17.4	13.1	24.5	0.485	0.429
Zambia	1970	Individual	3.5	5.8	8.5	15.5	13.6	10.0	43.1	0.618	0.795
Zimbabwe (formerly Rhodesia)	1969	Economically active person	3.1	4.9	8.3	15.7	12.0	11.0	45.0	0.623	0.860
	1969	Household	3.0	4.8	7.2	17.0	12.5	10.5	45.0	0.629	0.868
Asia											
Hong Kong	1971	Household	6.0	9.6	13.4	20.0	13.6	10.4	27.0	0.434	0.377
Republic of Korea	1970	Economically active person	6.0	10.0	14.5	21.5	16.5	12.5	19.0	0.400	0.278
	1970	Individual	6.0	10.5	14.5	21.5	16.5	11.0	20.0	0.395	0.276
	1970	Household	7.4	11.5	15.4	20.9	16.8	11.0	17.0	0.351	0.214

India	1961–64	Economically active person	5.0	11.0	13.0	19.0	13.0	12.5	26.5	0.441	0.390
	1964–65	Individual	6.8	10.5	13.8	19.3	14.1	11.1	24.4	0.406	0.325
	1964–65	Household	6.0	10.0	13.7	19.1	14.1	11.9	25.2	0.428	0.357
Iran	1971	Household	3.4	6.6	10.1	17.2	15.3	11.4	36.0	0.561	0.641
Lebanon	1960	Individual	5.0	8.0	10.0	16.0	16.0	11.0	34.0	0.521	0.566
Malaysia	1970	Household	3.7	7.3	11.9	19.3	14.6	12.5	30.7	0.520	0.522
Philippines	1971	Household	3.5	7.8	12.8	21.1	17.2	12.8	24.7	0.490	0.428
Sri Lanka	1973	Economically active person	4.0	9.5	15.0	23.5	16.0	8.0	24.0	0.432	0.349
	1973	Household	6.5	11.5	15.5	21.0	15.5	7.0	23.0	0.375	0.277
Thailand	1969	Household	3.9	6.8	11.8	20.6	18.1	14.6	24.2	0.504	0.452
Turkey	1968	Household	3.0	6.5	11.1	18.8	15.0	12.8	32.3	0.549	0.584
Latin America											
Argentina	1961	Economically active person	5.2	8.3	13.1	18.3	13.2	10.7	31.2	0.478	0.475
	1961	Household	7.0	10.3	13.1	17.6	12.9	9.7	29.4	0.425	0.398
Brazil	1960	Economically active person	4.0	7.0	10.0	20.4	18.0	11.6	29.0	0.520	0.510
	1970	Household	4.0	8.0	12.0	18.0	18.0	13.0	27.0	0.500	0.467
Chile	1968	Household	4.0	8.0	13.0	17.5	15.0	12.1	30.4	0.503	0.499
Colombia	1964	Economically active person	2.9	6.0	10.2	18.3	14.8	12.0	35.8	0.572	0.655
	1974	Household	4.0	6.5	13.0	18.0	15.0	12.0	31.5	0.520	0.533
Costa Rica	1971	Household	6.0	8.5	12.0	18.4	15.1	11.0	29.0	0.466	0.437
Ecuador	1970	Economically active person	2.9	4.7	6.4	16.5	18.0	14.0	37.5	0.625	0.777
El Salvador	1961	Economically active person	5.5	6.5	8.8	17.8	15.8	12.6	33.0	0.532	0.574
Honduras	1967–68	Household	3.2	4.1	7.7	17.5	16.9	14.6	36.0	0.612	0.735
Mexico	1969	Household	4.0	6.5	9.5	16.0	13.0	15.0	36.0	0.567	0.666
Panama	1970	Economically active person	2.5	5.7	12.3	18.9	15.4	11.8	33.4	0.558	0.608
Peru	1961	Economically active person	2.5	5.5	10.2	17.4	15.2	10.2	39.0	0.591	0.712
Puerto Rico	1963	Household	3.2	9.3	13.8	21.5	17.5	12.1	22.5	0.463	0.380
Uruguay	1967	Household	3.8	9.0	14.0	23.0	17.0	11.0	27.2	0.449	0.363
Venezuela	1962	Household	3.3	6.3	11.2	20.2	17.8	14.0	29.5	0.531	0.512
	1976	Economically active person	3.5	6.0	11.0	20.0	17.0	13.0		0.540	0.539

inequalities in income levels between individuals show up in consumption.

It is necessary to specify the particular concepts of income and of consumption that are used here. Whichever income unit may be under consideration, it will always refer to the totality of primary incomes, both monetary and non-monetary. Obviously the results would be devoid of significance if production for own consumption, which in many cases accounts for more than half of the total income of economically active persons or households with low incomes, were excluded.[5] Nevertheless, in most cases one form of non-monetary income has not been taken into account: the theoretical rent imputable to families owning their housing. (That omission, which occurs frequently in the estimates of income distribution not only for developing but also for developed countries, entails a bias of negligible importance where, as is often the case, the value of the housing is proportionate to the household's income.)

In the case of distributions by economically active persons, there is a risk of leaving out of account incomes from dividends, interest payments and rents, which are usually imputed to households rather than to such persons. In many cases, the incomes of economically active persons cover only wages and salaries and the mixed incomes of the self-employed. Such an omission is, by definition, impossible in the sources that concern, as is the case for many countries, the incomes of households. For the countries (excepting Ecuador and El Salvador) in respect of which the sources refer only to the incomes of economically active persons or of individuals, the data have been corrected to take into account unearned incomes (obtainable from the national accounts) if they were not already included. If there are no statistics on the distribution of unearned income among the economically active, 90 per cent of it has been imputed to the top decile, which seems reasonable in the case of those countries—in practice, all of them African—where only a very small number of persons are owners of interest-bearing securities, etc.

The household constitutes an intermediate income recipient unit, consideration of which is essential to an understanding of the transition from distribution by economically active persons to distribution by individuals. For example, if the number of economically active persons per household is constant (one or two persons), differences in the size of households according to income partly explain inequalities of income between individuals. If the size increases with average income, the coefficients of inequality for the distributions by economically active persons and by households will be equal, and higher than the coefficient for the distribution by individuals. If the size of the household is constant but the number of economically active persons per household varies (increasing as the average income grows), the distributions by households and by individuals will be similar but the distribution by economically active persons will be more equal. In practice the situation is more complex because the number of economically active persons and the size of households both vary; moreover, the variations are not continuous: the size of the household may grow and then diminish while income increases.

Whereas the distribution of incomes by economically active persons pertains solely to the formation of primary incomes, the disparities in income levels between individuals include the effects of redistribution. Households often benefit from social transfers according to the number and the ages of their constituent individuals, so that income distribution by individuals does not result solely from distribution by economically active persons and from the structure of the family. In a strict sense, a study of inequalities in income between individuals should take into account all transfers, whether positive or negative, from the public sector (deductions or payments in cash, services provided free of charge in matters of health, education, etc.). These transfers, which will be considered in Chapters 5 and 6, play a much less important role in developing countries than in developed countries having a market economy. In many countries they account for very small proportions of the primary incomes of households, and the distribution of incomes by households is almost the same after the transfers as before. In these circumstances it is legitimate to analyse, as will be done below, the distributions by households and by individuals by taking into account only the primary incomes, and to show the inequalities of income resulting solely from the primary incomes and the structure of the family. These inequalities do not correspond to the inequalities in expenditure. There are, in fact, two reasons why inequalities of consumption, including consumption from own production, should be less pronounced than inequalities of primary incomes. One of them arises out of transfers from the public sector and is sometimes negligible; the other one, which is always of some importance, results from savings, which grow with income, though it is often negative in the case of the lowest incomes. It has sometimes been held that the actual dispersion of standards of living is better reflected in inequalities of expenditure than in inequalities of income, which may overestimate it.[6] That point of view is partly well founded but it has to be qualified: when measuring the inequalities of expenditure by individuals, there is a risk of underestimating the dispersion of standards of living if, as is often the case, account is not taken of the services derived from family wealth acquired through savings, especially in the form of housing property.

Economically active persons and households

To make the statistics consistent, the first problem to be solved concerns the relationship between distribution by economically active persons and distribution by households. In many cases statistics of income distribution by economically active persons are available that are based either on nationally representative sample surveys or, more often, on estimates combining data drawn from various sources (national accounts, surveys of certain groups of economically active persons, statistics on the distribution of wages). For other countries only household budget surveys are available. It is therefore essential for purposes of international comparisons to make some assumptions with regard to the relationship between the distribution of income among economically active persons and its distribution among households.

The assumption made here results from a study of countries for which both distributions are known: Senegal, Tanzania, Zimbabwe; Argentina, Brazil, Colombia, Venezuela; India, Republic of Korea, Sri Lanka (table 4). If the countries for which the estimates refer to different years are excluded (Colombia, Venezuela), it is found that, except in the case of Zimbabwe, the distribution by economically active persons is always more concentrated than that by households, the mean difference between the two Gini coefficients amounting to 0.035. For Colombia the difference reaches 0.052. Yet the concentration did not lessen between 1964 and 1974;[7] it remained stable or increased very slightly, which corresponds to a difference for the same year falling between 0.03 and 0.05. In the case of Venezuela the difference does not exceed 0.009, although it appears that the concentration diminished a little between 1970 and 1976;[8] in 1976, the Gini coefficient for the distribution by households was certainly lower than it had been in 1962, and the difference estimated in 1976 would have reached 0.02–0.04. Thus for nine countries out of ten there is a mean difference of 0.035.

Contrary to what might have been expected, the number of economically active persons per household does not increase but falls with rises in the average income of the household. That result can be explained partly by certain characteristics of female work. The wives of farmers are mostly regarded as economically active. In towns, female work provides an indispensable supplement to poor families owing to the very low wages paid for unskilled work. On the other hand it is becoming less frequent among the richer households, especially those in the upper 5 per cent group, for whom the additional income that it brings is superfluous. That circumstance is linked also to the still low rate of enrolment of girls in secondary and higher education. In the large and poor families included in the first deciles, women and young people strive to supplement by their work the insufficient income of the head of the family. That is the case especially in rural environments, where a multiplication of sources of income for large families, accompanied by a diversification of work, leads to an increase of income in cash that tends to account for a growing proportion of household resources. The high activity rate on the part of the members of large and poor families contributes effectively to a reduction of income disparities between households and helps to explain why income inequalities are less pronounced by households than by economically active persons.[9]

This comparison of distributions by economically active persons and by households leads to an assumption that the Gini coefficient for the former is, on the average, 0.03 higher than it is for the latter. It is on that basis that tables 5 and 6 on the two distributions have been prepared. For the ten countries in respect of which both distributions are known, the Gini coefficients that have been found have been indicated; for the other countries, the Gini coefficient for the distribution that is not known has been estimated by increasing or diminishing by 0.03 the coefficient for the distribution that is known. Two homogeneous series have thus been obtained from which the bias inherent in the difference in income recipient units has been virtually eliminated.

Households and individuals

The shift from distribution by households to distribution by individuals is a more difficult one. Table 4 gives only four examples: India, Republic of Korea, Senegal, Tanzania. In Tanzania the two distributions are similar. In Senegal the distribution by households is more concentrated than the distribution by individuals (difference between the two Gini coefficients +0.023). The same applies to India (+0.022), whereas the reverse applies to the Republic of Korea (−0.024). The low significance of these results calls for a special analysis of the relationships between the two distributions.

The only satisfactory method of moving from the distribution of incomes by households to distribution by individuals requires information on the distribution of households by number of persons for each group of households falling within an income bracket. From that information, the income per person within each household is calculated. All individuals are then classed according to that income in order to obtain a distribution of incomes by individuals that will be comparable to the distribution by households since it will have been derived from the same sources.[10] That work has been done by Kuznets for two Asian countries.[11] It has been done here for Hong Kong and for Trinidad and Tobago.[12] In three cases the Gini coefficient is the same for both distributions, whereas in the case of Hong Kong it is markedly higher for the distribution by individuals (+0.05). But even with an equal Gini coefficient there are observable differences. Thus in Trinidad and Tobago the share of the first five deciles and the share of the tenth decile are greater for the distribution by individuals, the two features offsetting each other in a global indicator. When all the available information is assembled, it is

Table 5. Distribution of income among economically active persons in Africa, Asia and Latin America (Gini coefficients)

Africa

Country	Year	Gini coefficient
Benin[2]	1959	0.444
Chad[2]	1958	0.377
Congo[2]	1958	0.477
Gabon	1968	0.614
Ivory Coast	1970	0.517
Kenya	1969	0.604
Malawi[2]	1969	0.482
Senegal	1970	0.549
South Africa[2]	1965	0.593
Swaziland[1]	1974	0.667
Tanzania	1968	0.523
Togo[2]	1957	0.368
Tunisia	1970	0.485
Zambia[2]	1970	0.648
Zimbabwe (formerly Rhodesia)	1969	0.623

Asia

Country (territory)	Year	Gini coefficient
Hong Kong[3]	1971	0.464
India	1961–64	0.441
Iran[3]	1971	0.591
Rep. of Korea	1970	0.400
Lebanon[1]	1960	0.551
Malaysia[3]	1970	0.550
Philippines[3]	1971	0.520
Sri Lanka	1963	0.522
Thailand[3]	1973	0.432
Turkey[3]	1969	0.534
	1968	0.579

Latin America

Country (territory)	Year	Gini coefficient
Argentina	1961	0.478
Brazil	1960	0.520
Chile[3]	1970	0.560
Colombia	1968	0.533
Costa Rica	1964	0.572
Ecuador	1971	0.496
El Salvador	1970	0.625
Honduras	1961	0.532
Mexico[3]	1967–68	0.642
Panama	1969	0.597
Peru	1970	0.558
Puerto Rico[3]	1961	0.591
Uruguay[3]	1963	0.493
Venezuela	1967	0.479
	1962	0.561
	1976	0.540

[1] Assumptions: Ratio higher by 0.030 for the distribution by economically active persons than for the distribution by households. Similar ratios for the distribution by households and for the distribution by individuals. [2] According to the distribution by households. [3] According to the distribution by individuals.

Table 6. Distribution of income among households in Africa, Asia and Latin America (Gini coefficients)

Africa			Asia			Latin America		
Country	Year	Gini coefficient[1]	Country (territory)	Year	Gini coefficient[1]	Country (territory)	Year	Gini coefficient[1]
Benin[2]	1959	0.414	Hong Kong	1971	0.434	Argentina	1961	0.425
Congo[2]	1958	0.447	India	1964–65	0.428	Brazil	1960	0.500
Gabon[3]	1968	0.584	Iran	1971	0.561		1970	0.540
Ivory Coast[3]	1970	0.487	Rep. of Korea	1970	0.351	Chile	1968	0.503
Kenya[3]	1969	0.574	Lebanon[2]	1960	0.521	Colombia	1974	0.520
Malawi[2]	1969	0.452	Malaysia	1970	0.520	Costa Rica	1971	0.466
Senegal	1970	0.513	Philippines	1971	0.490	Ecuador[3]	1970	0.595
South Africa	1965	0.563	Sri Lanka	1963	0.486	El Salvador[3]	1961	0.502
Swaziland[2]	1974	0.637		1973	0.375	Honduras	1967–68	0.612
Tanzania	1968	0.509	Thailand	1969	0.504	Mexico	1969	0.567
Chad[2]	1958	0.347	Turkey	1968	0.549	Panama[3]	1970	0.528
Togo[2]	1957	0.338				Peru[3]	1961	0.561
Tunisia[3]	1970	0.455				Puerto Rico	1963	0.463
Zambia[2]	1970	0.618				Uruguay	1967	0.449
Zimbabwe (formerly Rhodesia)	1969	0.629				Venezuela	1962	0.531
							1976	0.510

[1] Assumptions: Similar ratios for the distribution by households and for the distribution by individuals. Ratio lower by 0.03 for the distribution by households than for the distribution by individuals. [2] According to the distribution by individuals. [3] According to the distribution by economically active persons.

33

found that in four cases the Gini coefficients are the same for the distribution by households and for the distribution by individuals; that in two cases the Gini coefficient is higher for the distribution by individuals than for the distribution by households; and that in the two other cases it is the other way round.

These results have discouraged the presentation of a series of Gini coefficients for the distribution by individuals on the basis of table 6: it seems that in most cases the Gini coefficients are the same, or approximately the same, for the distribution by households and for the distribution by individuals, and that the former may be taken, therefore, as referring also to the latter. Nevertheless, in certain countries there may be substantial differences in one direction or another. It is not possible to determine the direction without information on the distribution of households by number of persons for each income bracket.

The equality of the distribution by households and of the distribution by individuals, or the existence of only small differences, distinguishes the developing countries from the developed countries, in which, according to Kuznets, the distribution by individuals is less concentrated than the distribution by households:[11] as a result, when the distribution by households is considered there will be a bias in comparisons of developing with developed countries; in one case the real inequalities of income between individuals will be the same as the inequalities between households, whereas in another they will be markedly less pronounced, which leads to an underestimation of the real disparities of income between the two groups of countries.

The Kuznets hypothesis seems to be confirmed by analysis of the size of households as a function of income. In the developed countries average household size increases rapidly as one passes from the lower to the upper deciles. In the developing countries, on the other hand, household size increases slowly. Such is the case in the Philippines[11] and in Trinidad and Tobago, where household size even diminishes from the ninth to the tenth decile, while in Hong Kong the size is almost constant whatever the income of the household.[13]

These data show that the interactions between family structure and income distribution by households differ from country to country, and that the developing countries are marked in that regard by specific characteristics which in any event are not necessarily stable. The relatively large size of low-income households in many developing countries is linked to certain conditions. Several factors can contribute to a transformation of that family structure and to a reduction of the size of households, thus causing an increase in inequality at the level of households even if it does not increase at the level of individuals. The break-up of the traditional family unit and the proliferation of one-person households lead to a situation approaching that in the developed countries, where the size of households with low incomes is much smaller than that of other households and where, consequently, the distribution by individuals is markedly less concentrated than the distribution by households.

Among the factors that may serve to explain the transformations of the family structure, the first is linked to the process of urbanisation and industrialisation. In the traditional agricultural sector, the family is both a unit of production and a unit of consumption: it is an instrument of solidarity and the locus of redistribution of income between the young and the old, between the healthy and the sick and between the active and the unemployed. That system, which is adaptable to most activities of the traditional type, no longer serves its purpose when the family loses its economic independence and draws its resources from the wage employment of some of its members: at that point the link between the generations weakens and ultimately vanishes in consequence of the mobility of labour. The break-up occurs when the younger and usually celibate members migrate to towns to find employment and for purposes of study. The proliferation of one-person households is closely connected with the migration of the young and the process of industrialisation. The second explanatory factor is the increase in income per head as a result of economic development, on the assumption that the propensity of the adult members to form separate households increases as the family income rises. Lastly, social factors may combine with the purely economic factors. By modifying family living conditions and leading to a dispersion of its members, economic growth can change social values, weaken the sense of family solidarity and develop individualism.[14]

This analysis shows that only detailed information on the structure of households for each income bracket would make it possible to estimate for each country the effect of that structure on the distribution of incomes by households, and hence the relationship between the Gini coefficient for distribution by households and that for distribution by individuals. It would be too risky to estimate that relationship for one country from what can be observed in another, inasmuch as changes in family structures are highly complex and are not linked in a simple and mechanical way to variables such as national income per head and the degree of industrialisation and urbanisation.

Income distribution in Africa, Latin America and Asia.

The following paragraphs describe and analyse the three tables on the distribution of incomes that have been prepared. Table 4 has been prepared directly from the sources; it indicates the distribution of incomes according to the income recipient unit used in the sources for the first four quintiles (0–20th, 21st–40th, 41st–60th and 61st–80th percentiles), for the ninth decile (81st–90th percentile) and, in the last decile, for the last two groups of 5 per cent (91st–95th and 96th–100th percentiles), with two indicators of inequality: the Gini coefficient and the Theil index. Tables 5 and 6 give the Gini coefficient for the distribution by economically active persons and for the distribution by households; the estimates have been made on the basis of table 4 and of the hypotheses referred to above. The countries are listed by continent.

The characteristic feature in Africa is that it has two extreme situations: it shows both the most equal and the least equal distributions. With Gini coefficients that are below, or equal to, 0.41 (Chad, Togo), there are, on that continent, distributions that are less unequal than in some developed countries. Other countries (Congo, Malawi) are close to them. On the other hand some countries of eastern and southern Africa reach the maxima (0.6–0.64 in Kenya, Swaziland, Zambia, Zimbabwe) that have been found. South Africa likewise shows a high concentration (0.563). The only comparable country outside those regions is Gabon (0.614). In these six countries the share of the first two quintiles falls to an average of 8 per cent, that is, an average income equal to one-fifth of the national average income per head. The other countries (Ivory Coast, Senegal, Tanzania, Tunisia) show a markedly lower but nevertheless quite high concentration (of the order of 0.5). In the Ivory Coast and in Tunisia is to be noted the rather large share (38 per cent) of deciles 7, 8 and 9, whereas that share reaches only 28 to 30 per cent both in countries where income distribution is on the whole highly unequal (Zambia, Zimbabwe) and in countries where it is relatively equal such as Benin and the Congo. This feature corresponds to specific characteristics of the distribution: very small share of the first deciles, but formation of a middle class of planters in one case and of civil servants in the other, with incomes equal to, or larger than, the national average.

In Latin America, Argentina, Costa Rica and Uruguay are among the countries with a moderate concentration, at any rate at the dates indicated. The Gini coefficient for households and also for individuals does not exceed 0.466, while the Theil index does not exceed 0.437. These figures are higher than those found in the developed countries but the disparity is small (about 0.03) in relation to the developed countries where income distribution is most unequal. The disparity would be larger if account were taken of the redistribution of incomes, which plays a larger role in industrialised countries than in the developing countries. The share of households in the first two quintiles varies between 12 and 17 per cent, so that their income is approximately equivalent to one-third of the national average. The highest rates of concentration are reached in Ecuador, Honduras, Mexico and Peru, and, in 1970, in Brazil, with the Gini coefficient for the distribution by households reaching or surpassing 0.55. The share of the first two quintiles varies between 7 and 11 per cent, which is equivalent to an average income per household (and per individual) falling between a sixth and a quarter of the national average. The large sizes of the populations of Brazil and Mexico must be stressed: if Peru is added to them, the three countries account for two-thirds of the population of Latin America. The other countries (Chile, Colombia, Panama, El Salvador, Venezuela) are in many cases closer to Brazil and Mexico than to the first group of countries.

Asia also offers instances of relatively equal distribution of income. The Gini coefficient is lower in the Republic of Korea and in Sri Lanka than in several developed countries. In both cases there is a combination of agrarian reform, many measures of rural development and a high rate of enrolment in primary and secondary schools. Hong Kong approximates to that group (Gini coefficient 0.434), but in special circumstances, being the only country where agriculture is virtually non-existent. India likewise shows a moderate Gini coefficient, though the distribution there is to the advantage of the top 5 per cent, which explains why the Theil index for that country is much higher than it is for the Republic of Korea or for Sri Lanka: 0.357 instead of 0.214 and 0.277 respectively. The countries where income distribution is most unequal are Iran and Turkey, followed by Lebanon and Malaysia. Nevertheless, the cases of very high inequality of income (Gini coefficient exceeding 0.52) are fewer in Asia (three countries) than in Africa (six countries) and in Latin America (seven).

Distribution of incomes and GDP per head

With the help of this new series of homogeneous estimates, the countries can be classified by GDP per head in order to verify whether the new data confirm the conclusions of the previous studies summarised in Chapter 1. Tables 7 and 8 respectively show the income distributions found in the 39 developing countries and in eight developed countries. The developing countries are arranged by continent in view of the differences which, as was noted above, are linked to that factor.

Table 7 clearly reveals two facts: on the one hand, product per head undoubtedly exercises an influence since the average inter-regional Gini coefficients shift from 0.467 to 0.551 and 0.575 and then to 0.517 as income increases; on the other hand, the concentration of incomes varies so much among countries with roughly the same GNP per head that the Kuznets hypothesis serves to explain only a small part of the differences found between countries.

Among the poorest countries the Gini coefficient ranges from 0.368 (Togo) to 0.604 (Kenya). Kenya, it is true, had in 1969 a modern sector, which was almost non-existent in Togo in 1957. Yet that sector was still very marginal in Tanzania, where the Gini coefficient nevertheless reached 0.523. There are just as significant differences in the 200–330

Table 7. Distribution of income in developing countries, by major region and by income group (Gini coefficients and GDP per head)

Africa					Latin America					Asia				
Country	GDP per head (US dollars, 1970)	Gini coefficient Year¹	A²	H³	Country	GDP per head (US dollars, 1970)	Gini coefficient Year¹	A²	H³	Country	GDP per head (US dollars, 1970)	Gini coefficient Year¹	A²	H³

Group 1: GDP per head under 200 dollars: inter-regional average Gini coefficient for economically active persons 0.467.

Africa					Latin America					Asia				
Malawi	80	1969	0.482	0.452						India	110	1961–64	0.441	0.411
Chad	80	1958	0.377	0.347						Sri Lanka	110	1973	0.432	0.402
Benin	90	1959	0.444	0.414						Thailand	200	1969	0.534	0.504
Tanzania	100	1968	0.523	0.493										
Togo	140	1957	0.368	0.338										
Kenya	150	1969	0.604	0.574										
Average			*0.466*							*Average*			*0.469*	

Group 2: GDP per head 200–330 dollars: inter-regional average Gini coefficient for economically active persons 0.551.

Africa					Latin America					Asia				
Senegal	230	1970	0.549	0.519	Honduras	280	1967–68	0.642	0.612	Philippines	210	1971	0.520	0.490
Tunisia	250	1970	0.485	0.455	Ecuador	290	1970	0.625	0.595	Rep. of Korea	250	1970	0.400	0.370
Swaziland	260⁴	1974	0.667	0.637	El Salvador	300	1961	0.532	0.502	Turkey	310	1968	0.579	0.549
Zimbabwe	280	1969	0.623	0.593										
Congo	300	1958	0.477	0.477										
Ivory Coast	310	1970	0.517	0.487										
Average			*0.553*		*Average*			*0.600*		*Average*			*0.500*	

Group 3: GDP per head 331–700 dollars: inter-regional average Gini coefficient for economically active persons 0.575.

Country	GDP	Year			Country	GDP	Year			Country	GDP	Year		
Zambia	400	1970	0.648	0.618	Colombia	340	1974	0.550	0.520	Iran	380	1971	0.591	0.561
Gabon	630	1968	0.614	0.584	Brazil	420	1970	0.560	0.530	Malaysia	380	1970	0.550	0.520
					Peru	450	1961	0.591	0.561	Lebanon	590	1960	0.551	0.521
					Costa Rica	560	1971	0.496	0.466					
					Mexico	670	1969	0.597	0.567					
Average				*0.631*	*Average*				*0.559*	*Average*				*0.564*

Group 4: GDP per head over 700 dollars: inter-regional average Gini coefficient for economically active persons 0.517.

Country	GDP	Year			Country	GDP	Year			Country	GDP	Year		
South Africa	760	1965	0.593	0.563	Chile	720	1968	0.533	0.503	Hong Kong	970	1971	0.464	0.434
					Panama	730	1970	0.558	0.528					
					Uruguay	820	1967	0.479	0.449					
					Venezuela	980	1976	0.540	0.510					
					Argentina	1160	1961	0.478	0.448					
					Puerto Rico	1650	1963	0.493	0.463					
					Average				*0.513*					

Key: [1] Year of estimate of income distribution. [2] Distribution by economically active persons. [3] Distribution by households. [4] 1972.
Source: Gini coefficient: see above, tables 5 and 6. GDP per head: World Bank: *World Bank Atlas* (1972).

Table 8. Distribution of income in developed countries (Gini coefficients and GDP per head)

Country	GDP per head (US dollars), 1970	Gini coefficient	
		Year[1]	[2]
Japan	1 920	1971	0.407
United Kingdom	2 270	1973	0.344
Norway	2 860	1970	0.354
Federal Republic of Germany	2 930	1973	0.396
France	3 100	1970	0.416
Canada	3 700	1969	0.382
Sweden	4 040	1972	0.346
United States	4 760	1972	0.404
Average			*0.381*

[1] Year of estimate of the distribution of incomes. [2] Distribution by households.

Sources: Gini coefficients: For Japan, Wada: *Changes in the size distribution of income in postwar Japan* (1974), p. 22; for the other countries, Sawyer: "Income distribution in OECD countries" (1976), p. 17. GDP per head: *World Bank Atlas* (1972).

dollars income bracket. The lowest Gini coefficient amounted to 0.4 (Republic of Korea), while the highest exceeded 0.62 (Ecuador, Honduras, Swaziland, Zimbabwe). In the 331–700 dollars bracket the disparity ranged from 0.496 (Costa Rica) to 0.648 (Zambia). Lastly, among the countries with a GDP per head exceeding 700 dollars, Hong Kong had a Gini coefficient of 0.464 and South Africa of 0.593.

Table 7 shows the specificity of the Asian countries: for the same GDP per head the inequality in Asia is less than in African and Latin American countries. Within the regions, there are some notable differences: for nearly the same products per head the Congo and Tunisia have coefficients of about 0.48, while Zimbabwe has a coefficient of 0.623. The coefficients for Mexico and Peru exceed by 0.1 the coefficient for Costa Rica.

The σ/m values for the four income brackets (0.154, 0.136, 0.072, 0.083) point to a significant dispersion of the Gini coefficients in each case. That fact leads to the rejection of any simple model purporting to explain changes in the concentration of incomes solely in terms of product per head.

It is of interest to compare these results with earlier estimates. For that purpose, the two series that are most frequently quoted as points of reference (Paukert's and Ahluwalia's) have been chosen. If the countries are classified by gross domestic product per head and if the household is taken as the income recipient unit, which is the unit chosen for most of the countries in the two other series, we obtain the average Gini coefficients shown in table 9. Most of the countries fall into the same income brackets in the three series; the exceptions are due to the large differences

Table 9.   Distribution of incomes by households: indicator of inequality and GDP per head according to three sources

GDP per head (US dollars)	Gini coefficient			
	Paukert		Ahluwalia	Tables 7 and 8
Less developed countries				
Group 1 = under $ 200	0.419[1]	0.459[2]	0.438	0.437
	0.468[1]	0.506[2]	0.505	0.521
Group 2 = $ 200–330	0.499[1]			
Group 3 = $ 331–700	0.494		0.500	0.545
Group 4 = over $ 700	0.438		0.491	0.487
Developed countries	0.383		0.378	0.381

[1] For the groups: under $100; $100–200; $201–$300.   [2] For the groups: under $150; $150–$300.
Sources: Paukert: "Income distribution at different levels of development" (1973), pp. 114–115; Ahluwalia: "Income inequality" (1974).

sometimes found in GDP per head between the date of one estimate and another, and in the resulting shift of a country from a bracket in one series to a higher bracket in another.

The first finding that emerges from the comparison is the constancy of the figures for group 1 and for the developed countries. So far as group 4 is concerned, the average of the Paukert series results partly from the inclusion of Greece and Japan, which are countries with a moderate Gini coefficient that are not included in tables 7 and 8; their exclusion gives a figure of 0.465. There are thus estimates of the same orders of magnitude for the poorest countries and, at the other extreme, for the developed countries and those that are close to them. On the other hand the new series reveals a markedly higher concentration for the developing countries in groups 2 and 3, the maximum rising to 0.545 instead of 0.499 or 0.505; the maximum is, moreover, reached at a higher level, not in group 2 but in group 3. There is a difference of 0.108 instead of 0.08 or 0.067 between the maximum value and the minimum (or of 0.164 instead of 0.116 or 0.127 in the case of the developed countries). The preparation of a series of more homogeneous estimates has confirmed the Kuznets hypothesis on long-term changes in the distribution of incomes, but the sharp variations in the Gini coefficient within each income group show the limitations of that hypothesis for interpretations of changes in individual countries.

Since there are some obvious drawbacks to the interpretation of these changes on the basis of cross-section data, it has seemed desirable to use the new estimates for testing the Kuznets hypothesis with the available inter-temporal data, which are more satisfactory for that purpose. Any inter-temporal comparison must be based on comparable sources, but data of that kind are available for only a limited number of countries.

Estimates made at different dates by different methods entail margins of error that are wider than the observed variations, depriving the latter of significance. What are needed are estimates made on the basis of similar sources, which is rarely the case.

For Brazil two censuses carried out along the same lines point to an increase in the rate of concentration by 0.035 between 1960 and 1970. For Mexico the interval of time between the two surveys (1963 and 1968) is too short for any significant change to have emerged. The direct results of the surveys indicate a fall in the rate of concentration, but the corrected results bring out a variation in the opposite direction.[15] For Venezuela there was seemingly a slight reduction in the Gini coefficient between 1966 and 1976.[8] For Africa there are comparable estimates for 1958–60 and 1968–70 in respect of three countries: the Ivory Coast, Gabon and Senegal. In the Ivory Coast the Gini coefficient increased by about 0.03; in Gabon it showed a rise from 1956 to 1960 followed by a slight fall from 1960 to 1968 (from minus 0.01 to minus 0.02). In Senegal, too, there was a fall of minus 0.045 for the distribution by economically active persons. In the Republic of Korea the Gini coefficient seems to have increased by 0.022 between 1965 and 1971, with a sharp rise followed by a slight fall.[16] For Iran two comparable surveys show a marked rise in the Gini coefficient between 1965 and 1971 (plus 0.033). According to several surveys conducted from 1956 to 1971 in the Philippines, the Gini coefficient seems to have remained almost constant. In Sri Lanka, on the other hand, the concentration diminished sharply between 1963 and 1973 (minus 0.07).

These results must be interpreted with great prudence. The variations cannot be linked solely to changes in GDP per head during the period of observation: various events can explain certain differences. In Brazil an important change in economic policy in 1964 benefited incomes from capital. In Senegal a diminution in the number of foreign executive, supervisory and technical staff largely explains the fall in the Gini coefficient. In Sri Lanka the fall in the coefficient results from a whole series of socio-economic measures. Among the other countries referred to, the Republic of Korea, the Ivory Coast and Iran showed an upward movement whereas in Gabon and in Venezuela the movement was downward. It is significant that in 1970 the first three countries had a GDP of under 500 dollars per head whereas Gabon and Venezuela had already exceeded that level. This corroborates the Kuznets hypothesis on the relationship between GDP per head and the rate of concentration, provided that all other things are taken as equal. A measure of economic policy such as an agrarian reform scheme can appreciably reduce the rate of concentration in a country where it would tend to increase *pari passu* with GDP per head in the absence of such structural changes. It should be added that any single indicator of inequality is unsatisfactory. There can be significant changes in the distribution of incomes without any variation of the Gini coefficient. For example, in a number of countries the share of the 5 per cent at the top of the scale diminishes to the advantage of the group situated between the 80th and 90th percentiles between 1960 and 1970, while the Gini coefficient remains constant or even increases.

BIASES IN COMPARISONS BETWEEN DEVELOPED AND DEVELOPING COUNTRIES

The Kuznets hypothesis concerns not only the developing but also the developed countries, and the studies on the relationship between economic development and the distribution of incomes make use, like the present study, also of data relating to the developed countries. The comparisons that one is thus led to make between the two groups of countries are, however, apt to be vitiated by numerous biases that must be examined even though their correction can raise difficult problems.

The life cycle

The real inequalities between individuals should be calculated for their whole lifetime and not just for one year. A first bias comes from the fact that the difference between inequalities measured over a lifetime and inequalities observed in one year is not the same in both developing and developed countries.

Age

The incidence of age on disparities of income is much slighter in the developing countries than it is in the developed. As Paglin has shown,[17] if it is assumed that all the households falling within the same age group have the same income, the rate of concentration measured over a lifetime is nil even if there are more or less large differences in income as a function of age. Consequently, it can be considered that the rate of concentration C_a calculated on the basis of a distribution of households by age (assuming that the incomes of all the households falling within the same age group are constant) measures the inequality during the period of a year but not over a whole lifetime. The extent of inequality over a lifetime would be the difference between the inequality measured in one year C_a that is, $C - C_a$. The indicator chosen by Paglin, namely the Gini coefficient, is not decomposable. All that can be stated is that $C - C_a$ represents the difference between the observed overall distribution and the theoretical distribution that would be obtained if the factors of inequality other than age were eliminated. We have therefore used the Theil index, which is

43

Table 10. Indicators of inequality in the distribution of income overall and by age group in five countries

Country	Year	Recipient	Distribution by age groups			Overall distribution		T_a/T ratio
			Number of age groups	Gini coefficient (C_a)	Theil index (T_a)	Gini coefficient (C)	Theil index (T)	
Brazil	1970	Economically active person	8	0.183	0.0658	0.569	0.5983	0.110
Malaysia	1968	Economically active person						
Total population			6	0.133	0.0316	0.498	0.4691	0.067
			10	0.143	0.0355			0.076
Malays			6	0.109	0.0211	0.463	0.3850	0.055
			10	0.112	0.0222			0.058
Chinese			6	0.183	0.0633	0.483	0.4414	0.143
			10	0.188	0.0643			0.146
Mexico	1968	Family head	5	0.088	0.0132	0.532	0.5798	0.023
Philippines	1968	Family head	6	0.036	0.0033	0.493	0.4412	0.007
	1970 –71	Family head	6	0.091	0.0141	0.476	0.4237	0.033
United States	1972	Family head	6	0.112	0.0243	0.358	0.2159	0.113

Sources: Brazil: Langoni, "Income distribution and economic development in Brazil" (1975); Malaysia: Anand, *The size distribution of income in Malaysia* (1973); Mexico: van Ginneken, *Socio-economic groups and income distribution in Mexico* (1980), p. 41; Philippines: Encarnación, *Income distribution in the Philippines: The employed and the self-employed* (1974); and Kuznets, "Demographic aspects of the size distribution of income" (1976); United States: Paglin, "The measurement and trend of inequality" (1975).

decomposable and which enables us to calculate the percentage of overall inequality attributable to age.

Table 10 shows (as Kuznets had suggested on the basis of statistics referring to only two countries) that the contribution of age to inequalities is much lower in developing countries than it is in the United States. This conclusion seems to be weakened by the case of Brazil and, to a lesser extent, by that of Malaysia, where the relationship T_a/T approximates that which is found in the United States. Those relationships are not, however, comparable. In Brazil and in Malaysia the distribution is by economically active persons, not by heads of households as in the other countries; consequently, many young persons with low incomes who are not heads of families are included in one case and excluded in the other. The proportions of heads of families and of economically active persons under the age of 25 are very different: from 3 to 8 per cent for heads of families and from 28 to 30 per cent for economically active persons. It is probable that among the economically active persons aged under 25, those who are already heads of families are mostly those with the highest incomes. Consequently, it may be assumed that the ratios T_a/T for Brazil and Malaysia for the distribution by families would be reduced by about half, that is, 0.06 and 0.04.

Thus the age factor alone, without taking into account its interactions with other factors, serves to explain 11 per cent of the inequalities in the United States but only 3 to 4 per cent of the inequalities in the four comparatively undeveloped countries listed in table 10 (6 per cent in Brazil). Hence any comparison between developed and developing countries is biased. In the developed countries, the real inequalities measured over a lifetime are markedly lower than the inequalities measured over only a year. In the developing countries the inequalities are almost the same whatever the period chosen. Taking two imaginary countries that are representative of the two groups, in the developed country there is a Gini coefficient of 0.35 while in the developing country there is a Gini coefficient of 0.5; there is an apparent difference of 43 per cent. If the Gini coefficient were calculated over a lifetime, they would be 0.31 and 0.48 to 0.485 respectively, with the real difference reaching 55 to 57 per cent.

If the incomes of heads of families are considered in terms of age, the differences between the United States and the four other countries listed in table 10 are products of several factors. The proportion of young households is higher in the United States. Since those households have a lower income than the average their presence increases the disparities related to age, whereas the low proportion of such households in the developing countries reduces such inequality. (In the United States those young people have an income which, even though it may be much below the national average, is high enough in absolute terms to enable them to start a family; such is not the case in the developing countries.) In the developing countries the income of young people who work but cannot leave their families is added to the family head's. In those countries the proportion of old people, whose income is likewise below the national average, is comparatively small. Nevertheless their income diminishes less than in the United States, mainly because the share of non-wage incomes, which do not necessarily diminish with age, is greater and because the proportion of self-employed economically active persons, who continue to work after reaching the age of 65, is much larger.

The statistics concerning Malaysia reveal an interesting disaggregation by ethnic origin. The two indicators show considerable differences between Malays and Chinese: for C_a, 0.109 and 0.183; for T_a, 0.0211 and 0.0633. Yet the average income per economically active person is almost twice as high for the Chinese as for the Malays. The proportion of economically active persons who have not received any education is 22 per cent for the Chinese and 33 per cent for the Malays, while the proportion of economically active persons who have received a secondary or higher education is twice as high for the Chinese (26 per cent) as for the

Malays (13 per cent). The distribution of the economically active population shows also that Malays are relatively much more numerous in agriculture. All these data serve to show that as the rate of secondary and higher education rises and the average income increases and as the percentage of employment in agriculture diminishes, the share of the inequalities due to age increases. This analysis by ethnic origin thus confirms the interpretation suggested by the international comparison.

Life expectancy

The introduction of the life cycle concept reveals a second bias in comparisons between developed and developing countries: account must be taken of considerable differences in life expectancy. In the developed countries such differences exist also, but they are small, and the life expectancy even for the most underprivileged corresponds to the age of retirement. In the developing countries, on the other hand, there are very wide differences in life expectancy.

In Zimbabwe, where in 1969 the average income per economically active person amounted to 193 dollars for Africans and 3,150 dollars for non-Africans, the expectation of life varied from 37.5 years for Africans to 70.5 years for non-Africans. In South Africa the differences remain very large: 46.5 years for the Black population, 55.5 years for the Indian population and 67.5 years for the White population. In countries such as Algeria and Argentina a difference of 12 years has been found between a poor rural area and the capital city. The differences in life expectancy seem to be greater if there are wide disparities of income. This fact is hardly surprising since life expectancy depends partly on such factors as the standard of living, the quantity and quality of food consumed, housing conditions and medical care.

Statistics of distribution covering a year do not take these differences in life expectancy into account. If the difference in life expectancy reaches 15 years, it can have a very pronounced effect on inequalities of income received throughout a whole lifetime, as a simple example will show. In the example given in table 11, the unskilled workers have a life expectancy of 50 years and the supervisors of 65 years. The income expectations at the age of 21 (it being assumed that the distribution of ages at death is a normal one with an average of 50 years for workers and 65 for supervisors) amount to:

unskilled workers: $(70 \times 5) + (80 \times 10) + (90 \times 10) + (100 \times 5) = 2,550$;
supervisors: $(400 \times 10) + (600 \times 10) + (800 \times 10) + (750 \times 10) = 25,500$. The annual incomes obtained amount to $2,550/30 = 85$ and $25,500/45 = 567$, showing a disparity of 1 to 6.7 as against a disparity of 1 to 10 for the expected incomes.

Table 11.   Hypothetical annual incomes of workers and supervisors in different age groups

Category	Age (years)				
	21–25	26–35·	36–45	46–55	56–65
Workers	70	80	90	100	100
Supervisors	0	400	600	800	750

Inter-annual variations of low incomes

Thirdly, account must be taken of variations in income in relation to the level of income. In most of the poor countries the first five deciles are composed of farmers and agricultural workers or, in towns, of unemployed persons and the self-employed in the traditional sector, that is, economically active persons whose incomes vary from year to year. The average income of those five deciles taken together does not, of course, vary significantly from one year to another. Each year, the first decile comprises the most underprivileged persons, most of whom have a permanent income that is higher than the average income of that decile. Yet, although the share of those five deciles may be constant and, therefore, significant whatever year may be chosen for the estimate, there remains a hidden inequality between such economically active persons and those of the tenth decile. In the incomes under consideration the casual income component plays a role of importance in some cases, a negligible role in the case of skilled workers and of technical and supervisory staff, and no role at all in the case of public servants. The distribution by decile which shows for the tenth decile an average income ten times higher than the average income of the first five deciles does not take into account inter-annual fluctuations of income. It is clear that a constant annual income of 100 provides a greater degree of utility than an income which varies between 10 and 200 according to the year with an average equal to 100, especially for the poor group, for whom an income of 100 hardly ensures the means of subsistence. The income whose variation calculated over a lifetime is very high should be converted into a constant income throughout the life cycle. Any coefficient is, of course, arbitrary, but it does not seem to be unreasonable to suggest 0.8 or 0.9. In the developed countries, on the other hand, the inter-annual income variation does not depend on the level of income. The incomes of economically active persons are subject to comparable variations in the tenth decile and in the first deciles, so that there is no need to correct the estimates of concentration.

The influence of the differences in expectation of life and of the variations in low incomes has been calculated for four countries of Africa: the Ivory Coast, Tunisia, South Africa and Zimbabwe.

Sharp variations in expectation of life have been assumed for the first two countries (50, 55, 60 and 68 years for deciles 1–4, 5–6, 7–8, 9, 10) and very sharp variations for the last two countries (45, 50, 55, 60 and 61 years for the same groups) and a coefficient of 0.9 has been applied to take into account the larger variation in the incomes of the first five deciles. It has been found that the Gini coefficients of about 0.5 for the Ivory Coast and Tunisia and of 0.6 for South Africa and Zimbabwe increase by 0.032 and by 0.045 and that differences in life expectancy account for most of the increase. Whatever objections may be made to the method used, there remains a marked difference between the developed and the developing countries: the inequalities in life expectancy are much greater for the latter than for the former. Consequently, the incomes received in the developed countries correspond approximately to the profiles of income for the whole of active life at whatever level of income. In the developing countries the incomes received by economically active persons with low incomes, but not by the others, are smaller than those that would be estimated on the basis of income profiles for the whole life cycle.

Regional differences in cost of living

The method of using GDP per head in dollars and shares of cash income for the purpose of analysing the relationship between economic development and distribution of incomes is open to question.[18] In the general theory of distribution, much importance is given to real variables. Moreover, the effective disparities in standards of living cannot be expressed correctly otherwise than in terms of distribution of real incomes. The significance of nominal variations is in any case limited during periods of inflation. Shares of cash income may be only loosely related to real shares, thereby greatly reducing the value of international comparisons.

Experience shows that there are appreciable differences between one region and another in the cost of living, and particularly in the relative prices of food, which accounts for a large part of the consumption of the poorest groups. It is possible, therefore, that the differences found in the distribution of monetary incomes between countries are much influenced by disparities in relative prices, and that those differences would be revealed to be purely fictitious if one reasoned in real terms. Thus a fall in the prices of foodstuffs means a rise in the real incomes of the poor, which may not appear in a distribution of cash incomes. A correct analysis of the relationship between economic development and the distribution of incomes requires, therefore, that the links between development and relative prices shall not be overlooked.

Even in a developed economy there are regional differences in prices, but their incidence on the distribution of incomes is negligible for two reasons: the differences are small and there is relatively little regional variation in average incomes. In the developing countries, on the other hand, the differences are by no means negligible and they can be to the advantage or disadvantage of particular groups, most of whose members fall within particular income brackets. They can have an effect, therefore, on the distribution of incomes.

Three examples will show the extent of those variations. A comparable study of urban and rural costs of living in Ghana shows, for a rural level of 100, an urban level of 112 with weighting based on the structure of rural consumption and of 104 with weighting based on the structure of urban consumption. Thus urban households purchase relatively more goods that are proportionately less expensive for them. The advantageous urban goods are imported foodstuffs and transport services. In rural areas all goods produced locally are less expensive than in towns, whether they be, for example, agricultural produce or clothing or furniture.[19]

In Indonesia the index of prices (for 62 products) varies from 100 (Jakarta) to 155 (Kalimantan East) and to 79 (Nusatenggara West). In Java alone the variations drop from a maximum of 100 for the capital city to 87 at Jogjakarta.[20]

For Zambia two urban and rural price indices have been compiled. They are based on the structure of comsumption in urban and rural areas respectively. That fact explains the difference between the ratios of the two indices (1.2 in one case, 1.45 in the other), products of rural origin accounting for a larger part of the budget in rural than in urban areas. The cost of living would thus seem to be 20 per cent higher in urban than in rural areas, which are inhabited by most of the households comprised in the first three quintiles.[21]

These three examples show that there can be disparities ranging from 10 to 20 per cent between town and country.[22] Consequently the share of the first three quintiles in the distribution of incomes is usually underestimated. If the share amounts to 20 per cent, a 10 per cent correction to take account of differences in cost of living raises it to 21.6 per cent. That effect, though moderate, is not negligible and probably plays a role in most of the developing countries. If it is not taken into account, the rate of concentration will be overestimated, and accordingly so will the difference in inequality of income between developing and developed countries.

Undistributed corporate profits

The distribution of profits to households depends on the legal structure of undertakings and, in particular, on the degree of substitution

49

of incorporated companies for personal family undertakings. If they are self-financing, the large incorporated undertakings distribute less in the form of dividends to their shareholders. As the profits accrue in most cases to shareholders with high incomes, the retention of profits entails a reduction of those incomes and thus a reduction in inequality of distribution. It has been held that international comparisons lead to an overestimation of inequality in the poor countries by comparison with the rich countries where the concentration of undertakings is more advanced and where the retention of profits is more frequent. It has even been suggested that if the undistributed profits could be imputed to households all reduction of inequality of personal incomes which accompanies increases in GDP per head would vanish.[23] The facts are that in the poorest countries (those in which GDP per head falls below 100 dollars) the modern sector accounts for a very small part of national output and the undistributed profits of companies are negligible. In a country such as the United States, [24] on the other hand, undistributed profits amount to 4 per cent of the incomes of households. Since they are not usually taken into account in estimates of income distribution and are imputable mainly to households in the last quintile, there is underestimation of the concentration. In the developing countries with a GDP above 200 or 300 dollars per head, companies already play an important role, at any rate in the modern sector, and their undistributed profits can represent 2 to 4 per cent of incomes. For Malaysia undistributed profits have been estimated at 2.2 per cent of household incomes and they have been imputed entirely to the tenth decile, which thereby rises from 43.1 to 44.2 per cent.[25] For Colombia the same incomes have been estimated at 3 per cent, a proportion that seems likely to increase.[26] Since the ownership of stocks and shares in the developing countries is concentrated, the effect of underestimation as analysed here should be as important in the developing countries as in the developed countries, among which, it may be noted, the United States percentage exceeds the corresponding figures in France, in Italy and in the United Kingdom. Even so, the concentration of incomes in all those countries is underestimated relatively to the developing countries, where companies account for a very small part of output.

Resulting distortions

The taking into account of the various biases inherent in any comparison of income distribution in countries at different levels of development must lead to a qualified conclusion. In the case of very poor countries, it is possible that the effects of underestimation of concentration relating to the life cycle are balanced by the opposite effects due to the virtual absence of company savings and to differences between urban and rural costs of living. In the developing countries for which the Gini coefficients show the greatest differences from those for the developed countries, the effects of underestimation of concentration may prevail over the effect of overestimation relating to price differences. It can be stated that, for the countries in which GDP per head in 1970 lay between 300 and 1,000 dollars, the coefficients corrected to take account of all the biases that have been considered, that is, the coefficients corresponding to the real inequalities in standards of living, would tend to be higher than those that were estimated in the first part of the present chapter. The comparison of the series in table 7 and of those of Ahluwalia and Paukert has already shown that the use of more reliable data leads to higher average values for the Gini coefficient in the intermediate income brackets (GDP per head falling between 200 and 700 dollars). Furthermore, the analysis of the biases that are not taken into account in those series reveals an underestimation of the Gini coefficient for the countries at the intermediate-income level relatively to the others. It is permissible, therefore, to assert that the real disparity in average concentration of incomes between intermediate-income countries and the developed countries or the underdeveloped countries is higher than indicated in the series that are usually quoted.

Notes

[1] Jain: *Size distribution of income* (1975).

[2] Adelman and Morris: *An anatomy of patterns of income distribution in developing countries* (1971).

[3] Ahluwalia: "Income inequality" (1974).

[4] See Theil: *Economics and information theory* (1967); idem: *Statistical decomposition analysis, with application in the social and administrative sciences* (1972).

[5] Lecaillon and Germidis: *Inégalité des revenus et développement économique* (1977), pp. 62–63.

[6] See van Ginneken: *The regional and rural-urban income distribution in the Sudan* (1975); idem: *Rural and urban income inequalities in Indonesia, Mexico, Pakistan, Tanzania and Tunisia* (1976), pp. 11–23; Pyatt: "On international comparisons of inequality" (1977), pp. 71–75.

[7] Berry and Urrutia: *Income distribution in Colombia* (1976).

[8] Bourguignon: "Oil and income distribution in Venezuela, 1968–87" (1980).

[9] These various mechanisms have been brought to notice in several studies. See, for example, Lean: *The pattern of income distribution in West Malaysia, 1957–1970* (1974), p. 25; Henry: *A note on income distribution and poverty in Trinidad-and-Tobago* (1975), pp. 5, 31; Lecaillon and Germidis, op. cit., p. 64.

[10] The necessary information appears as follows:

Income bracket (monetary units per household)	Number of households										Total
	By size in terms of number of members										
	1	2	3	4	5	6	7	8	9	10 or more	
0–100	300	500	800	600	500	450	400	300	280	410	4 540
101–200	280	450	850	700	650	600	500	310	300	500	5 140
201–300	. . . .										
. . . .											

If the average income of the households within each bracket is known, for example, 80, 140, 245 monetary units, it suffices to divide that income by the number of persons per household to find that, in the first income bracket, there are—
300 persons whose income is equal to 80 units;
1,000 persons whose income is equal to 40 units;
2,400 persons whose income is equal to 27 units; and so on.
Similarly, in the second income bracket there are—
280 persons whose income is equal to 140 units;
900 persons whose income is equal to 70 units; etc.
There are two main drawbacks to this method. On the one hand, it is assumed that the average income of a household is the same whatever may be the number of persons in the household, whereas it is probable that that income increases with household size even if it remains, by definition, within the bracket considered. On the other hand, no account is taken of the ages of the members of the household nor of the economies of scale resulting from the household's size. For example, a household composed of two parents and six children is reckoned as being composed of eight persons, while a household composed of only two adults is reckoned as consisting of two persons; yet in fact a same income per person in the two households ensures a higher standard of living for the first one than for the second. A scale of adult-equivalents should be applied in order to compare incomes by adult-equivalent. The sources that have been used do not indicate the structure of the household for each household size and each income bracket. On the economies of scale achieved by large households, see van Ginneken: *Rural and urban income inequalities in Indonesia, Morocco, Pakistan, Tanzania and Tunisia* (1976) pp. 19–22.

[11] Kuznets: "Demographic aspects of the size distribution of income" (1976).

[12] Thanks to data assembled by Hsia and Chau—their *Industrialisation, employment and income distribution* (1978)—and by Henry: *A note on income distribution and poverty in Trinidad-and-Tobago* (1975).

[13] See for Trinidad and Tobago, Henry, op. cit., and for Hong Kong, Hsia and Chau, op. cit., pp. 66 et seq.

[14] These results have been found in Hong Kong by Hsia and Chau, op. cit., p. 23; in Japan by Wada: *Changes in the size distribution of income in postwar Japan* (1974), pp. 32, 37, 43, and *Impact of economic growth on the size distribution of income* (1975), pp. 26–27, 35, 42, 57, 73–74; in Trinidad and Tobago by Henry, op. cit., pp. 10–11. On the link between a rise in family income and the setting up of separate households, see Reder: "A partial survey of the theory of income size distribution" (1969), p. 246.

[15] See de Navarrete: "La distribución del ingreso en México" (1971).

[16] Mizoguchi, Kim and Chung: "Overtime changes of the size distribution of household income in Korea, 1963–71" (1976).

[17] Paglin: "The measurement and trend of inequality" (1975).

[18] See Beckerman: "Some reflections on redistribution with growth" (1977).

[19] Knight: "Rural-urban income comparisons and migration in Ghana" (1972).

[20] Lydall: *Employment and income distribution in developing countries, with special reference to Indonesia and Sri Lanka* (unpublished).

[21] See van der Hoeven: *Zambia's income distribution during the early seventies* (1977).

[22] For a similar conclusion relating to the Sudan, see van Ginneken: *The regional and rural-urban income distribution in the Sudan* (1976), p. 16.

[23] Pyatt, "On international comparisons of inequality" (1977), p. 73.

[24] See Pechman and Okner: *Who bears the tax burden?* (1974).

[25] Lean: *Employment and income distribution in West Malaysia* (1975).

[26] Bourguignon: *General equilibrium analysis of the Colombian income distribution* (1978).

INEQUALITY AND DUALISM

3

The general distribution of incomes is necessarily linked to the structure of the economy and, in particular, to the distribution of the labour force among the various sectors. As the conditions of production and of remuneration vary with the sector, there are likewise different distributions of people according to the sector, and population shifts between the sectors as a result of economic development react automatically on the general distribution of incomes.

Being constructed along those lines, the models referred to in Chapter 1 indicate that the general distribution of incomes depends on three principal factors: the levels of the relative average incomes in the various sectors of the economy; the relative importance of the sectors as measured by the proportions of the population which they employ; and the extent of the dispersion of incomes within each sector. These factors not only account for the system of distribution at a particular moment in time; they also enter into analyses of changes in that distribution over time: the intersectoral differences in income tend to set up population movements from the least remunerative sectors towards those that provide the highest incomes; the relative weights of the sectors undergo changes; and the intersectoral differences, as well as the dispersions of income within the sectors, may change in their turn.

In the developing countries, the differences in average income between industries or services are generally less marked than the disparity between agriculture and non-agricultural activities, which is the principal factor in urban-rural inequality. Hence the overriding importance that is attached to it in many studies.[1] In the early stages of development, that distinction largely tallies with the distinction between the traditional sector and the modern sector: it reflects that structural dualism of the economy which is held to be one of the fundamental causes of the general inequality of incomes.

DISPARITIES IN AVERAGE INCOMES BETWEEN THE RURAL AND THE URBAN SECTOR

In the highly developed countries, the inequality of cash incomes reflects well enough the disparities in real incomes between the main groups of the population. In the developing countries, on the other hand, that assimilation of cash to real incomes is much less clear-cut. In the comparisons between the urban and the rural population, the importance of production for own consumption in rural environments, the disparities in prices and cost of living between town and country and the sense of solidarity that links together the members of the larger families all introduce biases that are not to be overlooked in the relationship between statistically established incomes and the standards of living. Subject to these reservations, it is possible to furnish some indications on the extent and the causes of intersectoral income disparities.

Extent of disparities

Table 12 shows the available statistical information on intersectoral inequalities of income for 12 developing countries. It reveals that the disparities in average income between the non-agricultural sector and the agricultural sector vary between 203 and 252 (average agricultural income = 100) in seven non-African countries that have been considered, whereas they range from 394 to 885 in the five African countries. Among the latter, the smallest disparity is found in the Ivory Coast, which is the country in which cash crops are the most developed, whereas the largest disparities appear in Madagascar and in Swaziland, which are the poorest countries where subsistence agriculture predominates. Rural-urban disparities decline in line with reductions in agricultural employment, which accounts for 81–82 per cent of the economically active population in Madagascar and in Swaziland, for 66 per cent in the Ivory Coast and for about 50 per cent in the non-African countries (30.7 per cent in Colombia). The contrast between the African countries and the others is easy to explain: while the share of agriculture in the incomes is no greater, amounting roughly to an average of 35 per cent instead of 30 per cent, the share of agriculture in employment is much larger in the African countries.

These differences between continents are reflected with regard to intersectoral distribution (assuming the dispersion of incomes within each sector to be nil) in Gini coefficients ranging from an average of about 0.2 in the non-African countries to 0.33 in the Ivory Coast, 0.4 in Senegal and in Zambia, 0.43 in Madagascar and 0.48 in Swaziland. The Theil index shows the same variations: under 0.1 in the non-African countries and from 0.226 to 0.558 in the African countries. The share of the intersectoral income disparity in the Theil index for the overall distri-

Table 12. Distribution of incomes and indicators of inequality between the agricultural sector and the non-agricultural sector in 12 developing countries

Item	Ivory Coast 1970	Madagascar 1970	Senegal 1970	Swaziland 1974	Zambia 1972	Colombia 1972	Mexico 1968	Iran 1972	Rep. of Korea 1970	Malaysia 1967	Philippines 1961	Turkey 1970
Distribution of economically active persons (percentages):												
Agricultural sector	66	81.1	74	82	66.7	30.7	46.7	47.1	52.2	50.1	53	49.2
Non-agricultural sector	34	18.9	26	18	33.3	69.3	53.3	52.9	47.8	49.9	47	50.8
Distribution of incomes (percentages):												
Agricultural sector	33	37.8	35	34	27	15.7	26.7	30.4	30.3	28.8	32.5	31.8
Non-agricultural sector	67	62.2	65	66	73	84.3	73.3	69.6	69.7	71.2	67.5	68.2
Average income of non-agricultural sector (agricultural sector = 100)	394	706	532	885	541	239	245	203	252	248	234	208
Indices of inequality:												
Gini coefficient:												
Inter-sectoral distribution[1]	0.33	0.433	0.390	0.480	0.397	0.15	0.213	0.167	0.219	0.213	0.205	0.174
Overall distribution	0.517	.	0.549	0.667	0.648	0.55	0.597	0.591	0.400	0.550	0.520	0.579
Theil index:												
Inter-sectoral distribution,[1] (a)	0.226	0.452	0.334	0.558	0.329	0.06	0.094	0.058	0.098	0.098	0.085	0.062
Overall distribution, (b)	0.506	.	0.713	0.877	0.835	0.628	0.699	0.673	0.278	0.553	0.47	0.613
Ratio a/b	0.44	.	0.47	0.64	0.39	0.09	0.13	0.09	0.35	0.18	0.18	0.1

Key: . = Figure not available.
[1] The dispersion of incomes within each sector is assumed to be nil.

bution of incomes thus varies very widely: it is of the order of 10 per cent in Colombia, Mexico, Iran and Turkey; of 20 per cent in Malaysia and in the Philippines; 35 per cent in the Republic of Korea; 40 per cent in Zambia; 45 per cent in the Ivory Coast; and from 45 to 65 per cent in Madagascar, Senegal and Swaziland.

The Republic of Korea differs sharply from countries such as Colombia, Mexico, Iran and Turkey because the overall income inequality in that country is relatively low, so that the same intersectoral income disparity accounts for a much larger part of the overall Theil index.

Among the African countries, the Ivory Coast calls for special attention because it is the country where cash crops have been the most highly developed. A comparison with the opposite situation (Madagascar, Swaziland) shows that the intersectoral inequalities have not been increased by that policy: the Ivory Coast is, after Zambia, the African country where the part of the overall Theil index imputable to the income disparity between the agricultural sector and the non-agricultural sector is the smallest. In Zambia, employment in the non-agricultural sector is as important, relatively, as in the Ivory Coast, especially owing to the importance of Zambian mining; the share of agriculture in the national income is smaller because commercial farming is less developed. The development of cash crops is not, however, everywhere as advanced as in the Ivory Coast: it is less satisfactory in Senegal owing to the unremunerative character of the cultivation of groundnuts and to the relatively lower productivity of its agriculture.

Causes of disparities

The various factors accounting for inequality of incomes can be classified as economic, political or social.

In the first rank of the specifically economic causes of differences in income are the differences in productivity between agriculture and the rest of the economy. Measured by gross product per economically active person, the productivity of the non-agricultural sectors has been found to be 2.3 times higher than agricultural productivity in Pakistan, 3.8 times higher in Tunisia, 4.3 times higher in Iran and 5.7 times higher in Mexico.[2]

Such wide differences in productivity are due to the backwardness of production techniques in the traditional agricultural sector and to differences in such factors as the quantity of capital per worker, the levels of education and skill, the development of the economic infrastructure and of public services, the proximity to sources of supply and to markets, and the pull exercised on entrepreneurs, capital and labour by opportunities to expand economic activities.

Furthermore, irrespective of whether or not land is available to them in sufficient quantity, it is often difficult for rural workers to draw a stable and regular income from agriculture. Owing to the seasonal character of the work, agriculture often cannot provide opportunities of productive employment throughout the year; there is consequently an underemployment of the labour force which contributes to the maintenance of low incomes. That situation is aggravated in the case of production for export by the fluctuations of international markets, which generate a marked instability of agricultural incomes even though they can be supported from stabilisation funds.

Lastly, the inequality between urban and rural areas can result from a deterioration in the terms of trade for agricultural produce. When the quantity of agricultural produce required for the acquisition of a particular quantity of non-agricultural products increases over the years, the purchasing power of farmers diminishes relatively to that of town dwellers.[3]

To these economic causes of income disparities can be added causes of a political nature. In very many developing countries taxes are levied on exported agricultural produce or on goods purchased by farmers, and dues are payable to produce marketing boards. The burden of these deductions can be heavy. It has been calculated that in the Ivory Coast taxes and dues amounted to a minimum of 30 per cent of farmers' cash incomes, whereas such charges on non-agricultural activities amounted to some 25 per cent.[4] In Nigeria produce marketing fees and costs depress the producer prices to levels of 40 to 65 per cent of the world market prices for certain commodities.[5] This revenue is used largely for the financing of investments, but not necessarily in the agricultural sector.

In general, one of the reasons for low agricultural productivity and incomes lies in the unequal distribution of public expenditure among the various sectors of the economy. The development budget of the Fourth Five-year Plan in Iran, for example, allocated only 13.5 per cent of its total to agriculture, spending 66 per cent on industry. It seems, moreover, that the distribution of agricultural credit benefited the richer rural groups relatively more than the others, thereby increasing inequality within the rural areas themselves.[5]

Among the social factors bearing on the income disparities between town and country, reference must be made to the sense of solidarity lying behind transfers which lead to a private redistribution between the urban and rural sectors. The concept of transfer covers a wide variety of operations: remittances made by migrants for the subsistence of their families left behind in the villages; assistance given to new migrants or unemployed workers by families receiving them in the towns; assistance given by country folk to relatives established in towns. The inquiries that have been carried out have generally shown that a large proportion of migrants regularly send to their families in the villages substantial portions of their earnings, at any rate during the early phase of their establishment. It has also been found, however, that there are remittances from country to town for the benefit of migrants during the months following their departure. It is not always easy to evaluate the net results of these two-way transfers.

RELATIVE EFFECTS OF MIGRATION ON THE TWO SECTORS

The general distribution of incomes depends not only on the disparities of income between the sectors but also on the relative sizes of the populations at work in the sectors. The size of each sector's population changes under the effect of migrations, which, in the developing countries, consist of massive and continuous movements of persons and families from rural to urban areas.

Despite the social and human problems which they raise, these population movements are not systematically regarded as undesirable by development experts. According to many theoretical studies, development implies a transformation of an agricultural economy into an industrial and predominantly urban economy. Such transformation is feasible only at the cost of a progressive absorption of rural workers by an expanding industrial and urban sector. The movement of migrants from regions of low productivity and low incomes to areas of high productivity and incomes ensures a more efficient employment of human resources.

Intersectoral income disparities have an initial role to play in the redistribution of productive energies: they constitute the principal driving force behind migrations and one of the factors that should lead to a better equilibrium in the employment market. As a result, the relative importance of urban areas tends, of course, to increase and they exercise an ever growing influence on the general distribution of incomes.

Causes of migration

Most of the inquiries conducted in various parts of the world show that, while the motives of migrants are complex mixtures of reluctance to leave the countryside where they were born and of attraction to an urban environment, the economic factors seem to play a predominant role. Country people migrate because they have grounds for believing that they and their families will lead better lives elsewhere. A high rate of migration reflects pronounced inter-regional and intersectoral inequalities in economic or population growth: it is a process of dynamic adjustment.[6]

Population pressure, lack of land due sometimes to the system of tenure, difficulties in finding jobs in rural areas, low agricultural productivity and low incomes—all these are among the causes of migration that are most frequently mentioned. The problem of employment is often referred to in the inquiries, especially in the case of young men, who constitute the majority of migrants. The fact that, before leaving the countryside, many migrants were in employment merely shows that they did not have suitable work on the family farm or that they considered their earnings to be insufficient by comparison with what they hoped to obtain in the town. Employment and income are thus the two motives for migration that are given priority in most of the studies. Migrants are attracted mainly by the employment opportunities in towns, the higher level of earnings and possibilities of education and training in line with their aspirations. The presence of relations or friends in towns facilitates migrations, which, with migrants joining their relations and wives joining their husbands, assume a family character that extends and consolidates individual departures.[7]

A systematic analysis of migratory movements has been undertaken in several studies based especially on the Harris and Todaro model. In that model, the attraction exercised by the town on the rural population depends principally on the income disparity between the urban sector and the rural, on the cost of migration and on the probability of finding a job in the towns.[8]

If the income disparity between town and country exceeds a certain level, taking into account the cost of migration and all the monetary and non-monetary advantages and disadvantages of urban life, the influx of labour will cause a certain amount of urban unemployment. As a rule, the greater the disparity of income between town and country, the higher will be the rate of urban unemployment. For a given intersectoral income disparity, the creation of new jobs in the towns can lead paradoxically, by stimulating migration, to an increase in urban unemployment. That fact has been established in various countries, including for example Kenya.[9] It has been held nevertheless that there was an equilibrium rate of unemployment at which migration could be stopped, and that the rate in question could be lowered by a reduction of the income disparity between town and country. It is to be noted, however, that it is difficult to lower real urban wages below a certain minimum without adversely affecting the efficiency of the labour force.

The existence of a so-called "informal" sector can stimulate migration by facilitating the entry of country people into the urban economy. Moreover, when that sector expands and provides occupations for more than a negligible proportion of paid or self-employed labour, it re-establishes in the urban areas a type of dual economy which exercises an influence on the distribution of incomes. In a country such as Turkey it is the public sector that absorbs some of the migrants, who manage to find somewhat unproductive and poorly paid jobs in public undertakings in which they have family or village relations. In this extreme case, the volume and the growth of public employment are determined to some extent by the migratory influx and it is by no means certain that a situation of equilibrium can be established.[10]

Influence of migration on income distribution

Migration exercises an undoubted influence on the distribution of incomes, especially by unbalancing the urban employment market (a problem to which reference will be made again in the next chapter). Nevertheless, it is not easy to assess the net result of that influence because it is a complex one; and there is, in particular, nothing that could warrant an assertion that migration constitutes a major cause of aggravations of income inequalities in the early stages of economic development.

It can be said in a general way that migration has an effect on the overall dispersion of incomes either by modifying the income disparities between town and country (inter-regional or intersectoral disparities) or by modifying the dispersions of incomes in rural or urban areas respectively (intrasectoral dispersions).

Inter-regional and intersectoral income disparities

So far as income disparities between town and country, or, more generally, inter-regional income disparities are concerned, migration performs an important function in the course of economic development by facilitating the very structural adjustments that enable the inequalities to be kept within certain limits. It tends to reduce the marginal income differences and the inter-regional income disparities among the migrants. Since migrants, on the whole, move from areas of low incomes to areas of high incomes, in the long run the general dispersion of incomes should be reduced.[11]

Intrasectoral income dispersion

The influence exercised by migration on the dispersion of incomes in rural areas is uncertain. If productivity and income, especially in agriculture, do not diminish after the departure of migrants, it may be expected that the incomes of individuals who stay behind will rise, and consequently that there will be a diminution of inequality. Nevertheless, since migrants tend to be among the young and most active members of the population, their departure means a loss of human capital that can have unfavourable effects on agricultural productivity and stimulate more departures. Ultimately everything depends on the weight of the migrants' marginal contribution to total production in the agricultural sector (for if that contribution were small and if the migrants were underemployed, their departure would not be seriously felt); on the possibility for the people remaining behind to make up for the absence of the migrants, which depends partly on population growth in the agricultural sector; and on the technological changes that may be induced by the reduction in the supply of labour.[11]

In urban areas, migration leads in various ways to an increase in the dispersion of incomes. When the migratory influx exceeds the absorption capacities of the various occupations the migrants, who generally have few qualifications and little occupational experience, remain confined to poorly paid jobs, and their income remains lower than that of other workers. If there is a surplus of labour in those jobs, work will be paid at cheap rates, thereby modifying the distribution of incomes to the disadvantage of recipients of low incomes. The migrants doubtless succeed in due course in merging with the rest of the urban population so that the differences between them and the inhabitants of urban origin ultimately vanish; but as long as the migratory influx continues there will be a group of poorly paid new migrants and the disparities in average income between the immigrants and the previously established local population will be maintained: there will be two subgroups of population between which inequalities will endure.

During the first stages of development that situation may entail the formation in urban areas of a dual structure marked by the coexistence of strongly capital-intensive modern activities and of a sector of the traditional type. The dispersion of incomes can be more pronounced in the traditional urban sector than in the traditional rural sector, and the differences in income between the traditional urban sector and the modern urban sector can be considerable. Through the establishment of that dualism, migration contributes to an increase of income inequalities in the towns. In many cases the larger the towns or the faster their development, the greater is the dispersion of urban incomes.

In a word, migration contributes to a widening of the dispersion of urban incomes by industries, occupations or levels of education, while at the same time increasing the importance of urban areas relatively to rural areas. It explains in some measure why the inequality of incomes is often greater in towns than in the countryside and why the general dispersion of incomes tends to become accentuated during the early stages of development. For as long as there remains a large rural sector, it will take years of sustained economic growth for adjustments to urban dualism to be made and for poverty to be eliminated from the towns.[12]

INCOME DISPERSION IN THE RURAL SECTOR

Although the general dispersion of incomes depends both on disparities between the urban sector and the rural sector and on dispersion within each of these two sectors, most of the statistical breakdowns that have been made for various countries indicate that the role played by intersectoral inequalities is not always decisive. A determining factor in the general dispersion of incomes is inequality within the rural sector and within the urban sector. So far as the rural sector is concerned, it is the system of distribution of land on which stress is generally laid since the concentration of landed property normally must lead to a concentration of agricultural incomes. The influence of that factor of inequality is, however, combined with other factors that are connected mainly with trading for cash and with participation in a market economy.

Land ownership and the dispersion of agricultural incomes

The structure of landed property differs from one country to another: it is the result of a historical process in the course of which the development of institutions and customs interacts with demographic change and produces an employment structure that largely determines the distribution of agricultural incomes.[13]

In historical accounts of present-day land ownership, prominence has been given to the effects of population growth within a given institutional framework when the supply of land is limited.

When the surplus population in rural areas is not drained off by migration to the towns, there will be, at first, a progressive fragmentation of the land, which is often hastened by inheritance laws requiring strict equality in the division of inheritances among all the children or by sales attributable to migration, indebtedness and the cost of bringing up children. As a rule, the process of fragmentation has pernicious effects on agricultural productivity. At a later stage that situation leads to the simultaneous appearance of two extreme groups: a landless peasantry and big landowners. When a property becomes too small to sustain its owner, all he can do is sell it to someone who can afford to buy it. Landless peasants and big landowners thus appear on the scene together.

A distinction has to be drawn, however, between the extent of a holding and the size of a cultivation unit. It is possible, for example, for small landowners to rent lands to others with a view to forming cultivation units that are economically viable; they may also rent plots of land to large landowners. Conversely, the latter, for fear of land reform or of a land tax, may transfer ownership of some of their land to members of their family while reserving the use of such land for themselves. These various practices introduce a bias into the relationship between land concentration and concentration of agricultural incomes inasmuch as renting agreements bring about, in particular, a redistribution of land and of the income it provides.

Access to land determines access to employment and to the income that it provides. From that point of view, a distinction should be drawn among the economically active agricultural population between farmers and agricultural labourers.[14] Whether they be landowners or tenants, the farmers are responsible for a unit of production. Their essential characteristic is that they have the use of a piece of land. The extent of that right of use of land is of great importance by reason of the seasonal character of agricultural work.

Some farmers have holdings that are large enough to keep them fully occupied throughout the year; at peak periods they call in seasonal workers from outside the farm. Others have farms requiring their continuous presence but without having recourse, unless exceptionally, to outside workers. There remain the small farmers whose holdings are too small to occupy them fully throughout the year; they are, to some extent, underemployed workers but, because their farm requires a minimum of attendance from them, they are prevented from taking a supplementary job elsewhere. For this last group there is, by comparison with the other farmers, a sharp drop in income which may be out of proportion with the difference in the sizes of the farms.

Farmers thus make up a group that is by no means uniform, and it is clear that the dispersion of agricultural incomes depends partly on its composition, which varies from one country to another.

Working on another's land for a wage in cash or in kind or receiving a part of the harvest, agricultural labourers hold no title to the land which they cultivate. This category of persons is no more homogeneous than the other one. They depend for their employment on the existence of a demand for labour, at any rate during the periods of peak activity. Between those periods they are unemployed or must look for a source of income outside agriculture. The level and the dispersion of incomes depend, in the course of the year, on the number of days of paid work that are available. Those incomes are, therefore, usually very low and extremely variable. The development of this category of landless seasonal labourers thus contributes to the dispersion of incomes. This does not necessarily apply to wage earners on plantations when they have stable employment and when there is no supplementary activity enabling them to increase their earnings in varying proportions.

It must be concluded, therefore, that while the inequality of agricultural incomes increases under the effect of the concentration of land ownership, the extent of that inequality varies with the structure of employment resulting from the concentration of land ownership. Furthermore, the concentration of incomes is nearly always less pronounced than the concentration of land ownership because other factors may come into play.[15]

Commercialisation of agriculture and its integration in the market economy

In the course of economic development, agriculture is increasingly closely linked with other activities. In the rural areas themselves, there is non-agricultural employment in the traditional or modern types of activity. So long as the activities are crafts organised on a family basis, the form of distribution of income remains similar to the one found in family agriculture. Such is not the case with modern activities, especially in the service industries, providing incomes that are higher or more dispersed than those in the agricultural sector.

Of the greatest importance is the development of division of labour not only within rural areas but also between town and country. The large urban centres in touch with the outside world can supply the consumer and capital goods which the rural sector needs. If the rural sector is to have the cash resources required for trading, it must aim at producing goods that can be marketed. Cash trading, which goes hand in hand with the participation of rural activities in a market economy, alters the working conditions on farms, overturns the existing structures and increases the dispersion of incomes in the rural sector.

The growth of cash income, which is in the nature of a supplement to subsistence income, plays an essential role in changes in the distribution of incomes in rural environments. As trading between rural and urban areas expands, rural incomes become mixed, combining income in kind drawn from family food production for own consumption with income in cash drawn from production for the market. This income dualism may correspond to dualism on the farm itself, with a division of labour within the family group. In that situation, ownership of land or a recognised title to occupy land constitutes a fundamental prerequisite governing the possibility of producing for the market or for export. It may then be that the farmer, now possessing marketable products resulting, as is often the case, from land ownership or from a title to occupy land, will be able to allocate to himself an income markedly higher than that of the members of his family who are subject to his authority. If the basic remuneration remains an income in kind close to the minimum needed to support life and fairly equitably distributed, the surplus of resources in cash will be much less equitably distributed. That inadequate distribution of incomes in cash is generally held to be one of the operative factors in flights from the land.[16]

Data are available which allow the effect of the introduction of cash crops on farmers' income to be estimated. The disparity between average income from subsistence agriculture and from traditional agriculture for the market is of the order of 1 to 2 in Senegal, 1 to 2.4 in Colombia and 1 to 3.4 in the Ivory Coast and in Zambia, as well as in Malaysia.[17] The growth of income from cash crops alters the order of importance of the sources of income: without cash crops, the farmer's income remains far below that of an urban unskilled labourer, whereas with cash crops it often exceeds that labourer's income. (This comparison is of special interest inasmuch as the only paid employment which a farmer who migrates to a town can hope to find is that of an unskilled labourer.)

Nevertheless, the disparity in average income between subsistence agriculture and agriculture for the market increases the real differences in standards of living: the prices of food crops are often underestimated relatively to the prices of cash crops. The selling prices of food produce can rise abruptly if there are poor harvests. Lastly, cash crops place the grower in a situation of dependence on external demand, and the risks which that would entail are not taken into account in the foregoing comparison.

The progressive integration of the rural sector in the market economy likewise exercises an influence on the distribution of incomes through the effects of technology. Even under a homogeneous system of small farms, differences in land productivity and the diversity of production techniques lead to inequalities in standards of living between households. Modernisation and the adoption of new methods of production by the most progressive farmers, together with an enlargement of the size of farms, have been regarded as among the factors accounting for increases in the dispersion of incomes in the agricultural sector.[18] In fact, the relationship between the size of farms and productivity is a complex one: it depends on the types of crops and on the nature of the technical innovations. It is frequently the case that output per unit of land is greater on small farms than on large ones, making the distribution of incomes less unequal than that of land.[15]

In Japan, the increase in the dispersion of agricultural incomes that has been recorded since the Second World War appears to be due not to a greater concentration of land but to an increase in disparities in productivity per head following upon a change of course in the technical field: based until then especially on biological and chemical methods, agriculture has become increasingly mechanised, to the benefit of large farms thanks to economies of scale. Yet the sizes of farms have not been radically altered, either because of the limitations required by agrarian reform or because of a rise in the price of land.[19]

What has been happening, in a general way, has been an aggravation of income disparities independently of any change in the distribution of land, especially where the application of new techniques has required heavy capital investment. That is what has happened, for example, in Iran, where despite the agrarian reform of 1962 there was an increase of inequality among rural households due to the fact that credit facilities and the other kinds of assistance provided for by the reform have been of more benefit to the households that were already relatively well-off than to the others.[3] In Sri Lanka likewise, the progress achieved in the cultivation of rice has not, in general, prompted the big landowners to give up tenant farming and to work the land themselves with paid labour and the help of mechanisation. Considerable unemployment has had the

Table 13. Regional distribution of rural cash incomes in the Ivory Coast, 1970

Item	Region			
	I	II	III	IV
Average income (region IV = 100)	1 500	800	300	100
Percentage of the population	5	43	35	17

effect of increasing competition among the landless for tenancy rights even to small plots, and has transformed tenant farming into a form of cheap labour for the landlords. It is less advantageous to the landlords to work the land themselves with wage labour because tenancy gives them a stable supply of labour. Moreover, in the event of a crop failure they can transfer a part of the loss to the tenants. There are, however, cases of "disguised tenancy" under which the tenants are represented as being agricultural labourers, thereby enabling the landlord, who is supposed to work the land himself, to benefit from government loans and subsidies, transferring only a part of them to the tenants.[20]

In these different examples, access to the new techniques, or the nature of advances in agricultural methods, exercises a decisive influence, side by side with the distribution of landed property itself, on changes in the dispersion of incomes. It is to be noted, too, that rural unemployment and the diffusion of new techniques taken together appear to have worsened the position of non-land-owning cultivators such as tenant farmers and share-croppers.

In so far as the different regions of a country are unequally capable of developing marketable outputs, trading for cash is accompanied by an increase in regional income disparities, which constitutes an element of the general dispersion of incomes and of the dispersion of rural incomes in particular. Statistics of rural cash incomes for the Ivory Coast, for example, show wide geographical disparities: from an index of 100 for the region still living on production for own consumption to 1,500 for the region in which marketed crops are the most developed (table 13).

However, these figures overestimate the real income disparities because they do not take into account production for own consumption, which is approximately constant whatever may be the cash income of the cultivator. In the United Republic of Cameroon, in the case of wages alone, there were in 1971 disparities in average wages ranging between an index of 100 (south-west and north-east) and an index of 442 (coastal region, Douala), with intermediate values of about 170 (east, west), 227 (north) and 290 (centre, Yaoundé).[21]

Such disparities are characteristic of developing countries, the disparities in developed countries ranging from 1 to 2 and, in many cases, from 1 to only 1.5. In their extreme forms, these disparities explain the analyses of regional dualism or of a "closed economy" that have been applied to certain developing countries.

INCOME DISPERSION IN THE URBAN SECTOR

Most of the studies indicate that there is more inequality of incomes in the urban than in the rural sectors, though there are some exceptions to that finding. With industrialisation and urbanisation, the weight of the sector in which income distribution is most unequal increases, thereby contributing to an increase in the general dispersion of incomes. Other things being equal, changes in the dispersion of incomes in urban areas thus constitute a determining factor in long-term changes in the inequality of incomes.

The relationship between degree of urbanisation and inequality is not, however, a simple one. Various analyses reveal that the indices of concentration diminish as one moves from small towns to medium-sized ones and then increase in the large conurbations. There would thus appear to be a threshold corresponding to the optimum size of towns from the point of view of income dispersion.

There are various reasons for the increase in inequality after a certain degree of urbanisation has been reached. One of those most frequently mentioned is that the migratory flows tend to go to the larger towns, where there are greater opportunities for employment. As the migrants generally have few qualifications and are ready to take poorly paid jobs, there is an automatic increase in wage differentials. Furthermore, the surplus supply of labour feeds urban unemployment, and it is the volume of unemployment and the hours of work that are among the important causes of dispersion of incomes. (This question will be referred to again in Chapter 4.)

Industrial growth and the appearance of technologically advanced new industries are reflected in increases of productivity which sharpen the contrast with activities of the traditional type. The labour force is more homogeneous in small towns than in large ones, where activities and jobs are more diversified. That diversification is accompanied, as a rule, by an increase in the dispersion of incomes.[22]

Lastly, there is a difference between towns and rural areas in the nature of the incomes themselves. There is generally a separation between income derived from capital and labour in modern urban activities, whereas most of rural incomes are mixed. The functional distinction between profits and wages is more important in large towns than in small ones and partly accounts for changes in distribution in the former. Clearly, these influences are not independent of the occupational status of the income recipients and of their level of education. These two factors will be considered in the next chapter, the remainder of the present chapter being devoted to the roles played by the sector of activity and by functional distribution.[23]

Influence of the sector of activity

The sector of activity plays a role in urban disparities of income as it does in disparities between urban and rural areas. The disparities are, however, generally less pronounced between one activity and another in urban areas than they are between agricultural and non-agricultural activities. They are nevertheless due to similar causes, namely differences in productivity, which are themselves linked to the amount of capital per worker: the more the amount of capital in an industry, the higher do real incomes in that industry tend to be.

Table 14 shows, for Mexico, Hong Kong, Iran and Malaysia, the distribution of incomes of households or economically active persons by sector of activity, with the two indicators of inequality: Gini coefficient and Theil index. The non-agricultural activities are distributed among several sectors: manufacturing industries, construction and public works, transport, trade, services. Table 15 indicates the wage and salary disparities, by sector of activity, for the United Republic of Cameroon, Madagascar and Zambia. Several facts emerge from those figures.

As table 14 shows, it is (outside agriculture) in the textiles industry in Iran and in construction, public works and manufacturing elsewhere that average incomes are the lowest. (In Iran, the fact that the level of income in the textile industry is lower by one-third than the level in agriculture is due to the rate of wages paid to female labour employed in the production of carpets.) It is in the service industries, especially financial services and the public sector, that average incomes are the highest. Relatively to average income per economically active person (100), the maximum disparity is found in the service industries in Malaysia (168) and in Mexico (154), in the public sector and in transport in Iran (215 and 219) and in banking and insurance in Hong Kong (220). The proportion of skilled wage or salary earners is indeed much greater in the service industries than in the rest of the economy. There are also purely sectoral differences: for example, a higher average wage or salary in the service industries than in other industries for the same level of skill. In the urban economy, construction and public works are the least well paid, with an average income lower by a third or a half if not more than for the most highly paid jobs in the service industries. In the manufacturing industries incomes fall within the average income bracket for economically active persons (plus or minus 20 per cent) or above it (index of 150 in Mexico). These relatively large differences between urban activities are due in the

Table 14.   Distribution of incomes by sector of activity and indicators of inequality in Mexico,
Hong Kong, Iran and Malaysia

Item	Indexed average income	Percentage of households or of economically active persons	Percentage of incomes
Mexico (1968, households)			
Agriculture	57.3	46.7	26.7
Manufacturing industries	150.0	12.9	19.3
Construction and public works	93.3	5.5	5.1
Trade	120.2	14.7	17.7
Service industries	154.0	20.2	31.2
Gini coefficient: 0.230			
Theil index: 0.093			
Hong Kong (1971, households)			
Agriculture	53.4	2.9	1.5
Fisheries	167.5	1.4	2.3
Manufacturing industries	79.0	40.7	32.2
Water, electricity	124.8	0.6	0.7
Construction and public works	81.1	7.4	6.0
Transport	96.6	10.1	9.8
Trade	111.5	19.8	22.1
Banking, insurance	219.8	2.9	6.4
Public and personal services	133.9	14.2	19.0
Gini coefficient: 0.287			
Theil index: 0.042			
Iran (1965, economically active persons)			
Agriculture	63.9	47.1	30.4
Manufacturing industries (excluding textiles)	115.0	10.1	11.7
Textiles	42.2	9.1	3.8
Construction and public works	97.1	7.6	7.4
Transport	219.1	3.3	7.3
Trade	178.9	7.6	13.6
Service industries	150.1	10.4	15.5
Public sector	214.7	4.8	10.3
Gini coefficient: 0.275			
Theil index: 0.126			
Malaysia (1968, economically active persons)			
Agriculture	56.9	50.1	28.5
Mining, quarries	129.7	2.4	3.1
Manufacturing industries	109.8	9.2	10.0
Construction and public works	119.4	3.3	3.9
Transport	133.6	3.8	5.1
Trade	145.6	13.8	20.1
Service industries	167.8	17.4	29.3
Gini coefficient: 0.247			
Theil index: 0.105			

Sources: Mexico: van Ginneken, *Socio-economic groups and income distribution in Mexico* (1980), p. 43, table 9; Hong Kong: Hsia and Chau, *Industrialisation, employment and income distribution* (1978), p. 30; Iran: Skolka and Garzuel, *Changes in income distribution, employment and structure of the economy* (1976), p. 97; Malaysia: Lean, *Employment and income distribution in West Malaysia* (1975), p. 34.

Table 15.   Relative levels of wages and salaries by sector of activity in the United Republic of
Cameroon, in Madagascar and in Zambia

Sector	Average wage or salary (agriculture = 100)
United Republic of Cameroon (1971)	
Agriculture	100
Mining	275
Manufacturing industries	221
Construction and public works	215
Electricity, gas, water	354
Transport	267
Trade	354
Banking, insurance	585
Service industries	373
Madagascar (1965)	
Agriculture, domestic services	100
Mining	115
Manufacturing industries	188
Construction and public works	157
Electricity, water	384
Transport	307
Trade, banking, insurance	310
Service industries	227
Zambia (1970)[1]	
Agriculture	100
Mining, quarries	355
Manufacturing industries	202
Construction and public works	140
Transport	278
Banking, insurance	311
Service industries	220

[1] Africans' wages.

Sources: United Republic of Cameroon and Madagascar: Lecaillon and Germidis, *Inégalité des revenus et développement économique* (1977), pp. 152, 155; Zambia: van der Hoeven, *Zambia's income distribution during the early seventies* (1977), p. 38.

first place to the structure of employment, the proportion of skilled workers and of technical, supervisory and executive staff being directly related to the average income in the sector.

The wage and salary disparities in the United Republic of Cameroon, Madagascar and Zambia (table 15) show the same characteristics: minimum in agriculture, maximum in the service industries in general. Domestic services (100 in Madagascar), construction and public works (157 in Madagascar, 140 in Zambia), in which most of the jobs are unskilled, are close to agriculture, whereas the service industries pay wages or salaries that are three or four times higher than the wages paid in agriculture, the highest figures being in financial services: 310 in

Madagascar, 311 in Zambia and 585 in the United Republic of Cameroon. In Zambia the highest wages (355) are paid in the copper mines.

It is difficult to point to any general rules that are valid for all countries because the methods of classification of branches of activity and by large sectors can exercise an influence on the results of the statistical analysis. An overall review has to be confined, therefore, to the indications that appear most frequently in the studies by countries.

Incomes are usually higher in industry and in services, that is, in the most capital-intensive sectors, than in agriculture or in construction and public works. The service industries in the modern sector (trade, banking and even public administration) are in many cases those that pay the highest salaries. That situation, which can be explained on the ground of a lack of commercial and administrative structures or by the high risks that are run in some underdeveloped regions, contributes to the attracting of the available savings and of the élite of the population to those activities. While the creation of jobs can enable a part of the labour force to be absorbed, it is to be feared that too large a proportion of productive resources will be diverted from the production of goods that are essential for a general raising of the standard of living.[24]

The influence exercised on the general dispersion of urban incomes by income disparities between the different sectors is less than that exercised by the disparities within those sectors themselves. It is found in that respect that the dispersion is comparatively wide in the sectors in which average income is high and which are the more capital-intensive, and that it is narrow in the sectors with low incomes.[25] In other words, there is a positive correlation between the level of income and the degree of inequality. Thus the dispersion of incomes is greater in the service industries, banking and insurance than in manufacturing industry, public services and transport. According to some studies, the dispersion increases in the leading sectors, that is, in those that are most modern and rapidly expanding. Nevertheless, it is not possible to say whether that results from the capital-intensive character of the sectors in question and from the high skills of the employees or only from the rapidity of the sectors' growth.

In the case of the developing countries, the dispersion of incomes within each economic sector is correlated in a number of studies with the relative sizes of modern and traditional establishments.[26] The small establishments in which the work is done with simple hand tools pay wages that are low by comparison with the high wages paid in the larger establishments in which the amounts of capital invested per worker are substantial. This explanation shifts to the level of subsectors the analysis based on the dualism between the traditional sector and the modern sector. The less homogeneous the structure of an economic sector, the greater the dispersion of incomes. It is found that the modern character of production and the level of incomes are associated with the size of establishments because it is the large undertakings that can obtain the largest amounts of capital and pay the highest wages. Since the modern undertakings have a more skilled and more diversified labour force, the classification by sector and by branch of activity tallies with the classification by occupation and by level of skill (a question that will be referred to again below).

Influence of functional distribution

It is partly because the profits of undertakings in towns are more unequally distributed than the incomes of farms that the distribution of incomes is more unequal in towns than in the countryside. The influence exercised by the nature of incomes on their distribution has, however, been noted in studies especially in connection with the functional distinction between income from work (wages and salaries) and income from property and from enterprise (profits in the wide sense). In so far as economic development is accompanied by a modification of the relative shares of the factors of production in the national income, there are necessarily effects on the remuneration of the persons possessing those factors.

The distinction between wages and salaries on the one hand and profits on the other is characteristic especially of modern activities, in which in most cases capital is not provided by employed persons. The overall division between these two types of income is particularly decisive for income distribution among persons in the urban sector. That effect can be strengthened or thwarted by the influence of the subdistributions of incomes from capital and of incomes from labour.

Distribution between wages or salaries and profits

The effect of the distribution between wages and profits on the distribution of incomes is not wholly clear: the personal incomes of individuals and of households comprise different functional incomes. It is of importance to define at the outset the link between level of personal income and functional remuneration. That link arises out of a hierarchy of sources of personal incomes: it is usually accepted that the proportion of the incomes resulting from wage or salary employment begins by increasing with rises in the scale of incomes and is then stabilised before decreasing.

Those at the bottom of the scale of incomes are mainly part-time workers, small farmers, craftsmen and traders. Although often regarded as marginal in the industrialised countries, these categories are of considerable economic importance in the developing countries, where the traditional rural sector is predominant and where there is no sharp distinction between employment and unemployment. In practice, the first deciles of the distribution are composed of persons who have no full-time occupation and who are underemployed or are not employed very productively. At the intermediate steps there are the wage earners in regular employment but possessing little or no capital. Further up the scale of remuneration, incomes from property and from entrepreneurship account for growing proportions of the incomes of individuals, these incomes becoming preponderant at the top of the scale.

Leaving out of account the rural areas, where incomes are derived mainly from agriculture, it is obvious that other things being equal, an increase in the share of incomes from work to the detriment of incomes from capital or an increase in real wage or salary rates relatively to rates of profit will have an equalising effect on the distribution of personal incomes. Although incomes from capital are on the average higher than wages, the distribution of incomes from capital is in many cases more dispersed than the distribution of incomes from labour.

However, this line of reasoning cannot be followed without reservation in relation to the developing countries. It has been found, in particular, that in many of them the top income classes included, side by side with incomes from entrepreneurship,[27] many high wages or salaries. The dispersion of incomes from work then becomes particularly wide, taking into account the low levels of wages in the first deciles, and it is not certain that an increase in the share relating to incomes from work will automatically exercise an equalising influence.[28]

Distribution of income from capital

The distribution of income from capital depends basically on the distribution of property, and it is because property is highly concentrated that the inequality of income from capital is generally greater than that of income from work. The position varies widely from one country to another, and the lack of precise information is particularly thwarting in this regard.

According to the most commonly accepted analyses, it is, apart from landed agricultural property, the existence and the exploitation of extensive natural resources that make for the concentration of incomes. Property and incomes from lettings of housing are much less unequally distributed. As for the incomes of industrialists and financiers, their distribution is, of course, linked to the sizes of the undertakings, which themselves depend on the development and amount of accumulated capital. With regard to this last point, it is to be noted that, while the accumulation of capital increases in the long run the share of labour, it can generate at the same time a higher concentration of capital, which constitutes a factor of inequality. The enlargement of undertakings is reflected, in particular, in an increase in the profits of those that are incorporated companies and a reduction of the profits of undertakings under individual ownership; in so far as the capital of the former is held by rich owners of capital and the capital of the latter by small entrepreneurs, there can be no doubt about the trend towards concentration. Account must be taken, lastly, of the fact that in some developing countries the ownership and control of modern undertakings are, to a greater or lesser extent, in the hands of foreign interests and of multinational enterprises.

With regard to the relationship between the concentration of ownership of capital and of undertakings and the concentration of incomes, it has been pointed out that in many cases the profits of incorporated undertakings are not distributed to the shareholders but are used to finance investments directly. Those profits, which form part of the national income and are taken into account in the functional distribution, are excluded from the distribution among persons: they do not enter into the current incomes of households, so that there is a dissociation between the concentration of capital and the inequality of incomes. In other words, the development of the savings of incorporated undertakings and of self-financing makes the concentration of incomes less apparent unless capital gains are reintegrated into the incomes of individuals (this question was referred to at the end of chapter 2).

Distribution of income from work

The distribution of income from work depends partly on the nature of the supply of labour, which will be considered in the next chapter. The structure of wages depends also on the general circumstances attending the establishment of relationships between the supply of, and the demand for, the services of the various categories of workers.

Several studies lay stress on the fact that the wage disparities between skilled and unskilled workers in the non-agricultural sectors will be widened as long as there remains a surplus supply of labour expressed in a migratory outflow from the rural areas towards the towns.[29] In a general way, those disparities may be due to differences in the rate of growth of the demand for labour or to differences in the elasticity of demand. In an economy marked by a surplus of labour, even if the rate of growth of demand is the same for the two categories of worker, the wage disparities will broaden for the simple reason that the supply of unskilled labour is almost infinitely elastic whereas the supply of skilled labour remains inelastic in the medium term.[30]

The foregoing discussion calls for some elaboration.

When economic development is centred on the non-agricultural and mainly urban sectors, the expansion of those sectors must be sufficiently fast to entail an appreciable reduction of the surplus population in the rural areas. However, as long as the modern non-agricultural sectors account for only a small proportion of total employment, even a rapid expansion may remain insufficient to absorb the surplus supply arising out of population growth. In other words, in countries of rapid population growth the rate at which modern and urban activities must expand in order to absorb the surplus of labour may exceed what is physically possible; hence the need to seek a type of growth that will create jobs throughout the economy.

The technical characteristics of the modern sector are often such that any acceleration of growth will first be reflected in an increase in the demand for skilled labour. This differential expansion of demand and the relative inelasticity of the supply of skilled labour leads to a widening of the range of wages. Modern business and services can thus remain isolated from the rest of the economy and pay high wages which cause a break of continuity in the distribution of incomes.

A rapid growth of population and an increase in the number of children per family can have similar consequences in so far as for a given family income, the amount spent on education per child is inversely proportional to the number of children. When quantity thus tends to take the place of quality, the number of unskilled workers will increase relatively to the number of skilled workers, thereby exercising a further influence in the direction of an increase of inequality in the distribution of wages. Such trends have been traced, in particular, in some parts of Latin America, where the dispersion of incomes is especially wide and where there is a high rate of population growth.[31]

The situation will be different when the economy crosses the threshold at which, the surplus labour having been absorbed, labour in general becomes scarce. The supply of unskilled labour no longer being infinitely elastic, the wage disparities will now begin to lessen. The experience of some countries in Asia tends to prove that in those circumstances the wages of unskilled workers rise faster than those of skilled workers; that the wages of young people rise faster than those of adults; and that the wages of workers in small establishments rise faster than those of workers in large undertakings. In the long run, the growing cost of unskilled labour will force the adoption of labour-saving methods, thereby contributing to a reduction of the dispersion by establishment of the capital used per worker.[32]

Taken as a whole, the disparities of remuneration between categories of workers and within each category diminish in the non-agricultural sectors, and it is from the closing up of the structure of wages that a general reduction of inequalities of income between households would result once a certain level of development had been reached.

In explanation of the general dispersion of incomes, the foregoing analysis has laid stress on the general relationships between labour supply

75

and demand and on the volume of employment. It would be imprudent, however, to leave the analysis at that point. It has been found that disparities in remuneration between skilled and unskilled workers are not incompatible with considerable unemployment among workers who have reached a certain level of education. The supply of skilled labour is, therefore, not necessarily inelastic, and a mechanical explanation in terms of supply and demand does not always appear to suffice to account for the dispersion of wages. The differences in levels of education that warrant differences in remuneration are determined partly by socio-cultural factors, which, moreover, vary from one country to another. The analysis must therefore be broadened and the factors accounting for income inequalities must be systematically reviewed.

Notes

[1] See Skolka and Garzuel: *Changes in income distribution, employment and structure of the economy* (1976), p. 10; Lean: *Employment and income distribution in West Malaysia* (1975), p. 42; Szal and van der Hoeven: *Inequality and basic needs in Swaziland* (1976), p. 11; Oberai: *An analysis of migration to Greater Khartoum (Sudan)* (1975), p. 12; Lecaillon and Germidis: *Inégalité des revenus et développement économique* (1977), p. 83.

[2] van Ginneken: *Rural and urban income inequalities in Indonesia, Mexico, Pakistan and Tunisia* (1976), pp. 39–40; Skolka and Garzuel, op. cit., p. 10; Mehran: *Income distribution in Iran* (1975), p. 14.

[3] Mehran, op. cit., pp. 14–15.

[4] Figures quoted by Lecaillon and Germidis: *Inégalité des revenus et développement économique* (1977). p. 217.

[5] Fapohunda, Reijmerink and van Dijk: *Urban development, income distribution and employment in Lagos* (1975).

[6] Oberai: *An analysis of migration to Greater Khartoum (Sudan)* (1975), p. 10.

[7] Among the studies in which these aspects of migration are examined reference may be made to Lecaillon and Germidis: *Inégalité des revenus et développement économique* (1977), pp. 185–195; Oberai, op. cit., pp. 9–10; Fapohunda et al., op. cit., pp. 2/8 et seq.; Szal and van der Hoeven: *Inequality and basic needs in Swaziland* (1976), pp. 11–12; and Miller: *International migration of Turkish workers* (1976), pp. 13 et seq.

[8] Harris and Todaro: "Migration, unemployment and development" (1970); Todaro: *Internal migration in developing countries* (1976).

[9] See Todaro: "Income expectations, rural-urban migration and employment in Africa" (1971), pp. 398–400.

[10] Miller: *The dynamics of human resources development in Turkey and their implications for employment and income distribution* (1975), p. 44.

[11] Oberai: *An analysis of migration to Greater Khartoum (Sudan)* (1975), pp. 34–36.

[12] Hsia and Chau: *Industrialisation, employment and income distribution* (1978), pp. 14–16.

[13] See on this question van Ginneken: *Rural and urban income inequalities in Indonesia, Mexico, Pakistan and Tunisia* (1976), pp. 40–42; Farbman: *Sectoral employment and income distribution in rural India* (1975), pp. 45–49; Miller: *Aspects of income distribution in Turkey* (1975), pp. 23–36.

[14] Farbman, op. cit., pp. 11–16, 27–32.

[15] van Ginneken: *Rural and urban income inequalities in Indonesia, Mexico, Pakistan and Tunisia* (1976), pp. 40–42.

[16] Lecaillon and Germidis: "Income differentials and the dynamics of development" (1976), pp. 27–42.

[17] Ivory Coast and Senegal: Lecaillon and Germidis: *Inégalité des revenus et développement économique* (1977), pp. 124–135, and Morrisson, unpublished study prepared for the Development

Research Center of the World Bank (1974); Colombia: Bourguignon, *General equilibrium analysis of the Colombian income distribution* (1978), p. 32; Zambia: van der Hoeven, *Zambia's income distribution during the early seventies* (1977), pp. 34–43; Malaysia: Lean, *Employment and income distribution in West Malaysia* (1975).

[18] Kuznets: "Quantitative aspects of the economic growth of nations: VIII. Distribution of income by size" (1963), p. 67.

[19] Wada: *Impact of economic growth on the size distribution of income* (1975), pp. 91 et seq.

[20] Gooneratne: *Land tenure, government policies and income distribution in Sri Lanka* (1979), pp. 16, 42.

[21] Lecaillon and Germidis: *Inégalité des revenus et développement économique* (1977), pp. 106, 82.

[22] Mehran: *Income distribution in Iran* (1975), pp. 25–27.

[23] On the relationship between the degree of urbanisation and the inequality of incomes and on the factors referred to here, see Miller: *Aspects of income distribution in Turkey* (1975), pp. 16–19; and van Ginneken: *Rural and urban income inequalities in Indonesia, Mexico, Pakistan and Tunisia* (1976), pp. 42–45.

[24] Lecaillon and Germidis, op. cit., pp. 139–140.

[25] Hsia and Chau: *Industrialisation, employment and income distribution* (1978), p. 33.

[26] Wada: *Impact of economic growth on the size distribution of income* (1975), pp. 114–124.

[27] See ILO: *Household income and expenditure statistics*, No. 2: *1960–1972*, Part 1: *Africa, Asia, Latin America*, and No. 3: *1968–1976*.

[28] See Carnoy et al.: *Can educational policy equalise income distribution in Latin America?* (1979), pp. 5–7; Mangahas: *Income inequality in the Philippines* (1975), pp. 3–4; van Ginneken: *The regional and rural-urban income distribution in the Sudan* (1975), pp. 17–19; Lean: *The pattern of income distribution in West Malaysia, 1975–1970* (1974), pp. 48–50.

[29] Wada: *Impact of economic growth on the size distribution of income* (1975), p. 126.

[30] Kogut and Langoni: "Population growth, income distribution and economic development" (1975), pp. 326–330.

[31] ibid., p. 326–327.

[32] Wada: *Impact of economic growth on the size distribution of income* (1975), pp. 125–148; Hsia and Chau: *Industrialisation, employment and income distribution* (1978), pp. 129–133.

THE FACTORS OF INEQUALITY

4

The research carried out in the framework of the ILO's World Employment Programme has made it possible to bring to light a large number of factors—geographic, demographic, economic, social, cultural—that can account for the way in which incomes are distributed among individual persons or among households. These factors, which are partly independent of the structural dualism characterising the first stages of development and which can endure after that dualism has disappeared, are closely interlinked. Their effects, which are partly overlapping, may be cumulative or substitutive, so that it is not always possible to identify those that are in fact decisive. The purpose of the present chapter is to review them systematically, avoiding repetitiveness so far as possible.

The recipients of income can be considered individually as economically active persons. They possess a number of characteristics (age, sex, ethnic origin, nationality, etc.) that inevitably exercise an influence on the levels of incomes and on their dispersions. Some of those characteristics (state of health, level of education), which are commonly associated with the concept of "human capital", can become the subjects of action designed to reduce the inequalities. These inequalities are, however, determined not only by the personal characteristics of individuals but also by the characteristics of their employment (occupation, employment status). Moreover these two constantly interacting categories of factors exert their influence only in so far as the individuals concerned can work regularly: in the developing countries, the effects of unemployment and underemployment on the distribution of incomes are not to be overlooked.

PERSONAL CHARACTERISTICS

Among personal characteristics, there are many that can exercise an influence on the activities and the incomes of individuals. They include sex, age, ethnic origin or nationality, state of health and level of education.

Sex and age

In every country, whatever may be the stage of its development, the distribution of incomes among economically active persons is subject to the influence of differences of remuneration according to sex. Thus the dispersion of male persons' incomes sometimes differs from that of female persons' incomes, the decisive factor, from the point of view of general inequality, being the disparity in average incomes between the sexes; the difference in the underdeveloped countries is in the ratio of approximately 1 to 2 to the advantage of the men.

There have been many analyses of that situation. It is commonly recognised that the disparities of remuneration between men and women are due both to differences in activities and to discriminatory practices. In many cases, women fill the least well paid jobs because their level of education and training is lower than that of men. The differences in qualifications, which determine to some extent the disparities of income between the sexes, are themselves due to woman's status in society.

The access of women to the employment market often depends on custom, which may confine them to domestic work or, on the contrary, allow them to have a separate occupation. The volume of supply of female labour is thus variable, as is the proportion of women in the economically active population. Moreover, the remuneration that women are ready to accept is not independent of their family situation, especially when it constitutes only a supplementary income for the household. What has to be stressed is that behaviour is not immutable and can change according to the amount of the income, that is, it can change with economic development. In some cases, a rise in the household's standard of living will spare women from having to engage in a remunerated occupation; in other cases, such an occupation will be regarded as providing an improvement in status. It is clear that these different reactions will exercise an influence on the average disparities of remuneration between men and women and on the proportion of women in the economically active population; they will affect the general dispersion of incomes.

In the same way, there is a relationship between age, experience and training for a job, just as there is a relationship (which may be a reverse one) between age and level of education. On the whole, persons aged over 25 (from 25 to 50 years of age) earn more than young people (under 25 years of age), who, having recently come onto the job market, have no regular or definite job and whose services are not fully utilised. Age thus appears as one of the principal factors making for differences in earnings within the same sector of the economy or the same occupation. That source of inequality nevertheless disappears over a lifetime, as was seen in Chapter 2.

Table 16. Distribution of incomes by ethnic origin in five countries

Country, group	Percentage of population concerned	Percentage of income from wages or salaries	Indexed average income from wages or salaries
Ivory Coast (1971, employees, public sector)			
African aliens	41.7	16.8	100
Nationals	54.8	54.0	260
Europeans	3.5	29.2	2 085
Swaziland (1974, individuals)			
Swazis	97.5	77	100
Non-Swazis	2.5	23	1 164
Zambia (1970, employees)			
Africans	92	68	100
Non-Africans	8	32	540
Malaysia (1968, economically active persons)			
Malays	69.8	53.2	100
Chinese	19.6	32.4	216
Indians	10.2	13.1	174
Others	0.4	1.3	640
Singapore (1973, households)			
Indians, Pakistanis	6	3.9	100
Malays	15	10.5	107
Chinese	76	78.8	159
Others	3	6.8	348

Sources: Ivory Coast: Lecaillon and Germidis, *Inégalité des revenus et développement économique* (1977), p. 171; Swaziland: Szal and van der Hoeven, *Inequality and basic needs in Swaziland* (1976), p. 10; Zambia: van der Hoeven, *Zambia's income distribution during the early seventies* (1977), p. 38; Malaysia: Lean, *Employment and income distribution in West Malaysia* (1975), p. 47; Singapore: Pang, "Growth, inequality and race in Singapore" (1975).

In the general dispersion of incomes there are three factors that come into play: the disparity in average incomes between young and adult workers, the age composition of the economically active population and the dispersion of incomes within each group. The ultimate effect of these factors cannot be determined *a priori* because it depends on the way in which they are combined in a country at a given moment.

Ethnic origin and nationality

The disparities of income between persons of different ethnic origins and nationalities, which are among the most visible and most keenly felt manifestations of inequality of incomes, are found in various degrees in all parts of the world. Table 16 provides in that respect a series of figures for three African and two Asian countries.

Table 17. Indicators of inequality in income distribution in the same five countries as in table 16

Country	Gini coefficient		Theil index	
	Distribution by group	Overall distribution	Distribution by group	Overall distribution
Ivory Coast	0.390	. . .	0.459	. . .
Swaziland	0.205	0.637	0.329	0.844
Zambia	0.240	. . .	0.238	. . .
Malaysia	0.175	0.492	0.066	0.438
Singapore	0.094	0.400	0.030	. . .

Key: . . . = Figure not available.
Sources: as for table 16.

In Africa, one of the causes of the disparities found in many countries lies in the fact that most of the managers and heads of large undertakings are of European extraction. Among the countries shown in tables 16 and 17, the Ivory Coast is in a situation of its own that accounts for the distribution of earnings. The agricultural labourers, who are the worst paid workers, are Africans but are not, in a majority of cases, nationals of the Ivory Coast. Such nationals constitute the greater number of labourers in the non-agricultural sector and of skilled wage earners, but there are few of them among the supervisors except in the public sector. It is the Europeans who constitute the majority of supervisors in the private sector.

The distribution by ethnic origin thus largely coincides with the distribution by level of qualifications, which explains very wide disparities: the average remuneration of the Europeans is more than 20 times that of the Africans who are not nationals of the Ivory Coast. The Gini coefficient by groups corresponding to that distribution of remuneration is a high one (0.39). In the case of the United Republic of Cameroon,[1] where the distribution of remuneration is close to the one obtaining in the Ivory Coast, it can be estimated that the disparities associated with ethnic origin account for about three-quarters of the Theil index for the total distribution of wages and salaries.

The disparities are more moderate in Swaziland, as well as in Zambia, where the index of 100 refers not only to recent immigrant Africans but to all Africans. The average disparity between Africans and Europeans is in the ratio of 1 to 11.6 in Swaziland and 1 to 5.4 in Zambia. The corresponding Gini coefficients are 0.205 and 0.24. While the disparity is smaller in Zambia, the number of non-Africans is much greater (8 per cent as against 2.5 per cent). In these countries the salaried Europeans (nearly all of them supervisors) receive between a quarter and a third of the total wages and salaries bill.

In the two Asian countries shown in tables 16 and 17, the income disparities are appreciably smaller. In Malaysia all the ethnic groups concerned (excluding the "others", who constitute a negligible proportion of the population) are of Asian origin. The proportion of Chinese is much greater in certain categories (non-agricultural employers, as well as technical, supervisory and executive staff) than it is, on the average, in the economically active population as a whole. Thus they receive about a third of the incomes while accounting for no more than a fifth of the economically active persons. The Gini coefficient corresponding to the income disparities between Chinese, Malays and to a lesser extent Indians is 0.175; these disparities account for about 15 per cent of the Theil index figure for the total distribution of incomes. The position is slightly overestimated in that only cash income per economically active person, which represents a larger share of total income for the Chinese than for the Malays, is taken into account.

In Singapore the disparities are smaller than in Malaysia, the Gini and Theil indices (0.094 and 0.03) being lower by half. For the overall distribution the Gini coefficient is also lower, though by only a little, in Singapore than in Malaysia, from which it may be inferred that the share of inequalities due to ethnic origin is about twice as small there. This fact can be explained in terms of the occupational mix within each ethnic group: thus in the group with the lowest average income there are unskilled labourers but also lawyers, physicians, supervisors and directors of undertakings. In that sense, the situation in Singapore is the opposite of the situations found in Africa.

The fact that ethnically diversified communities seem to be less egalitarian than communities whose members are predominantly of the same race raises the question of the origin of the disparities that have been found. Some differences might be explained in terms of cultural outlook: the attitude towards risk-taking and expenditure of effort and economic motivation in general suffice in many cases to explain the performances of certain groups, or the fact that minorities of immigrants are more successful than the majority of a country's nationals in some occupations. As a result there is often a stratification of jobs with its disparities of income and a specialisation of ethnic groups in certain activities in preference to others. There is, for example, the case of Singapore, where the Chinese dominate industry and commerce while the Malays are concentrated in the public sector, transport and communications, with the Indians and Pakistanis working mainly in the service industries and in trade. Such stratification naturally tends to endure because the dominant group in a sector gives priority, as a rule, to workers of the same ethnic origin for the available jobs. Forms of discrimination and obstacles to mobility can thus make their appearance. Dominating groups and underprivileged groups will co-exist in the community with persisting disparities in levels of income.

It would be an over-simplification, however, to attribute those disparities solely to the factor of ethnic origin, which covers in practice a large number of other explanatory factors, including in particular the level of education and skill, specialisation and the range of occupations. Experience seems to show, moreover, that in the long run the concentration of certain ethnic groups in particular kinds of employment gradually weakens with the spread of education and under the effect of the process of development itself, which creates new kinds of specialisation and new types of employment.[2]

The presence of a large ethnic group of foreign origin, whose members retain their links with their country of origin, will have certain consequences. The most typical case in the developing countries is that of European or North American managers and technicians employed in private undertakings or seconded to a government under technical co-operation arrangements.

The remuneration of that staff, being established on the scales in force in the countries of origin, is appreciably higher than that of the local workers, on which it can exercise a pulling influence: on the whole, anything that stimulates imitation by putting persons from unequally developed countries in touch with one another leads to pressure for wage and salary increases in the less advanced country. In the developing countries that pressure acts as a factor in the widening of income ranges since the benchmark is taken from economies having higher standards of living and levels of income. In such cases the widening of the range of wages and salaries is not necessarily justifiable on economic grounds from the point of view of the local economy's productivity; it is potentially inflationary.[3]

The presence of an ethnic group with high incomes exercises an influence also on the structure of demand for consumer goods. If the products demanded by that group are of foreign origin, the corresponding imports can raise a foreign exchange problem. In a general way, the more mixed the community and the more diversified the living habits the more diversified also will be the structure of production.

Health

Health and productivity

An individual's or group's state of health and level of income are related. The link between the two is productivity.[4] The nature of that relationship and its effects on the general distribution of incomes and welfare nevertheless do raise certain questions.

The nature of the connection between state of health, productivity and income will depend upon the nature of the production function and on the supply of the various factors of production. The health of individuals is a feature of the supply of labour: its effect on production depends on the employment of labour and on the way in which labour is combined with the other factors of production.[5]

It can be assumed that, in the short run and with given methods of production and a given technology, an improvement in health will lead, particularly in the case of manual work, to an increase in labour productivity as measured by output per head and per day. It will generate, too, a potential increase in the supply of labour resulting, on the one hand, from an increase in the number of persons fit to work and, on the other hand, from a diminution in the number of days lost on account of sickness. That potential increase will be reflected in an increase in total production only if labour is scarce. Where there is much unemployment or underemployment, there is little likelihood that those favourable effects will come about. Such a situation is a frequent one in the developing countries, except in the course of intense agricultural activity during which the seasonal demand for labour expands or where certain categories of skilled labour are in insufficient supply.

In the long run, an improvement in health can contribute more to the advancement of productivity in so far as it encourages innovations, which depend not only upon the physical strength of individuals but also on their gift for foreseeing the future and for taking risks. Just as better health makes for that type of behaviour, it enables children to benefit more from education, likewise enabling persons who have acquired an occupational skill to exercise it effectively. It reduces absenteeism from work and instability of the labour force and promotes a better utilisation of the stock of abilities available in the economy. In these circumstances a question that arises is whether an increase in production and the resulting increase in income can modify the distribution of that income. This question will be referred to again below.

Access to medical care

The share of private expenditure in the total expenditure on health is larger in the developing countries than in the richer countries, as is indicated in table 18: the system of public medical care, making much use of Western techniques, plays a smaller role in the whole apparatus of medical care, with the traditional methods and medical care in the home continuing to play a large role. Moreover, public expenditure on health is in most cases excessively concentrated on the towns to the detriment of rural areas. Nevertheless it is found in various countries that the first four quintiles of the population (in the increasing order of income) make use of

Table 18. Expenditure on health as a percentage of the gross domestic product in developed and developing countries (estimates)

Country	Type of expenditure	
	Public	Private
Developed countries (1973–75)		
Australia	5.0	1.5
Belgium	4.2	0.8
Canada	5.1	1.7
Netherlands	5.1	2.2
Sweden	6.7	0.6
United Kingdom	5.1	2.2
United States	2.4	3.9
Developing countries (1970)		
Ghana	1.1	2.9
Honduras	1.9	3.2
India	0.4	2.1
Pakistan	0.9	1.5
Philippines	0.4	1.5
Sri Lanka	1.8	1.2
Sudan	2.2	1.5

Source: Richards, *Some distributional issues in planning for basic needs health care* (1979), p. 3.

the public system of medical care in proportion to their sizes, though not necessarily proportionately to their needs. As a result, in so far as private expenditure on health increases *pari passu* with income, the public expenditure cannot counterbalance the disequilibrium in the distribution of medical care.[6]

However, the inequality of access to health care cannot be explained solely in terms of an insufficient amount or poor distribution of the public expenditure. Other factors that must not be overlooked include individual attitudes towards sickness, will to look after one's health, and choice between traditional and modern medicine. Attitudes vary with the cultural environment and according to the social group and the degree of acceptance of the outside world; hence they are not independent of possession of information and, more generally, of the level of education.

Education

Although education is a field that has been thoroughly explored in the theory of distribution, there nevertheless remain many disagreements of interpretation.

In its simplest form, the theory rests on two general observations: the incomes of individuals rise with the level of the education they have received; and the more unequally education is distributed, the greater will be the inequality of income. From the empirical relationship between income and level of education, an easy step is taken to a causal explanation which automatically entails a political implication: the equalisation of incomes presupposes an equalisation of levels of education. In that simplified form, the theory does not take account of natural endowments. Although there has been no specific research on that aspect of the question under the World Employment Programme, reference should nevertheless be made to an important discussion that has taken place on the possible influence of genetic factors.[7]

In the pages that follow we will define the characteristics and the nature of the relationship between education and distribution of incomes in the developing countries.

There is a high degree of correlation between income and level of education, as is borne out by most of the studies carried out under the World Employment Programme. The highest incomes are found in the occupations requiring the highest degree of education and of skill. Our studies with decomposition of indicators of inequality show that education is in many cases the most important among the factors linked with inequality of income (which also include rural or urban environment, economic sector, age and occupation). The same holds good for the dispersion of urban incomes and for inequality between wage or salary earners and the self-employed.[8]

It appears that there are two distinct, though connected, aspects of the relationship between education and the distribution of incomes.

On the one hand, a higher level of education improves the earning capacity of individuals: it is reflected in their average income and profile of remuneration in the course of their careers. The theory of human capital rests on that finding. If the inertia of socio-economic relations is accepted, it can be expected that the effect of education on earnings will be sufficiently stable to enable sensible decisions to be taken with respect to investments in intellectual training. Many statistical surveys make it possible to evaluate the returns on those investments: they show clearly that education is a productive asset.[9] According to an extreme explanation of the relationship found between level of education and income, educated workers earn more than others because the knowledge that they have acquired has made them more productive.[10] In any case education acts here as a factor in the dispersion of incomes in so far as it is itself unequally distributed.

On the other hand, education can be a factor of inequality between individuals who have reached the same level of education. In other words there can be greater inequality of remuneration among persons who possess a high level of education than among those who have had little schooling. This is due partly to the fact that education is not a homogeneous factor. The quality of education received is itself unequal and gives rise to discrimination that can endure throughout working life owing to imperfections in the employment market or to the effects of relative academic prestige in securing salary increases that are unrelated to productivity. [11]

The differences can be due partly to other factors (innate abilities, personal motivation, family relationships, experience) that cannot always be completely dissociated from education. Thus earnings rise not only with education but also with age and experience, with the result that in econometric studies the correlation between age, education and income weakens in the case of the older and better educated groups. [9] The nature of that correlation is not altogether clear.

Can it be inferred from the correlation between level of education and level of income that education has a causal effect on distribution? The question has been much debated: divergent interpretations, based on different analyses of the working of the employment market, have been proposed. [12]

According to the theory of human capital, the productive abilities of individuals depend upon the amount of the investments in health improvement, in education, in training, and so forth. Under the principles of neo-classical economic theory, productivity determines earnings. Consequently a better education must generate a higher income. A causal relationship is established between the personal characteristics of individuals, that is, the supply of labour, and the distribution of incomes. Any modification of the distribution of personal characteristics must therefore entail a modification of the distribution of incomes. The tendency for disparities of remuneration to narrow in the more advanced economies can be explained in particular by the diffusion of education, the increase in the number of qualified personnel bringing with it increased competition and causing a relative fall in the higher wage and salary brackets.

One of the debated points in the argument is that the level of education can be correlated with income though without thereby having an effect on productivity. Such is the case where employers, in default of sufficient information on the abilities of the suppliers of labour, make use of the number of years of schooling (or the level of school certificates), as a criterion of selection when taking on staff; in that case there is a close correlation between number of years of schooling and income, though without any obvious contribution of schooling to performance. In a more general way, to explain distribution in terms of the education and presumed productivity of the workers is to take account only of the characteristics of labour supply and to ignore the possible influence of demand, that is, the characteristics of the jobs.

According to another school of thought, productivity is thus an attribute not of workers but of jobs, and depends especially upon the quantity and the quality of the equipment placed at the workers' disposal. Personal characteristics (age, sex, state of health, education) constitute only selection criteria enabling employers to choose the workers best fitted for the existing jobs. The best educated workers will be better placed than the others to hold the most productive and best remunerated jobs, but it is clear that if productivity is an attribute of the jobs the structure of incomes will depend not upon the distribution of education but upon the structure of those jobs.

Viewed from that angle, modifications of the distribution of incomes presuppose modifications not of the education or other personal characteristics of the workers but of various features of the economy. If the diffusion of education generates a surplus supply of labour at a higher level of education, the tendency of wages and salaries to fall will affect all categories of workers because the surplus number of educated workers will take the place of the less educated workers in the jobs previously held by them. The disparities in wages and salaries will remain, however, if there are no changes in the productivity differences between jobs.

Reference must be made also to studies based on the theory of segmentation of the labour market. Contrary to the more classical hypotheses that workers have a wide choice of jobs and of types of training whereas employers assess their abilities after taking their personal characteristics into account, those studies postulate that the labour market is segmented and that the economically active population is divided into permanent groups distinguished by enduring common characteristics: the members of a group have a specific career profile depending neither upon their personal choices nor upon the judgment of the employers but upon the structure of the employment market.

Remuneration varies from one sector of the employment market to another for political and social reasons. In every version of that theory, the structure of earnings is governed by variables distinct from the individual productivity of the workers (customs and social considerations, organisation of production, monopoly power, class system, discrimination); it is not determined by the distribution of productivity and is not even necessarily linked to that distribution. The existence of a correlation between level of education and amount of income does not in any way imply that a better education generates higher productivity. The relationship between workers' characteristics and remuneration is not economic but "socio-institutional". The distribution of productivity can change, therefore, without any corresponding effect on income distribution, which will be modified neither by changes in employment structure nor by improvements in the education and other personal characteristics of the workers but only in consequence of changes in the relative power of groups, giving to the members of one group the possibility of obtaining an increase in remuneration relatively to the wages of the other groups.

This theory has been supported by reference to the experience of certain countries of Latin America (Brazil, Chile, Mexico, Peru), which indicates that equalisation of education is not automatically accompanied by equalisation of incomes.[13] Other studies have shown, however, that when the equalisation of education was not accompanied by equalisation of income, the reason lay in the fact that the equalising effect of education was counterbalanced by the opposing influence of other factors. The income-equalising effect of education does exist: in Colombia, in Mexico and in Peru, the rate of return from education has diminished to a significant extent with the increase in the relative supply of educated workers,[14] so that the theory of human capital would appear to remain generally valid in its application to developing countries.

The studies relating to certain countries of Asia (Philippines, Sri Lanka) indicate, however, that the general distribution of incomes from work depends upon the distribution not of education but of jobs. If a larger investment in education leads, in association with age, to higher wages, it is because a better education and a better exercise of intellectual attainments open up the possibility of gaining access to the jobs providing the highest remuneration. In that sense, the model which makes productivity an attribute of the job would seem to provide the best description of the working of the labour market. It would seem, therefore, that in the end, it is the structure of employment that determines both the structure of the "output" of the educational system and the distribution of incomes.

If the situation is viewed from that angle, it is not to be expected that the spread of education could contribute significantly to the equalisation of incomes. Nor could it contribute to an equalisation of opportunities owing to the handicaps of the children of poor families, who, as can be observed in countries such as India, the Philippines, Sri Lanka and Thailand, begin their schooling later than do the children of other groups and derive less benefit from it.[15]

These analyses differ in the importance (decisive in the case of some of them, insignificant in the case of others) that they attach to education in order to explain and modify the dispersion of incomes. They show that in the present state of research it is extremely difficult to sift out the exact nature of the relationship between education and income distribution in the developing countries.

OCCUPATION AND EMPLOYMENT STATUS

Socio-economic groups and income distribution

Occupation and employment status play an important role in income distribution. In many cases that role corresponds to a stratification of socio-occupational categories. The relationship between income distribution and socio-occupational stratification is particularly clear in the developing countries, where there are often pronounced differences of social status and of standard of living corresponding to differences in occupation and employment status. To enter into certain occupations is, in many cases, to achieve a certain economic and social status. Given the level of education and skill that is generally required, it is not surprising that income, social status and education should be interdependent characteristics of the various socio-economic groups.

Although incomes and occupations do not rigorously correspond, nearly everywhere one finds at the top employers and managers and the members of the professions, who are followed by clerical and sales staffs and skilled workers and then by unskilled workers in the non-agricultural sectors, farmers and seasonal workers. In other words high levels of income imply possession of an element of material or human capital. The

Typology of economically active persons

Category	Code
Wage and salary earners:	
Unskilled in the agricultural sector	SIA
Unskilled in the non-agricultural sector	SIB
Skilled	S2
Executive, supervisory and technical staff	S3
Self-employed, agricultural sector:	
Farmers in the traditional sector engaged in subsistence agriculture mainly for own consumption	IA1
Farmers in the traditional sector producing for the market (traditional commercial agriculture)	IA2
Farmers in the modern sector	IA3
Self-employed, non-agricultural sector:	
Craftsmen and traders (without employees)	IB1
Craftsmen and traders (employers)	IB2
Heads of modern undertakings	IB3

relative scarcity of capital in developing countries is often given as one of the causes of inequality of incomes, which may be increased where there is a positive correlation between the average level of income and the degree of inequality in each category.[16]

In these circumstances, it may be of interest to set out a detailed typology of economically active persons in ten categories. It serves to show that, in the total inequality of incomes, the share resulting from differences in average income among economically active persons is much larger in the developing than in the developed countries. This typology is based on a fundamental distinction between the wage and salary earners, the self-employed in the agricultural sector and the self-employed in the non-agricultural sector. These three broad and very heterogeneous categories are subdivided as shown on the previous page.

This typology is applied in tables 19 and 20 to seven countries or territories: the Ivory Coast, Senegal, Swaziland, Zambia, Colombia, Hong Kong and Malaysia. In the case of Hong Kong and Malaysia the available statistics preclude any very detailed breakdown; where that is possible, it is found that there are considerable differences in income according to the categories.

Between the subsistence farmers (IA1) and the salaried managers (S3) or the heads of modern undertakings and the salaried managers (IB3, S3), the disparity in average income is in the ratio of 1 to 27 in the Ivory Coast, 1 to 34 in Senegal, 1 to 32 in Swaziland, 1 to 58 in Zambia (upper category: non-Africans only), 1 to 20 in Colombia and 1 to 10 in Malaysia. Between the three categories of wage and salary earners (S1, S2, S3), there are also wide disparities. They reach their maximum where unskilled workers are relatively numerous; thus the income disparity between the first category and the third is in the ratio of 1 to 10 in Senegal but 1 to 30 in the Ivory Coast, unskilled workers accounting for the overwhelming majority of wage and salary earners in the Ivory Coast but for a smaller part in Senegal.

Table 19. Distribution of incomes by socio-occupational categories in seven countries or territories

Country or territory and category	Percentage of economically active persons	Percentage of income	Indexed average income
Ivory Coast (1970)			
IA1	27.8	11.0	100
IA2	18.5	25.7	347
IB1, IB2	8.8	10.4	295
IB3	0.6	3.0	1 250
S1	33.6	12.2	90
S2	8.9	17.9	500
S3	1.8	19.8	2 750

Table 19 *(cont.)*

Country or territory and category	Percentage of economically active persons	Percentage of income	Indexed average income
Senegal (1970)			
IA1	66.7	28.7	100
IA2	7.3	6.3	200
IB1	10.3	8.3	186
IB2	2.2	4.8	507
IB3	0.6	5.5	2 130
S1	7.8	10.3	330
S2	3.8	17.1	1 046
S3	1.3	19.0	3 395
Swaziland (1974)			
IA1	62.0	18.0	100
S1A	20.0	16.0	275
S1B	7.0	12.5	620
IB1, IB2, S2	8.5	30.5	1 240
IB3, S3	2.5	23.0	3 170
Zambia (1972)			
IA1	50.7	12.9	100
IA2	16.0	14.1	347
IB1	3.3	1.6	183
S1B	3.1	1.5	188
IB2, S1B, S2, IB3[1], S3[1]	24.3	31.5	512
IB3[2], S3[2]	2.6	38.4	5 813
Colombia (1972)			
IA1	19.74	6.70	100
IA2	10.95	8.97	241
IB1	5.50	1.89	100
IB2	15.45	9.80	185
S1	24.47	8.37	100
S2	17.50	20.21	338
IB3, S3	6.39	44.06	2 030
Hong Kong (1971)			
S1	20.8	13.6	100
S2, S3[3]	46.2	51.7	171
IB1	28.8	24.0	127
IB2, IB3	4.2	10.7	391
Malaysia (1967)			
IA1	40.7	15.7	100
IA2	9.0	11.5	331
IB1, SB2, S1	39.6	44.7	292
IB2	9.1	21.8	622
IB3, S3	1.6	6.3	1 020

[1] Africans [2] Non-Africans [3] Including the professions, for which the figures are the following: 1.5; 3.8; 380.

Sources: Ivory Coast, Senegal: Lecaillon and Germidis, *Inégalité des revenus et développement économique* (1977), pp. 124–135, and C. Morrisson, unpublished study prepared for the Development Research Center of the World Bank (1974); Swaziland: Szal and van der Hoeven, *Inequality and basic needs in Swaziland* (1976), pp. 6–15; Zambia: van der Hoeven, *Zambia's income distribution during the early seventies* (1977), pp. 34–43; Colombia: Bourguignon, *General equilibrium analysis of the Colombian income distribution* (1978), p. 32; Hong Kong: Hsia and Chau, *Industrialisation, employment and income distribution* (1978), pp. 47–61; Malaysia: Lean, *Employment and income distribution in West Malaysia* (1975), pp. 20–37.

Table 20. Indicators of inequality in income distribution in the same seven countries and territories as in table 19

Country or territory	Gini coefficient		Theil index		Ratio a/b
	Distribution by categories	Overall distribution	Distribution by categories (a)	Overall distribution (b)	
Ivory Coast	0.475	0.520	0.524	0.590	0.89
Senegal	0.498	0.526	0.685	0.750	0.91
Swaziland	0.579	0.637	0.714	0.844	0.85
Zambia	0.577	0.650	0.899	1.163	0.85
Colombia	0.520	0.570	0.635	0.665	0.95
Hong Kong	0.158	0.439	0.057	0.418	0.14
Malaysia	0.332	0.492	0.210	0.438	0.48

A distinguishing feature of the African countries is that there are wide disparities of income between the categories, and consequently high corresponding Gini coefficients by category (the dispersion of incomes within each category being assumed to be nil), ranging from 0.475 in the Ivory Coast to 0.579 in Swaziland. In Colombia the disparity in average income between the extremes is less wide, but since the group of heads of modern undertakings and of executive, supervisory and technical staff (IB3, S3) is larger (6.4 per cent of the economically active population instead of 2–3 per cent) and since its share of the incomes reaches 44 per cent, there is also a high Gini coefficient (0.52). The coefficient is appreciably lower in Hong Kong and in Malaysia; there the disparities of income between the categories are slighter (in a ratio of 1 to 4 in the first case and of 1 to 10 in the second), with resulting Gini coefficients of 0.158 and 0.332.

The difference between the Gini coefficient for the general distribution of incomes among economically active persons and the same coefficient for the distribution by categories corresponds to the difference between the actual general distribution and what that distribution would be if there were a strictly equal distribution within each category. It is found that the difference is slight in the four African countries and in Colombia; it increases in Malaysia and reaches its maximum in Hong Kong (0.158 instead of 0.439). As a country develops (Hong Kong has a higher product per head than that of the six other countries), the dispersion of incomes within each group plays an increasingly important role in the total concentration of incomes (as is borne out by the example of France, where the two Gini coefficients are 0.3 and 0.43 respectively, even with a detailed breakdown into eight groups).

The relationship between the Theil index for the distribution by categories and that index for the overall distribution of incomes is even more significant inasmuch as it expresses the percentage of the overall index that can be explained in terms of the differences in average income between the categories.[17] In the four African countries and in Colombia, the ratio varies between 0.85 and 0.95. Even if account is taken of the underestimation of the overall index,[18] these figures signify that the income disparities between socio-economic groups alone explain about 75 per cent of the total inequality of incomes in those countries. The ratio falls to 0.48 in Malaysia and sinks to 0.14 in Hong Kong, which for several reasons is not representative of developing countries (virtual absence of agriculture and higher product per head than in most of those countries). Even for Malaysia, there is underestimation of the Theil index for the distribution by categories because the unskilled workers (S1) have been grouped with the employer craftsmen and traders (IB2), whose average incomes vary at least from 1 to 2, if not from 1 to 3.

In these circumstances, it may be concluded that the disparities in average income between socio-economic groups account for 60 to 80 per cent of the inequality of incomes in the developing countries, which is a much higher proportion than that which is reached in the developed countries (in France the ratio does not exceed 0.55 despite a more detailed breakdown into groups).

This conclusion is of interest in two ways. On the one hand, it is easier to explain the concentration of incomes in the developing countries than in the richer countries: the disparities in income between the socio-economic groups are linked directly to the structure of the gross domestic product (share of agriculture, for example, or of wages), to the sectoral distribution of the economically active population, to the differences in productivity between subsistence agriculture and traditional cultivation of cash crops, to techniques of production and to differences in the ratio of capital to economically active persons according to the sectors. On the other hand, it is not possible to discern from annual family budget surveys based on large samples the variations, which are very small in the short run, in the rate of concentration of incomes; whereas with national accounts and surveys of the economically active population, it is possible to trace annual variations in average income disparities by socio-economic group. It is likewise easier to estimate the effect of a measure of economic policy and of a fluctuation in the price of a cash crop on the average income of a group than on the overall rate of concentration of incomes. For all these reasons, estimating distribution by groups provides one of the best ways of studying the overall distribution of incomes.

Wage or salary earners and persons working on some other basis

One of the most characteristic classifications of categories in the stratification of occupations is that of wage or salary earners on the one hand, and people working on some other basis. The latter category includes employers, own-account workers and unpaid family workers; it is thus a heterogeneous category within which the dispersion of incomes plays an important role.

In broad terms, it may be said that employers and employees are representative of modern economic activities and that people working on their own account and unpaid family workers are representative of traditional activities. Employers and employees constitute the employment market. The relationship between employer and employee implies a contractual agreement laying down the hours of work and the rate of pay: the work provides both parties with a certain income. In many cases traditional economic activities are organised around the family, which is a unit of production in which self-employment and the work of the members of the family take the place of the employer-employee relationship; this type of employment is characterised by its risk and by the great variability of incomes. The progressive substitution of wage-earning for self-employment in the course of economic development exercises an influence on the general dispersion of incomes, in view of the income disparities between the two groups and the degree of concentration within each of them.

Disparities between the two groups

Table 21 indicates the distribution of incomes between employees and the self-employed in eight countries or territories. It shows that the disparities are both considerable and irregular. In two cases (Hong Kong and Turkey), the average income of employees, with an index of 85 or 65, is lower than that of the self-employed (index 100), which is due to the large amount of employers' incomes in the latter total. In the Philippines, the disparity is moderate: 133 instead of 100; consequently the Gini coefficient for the distribution between employees and self-employed is only 0.072 and the disparity accounts for only a negligible part (2 per cent) of the Theil index for the overall distribution. On the other hand the disparity in average income between employees and self-employed has a significant effect in four African countries: in the United Republic of Cameroon and in Madagascar, the index for average income of employees is about 250, while it reaches or exceeds 500 in Senegal and Swaziland. In these countries wages provide the best incomes, and their recipients fall automatically into the upper deciles. In the United Republic of Cameroon, as in Madagascar and Senegal, the proportion of employees is small (from 13 to 16 per cent), but that category receives from 28 to 46 per cent of the total income. There is a different situation in the Ivory Coast, where the disparity is small and where the average income of employees does not exceed the index of 139. More than half of

Table 21. Distribution of incomes between employees and self-employed persons in eight countries or territories and indicators of inequality

Item	United Republic of Cameroon 1960	Ivory Coast 1970	Madagascar 1970	Senegal 1970	Swaziland 1974	Hong Kong 1971	Philippines 1961	Turkey 1970
Distribution of economically active persons (percentages):								
Employees	13.5	27	16.1	12.9	30	65.5	43.7	45.3
Self-employed	86.5	73	83.9	87.1	70	34.5	56.3	54.7
Distribution of incomes (percentages):								
Employees	28	33.9	33.7	46.4	68.3	61.5	50.9	34.9
Self-employed	72	66.1	66.3	53.6	31.7	38.5	49.1	65.1
Average income of employees (self-employed = 100)	249	139	265	585	501	85	133	65
Indicators of inequality:								
Gini coefficient								
Distribution between employees and self-employed	0.145	0.069	0.176	0.335	0.383	0.040	0.072	0.104
Overall distribution	...	0.520	...	0.526	0.637	0.439	0.493	0.553
Theil index:								
Distribution between employees and self-employed, (a)	0.072	0.012	0.093	0.334	0.311	0.004	0.010	0.022
Overall distribution, (b)	...	0.590	...	0.750	0.844	0.418	0.442	0.642
Ratio a to b	...	0.02	...	0.45	0.37	0.001	0.02	0.03

Key: . . . = Figures not available.

Sources: United Republic of Cameroon, Ivory Coast, Madagascar: Lecaillon and Germidis, *Inégalité des revenus et développement économique* (1977), pp. 39, 75, 83 and 92; Senegal: Morrisson, unpublished study prepared for the Development Research Center of the World Bank (1974); Swaziland: Szal and van der Hoeven, *Inequality and basic needs in Swaziland* (1976), pp. 6–15; Hong Kong: Hsia and Chau, *Industrialisation, employment and income distribution* (1978), pp. 58–61; Philippines: Morrisson, op. cit.; Turkey: Ecevit and Ozötün, *The changing structural distribution of income and employment in Turkey and Kuznets' hypothesis* (1975).

97

Table 22.   Indices of inequality in the distribution of incomes within socio-occupational categories in eight countries or territories

Country	Category	Gini coefficient	Theil index
United Republic of Cameroon (1971)	Employees	0.517	0.592
Zambia (1972–74)	Rural sector	0.390	0.299
	Urban sector	0.530	0.508
	Traditional	0.285	0.134
	Modern	0.290	0.138
Brazil (1969)	Employees	0.419	0.361
Republic of Korea (1970)	Employees	0.381	0.238
	Self-employed		
	Agricultural sector	0.248	0.097
	Non-agricultural sector	0.380	0.272
Hong Kong (1971)	Distribution A		
	Employees		
	Unskilled	0.320	0.177
	Semi-skilled, skilled	0.310	0.165
	Clerical	0.360	0.222
	Supervisors	0.440	0.330
	Self-employed		
	Professional	0.510	0.434
	Others	0.550	0.525
	Distribution B		
	Employers	0.493	0.446
	Self-employed	0.401	0.301
	Employees	0.417	0.366
	Workers at home, retired	0.394	0.284
India (1965)	Farmers and agricultural labourers	0.370	
	Transport workers	0.300	
	Service workers	0.240	
	Craftsmen and non-agricultural labourers	0.280	
Malaysia	Professional, technical and related	0.426	0.325
	Administration, executive and managerial	0.429	0.312
	Clerical	0.390	0.291
	Sales and related	0.467	0.441
	Farmers	0.293	0.189
	Mines, quarrymen and related	0.330	0.299
	Transport and communications	0.353	0.329
	Services	0.430	0.406

Table 22 *(cont.)*

Country	Category	Gini coefficient	Theil index
	Craftsmen, production process workers, labourers	0.347	0.323
Turkey (1968)	Employees		
	Private sector	0.395	0.275
	Public sector	0.339	0.175
	Self-employed		
	Agricultural sector	0.590	0.758
	Non-agricultural sector	0.573	0.626

Sources: United Republic of Cameroon: Lecaillon and Germidis, *Inégalité des revenus et développement économique* (1977), p. 152; Zambia: van der Hoeven, *Zambia's income distribution during the early seventies* (1977), pp. 21–30; Brazil: Morley, *Changes in employment and the distribution of income during the Brazilian "miracle"* (1976); Republic of Korea: Skolka and Garzuel, *Income distribution by size, employment and the structure of the economy* (1978), p. 90; Hong Kong: Hsia and Chau, *Industrialisation, employment and income distribution* (1978), pp. 47–61; India: Farbman, *Sectoral employment and income distribution in rural India* (1975), p. 32; Malaysia: Lean, *Employment and income distribution in West Malaysia* (1975), p. 28; Turkey: Miller, *Aspects of income distribution in Turkey* (1975), pp. 19–23.

those employees are agricultural labourers, mostly immigrants, whose low wages fall below the incomes of plantation workers. The Gini coefficient for the distribution between employees and self-employed is 0.069 and the disparity between the two categories accounts for only 2 per cent of the Theil index for the overall distribution. At the other extreme, this disparity shows a Gini coefficient of about 0.35 in Senegal and in Swaziland and accounts for, respectively, 45 and 37 per cent of the Theil index for the overall distribution. In the absence of data on overall distribution in the United Republic of Cameroon and in Madagascar, it is not possible to estimate the contribution of the disparity between employees and the self-employed to the total concentration of incomes, but the Gini coefficients (0.145 and 0.176) for the distribution between employees and the self-employed places those countries between the Ivory Coast, on the one hand, and Senegal and Swaziland on the other.

Dispersion within each group

Since the concentration of incomes results both from the disparities in average income between the groups and from the dispersion of incomes within each group, an analysis of that dispersion must be added to the foregoing analysis.

Table 22, which brings together the data relating to eight countries or territories, makes it possible to discern certain constant characteristics of distribution, especially for the employees' group or for some of its subgroups. In several countries the Gini coefficient for the distribution of earnings varies between 0.38 and 0.42; such is the case in Brazil, in the Republic of Korea and in Turkey (private sector). For the subgroups the index is lower, the dispersion of incomes being necessarily narrower than for employees as a whole. That can be easily checked in the case of Hong Kong, where the Gini coefficient, which reaches 0.417 for the employees as a whole, is 0.32 for labourers, 0.31 for semi-skilled and skilled workers, 0.36 for employees and 0.44 for executive, supervisory and technical staff. These data confirm, moreover, that the concentration of incomes increases with increases in average wages. The Gini coefficients for employees in Malaysia tally approximately with those for Hong Kong, viz. 0.426 for professional, technical and related personnel, 0.39 for clerical staff and 0.33 for miners and quarrymen. For smaller categories (sales, transport, services), the indices are less significant.

In the case of the self-employed, there are wide differences according to the country. For example, the indices for the self-employed in the agricultural sector and in the non-agricultural sector are respectively 0.248 and 0.38 in the Republic of Korea, but 0.59 and 0.573 in Turkey. The first group corresponds to farmers, for whom the Gini coefficient is 0.293 in Malaysia. The dispersion of incomes among farmers depends closely on the structure of land use and ownership. Thus in Turkey 8.7 per cent of the farmers own 42.4 per cent of the land and 77.7 per cent of them only 34.1 per cent of the land (index of concentration: 0.481).[19] The agrarian concentration is less pronounced in the Republic of Korea, where the richer 6.1 per cent of households owned 17.6 per cent of the land in 1964 (index of concentration: 0.365).[20] In the Republic of Korea the dispersion of incomes of the self-employed is much wider in the non-agricultural than in the agricultural sector, although the Gini coefficient of 0.38 is a minimum by comparison with the other countries, where it invariably exceeds 0.4. Among the self-employed, too, distinctions must be made between several subgroups, for example between the small craftsmen and traders, on the one hand, and the employers on the other. The concentration of incomes seems to be much lower for the first of these subgroups than it is for the second. Thus in Hong Kong the Gini coefficient amounts to 0.493 for the employers and to 0.041 for the craftsmen and traders in the group of self-employed. In Malaysia, where craftsmen are coupled with non-agricultural workers, the index is 0.347, whereas it reaches 0.429 in the administrative, executive and managerial occupations and it is probable that the index would be even higher for general managers alone.

Several points emerge from the data set out in table 22. The distribution of earnings is relatively stable as between one country and

Table 23. Range of earnings (indices) of employees in the Ivory Coast, Nigeria, Hong Kong and the United Republic of Cameroon

Country and sector	Unskilled employees (= 100) S1	Skilled employees S2	Technicians, managers S3
Ivory Coast (1971)			
Private and semi-public sector	100 176[2]	270–400	750–1 800
Nigeria (1971–72)			
Industry	100	190	500–1 700
Public sector	100		500–1 300
United Republic of Cameroon[1] (1965)	100 130[2]	220–400	450–1 450
Hong Kong (1971)	100	180–200	365–535

[1] Douala.   [2] Semi-skilled employees.
Sources: United Republic of Cameroon, Ivory Coast: Lecaillon and Germidis, *Inégalité des revenus et développement économique* (1977), pp. 145, 153; Nigeria: Fapohunda et al., *Urban development, income distribution and employment in Lagos* (1975), pp. 3/20–3/21; Hong Kong: Hsia and Chau, *Industrialisation, employment and income distribution* (1978), p. 48.

another. It is more equal in the public sector than in the private according to the figures relating to Turkey, the Ivory Coast (see table 23 concerning the range of earnings; the scale of wages and salaries in the public sector ranges from 100 to 900) and Nigeria. Distribution also seems to be more equal in the countries that are comparatively advanced in the field of education, such as the Republic of Korea and Hong Kong.[21] As for the distribution of the incomes of the self-employed in the agricultural sector, it can vary widely according to the structure of land ownership and the system of land tenure; depending on the country, it can be either much more or much less concentrated than the distribution of earnings. In the non-agricultural sector the distribution of the incomes of the self-employed is more equal than that of employees' earnings (or, by way of exception, just as concentrated). Lastly, the subgroups of employees and of self-employed in the non-agricultural sector show a growing dispersion of incomes as average income increases.

Changes in employment status in the course of development

The changes in employment status that occur in the course of economic development are held to exercise a tangible influence on the general distribution of incomes. For many self-employed workers and family helps, a paid job represents a gain in security and an advancement in the scale of incomes. One of the essential characteristics of economic development from the angle of the employment status of economically active persons is thus the progressive substitution of remunerated employment for work on own account. This change is, of course, linked to rural-urban migration, to an extension of the modern sector to the detriment of traditional economic activities and to a shift of the labour force from agriculture to non-agricultural activities. There is a close connection between changes in employment status and intersectoral transfers of population. As was noted in Chapter 1, there is a high degree of negative correlation between the proportion of farmers and the proportion of employees in the economically active population.

Ever since the first of the studies by Kuznets, it has been accepted that these transformations exercise an influence which, as a rule, promotes greater equality: the size of the group whose incomes are the most dispersed, which is that of the self-employed taken as a whole, diminishes to the advantage of the group in which distribution is most equal, namely that of employees. That consequence nevertheless rarely appears during the first stages of development, in the course of which the relative situation of employees can deteriorate, with wages and salaries rising more slowly than the rate of increase in the number of employees.[22] It is only after a certain threshold of expansion in the number of employees corresponding to a certain degree of concentration of the units of production has been reached that the situation is stabilised or the trend is reversed. Once that threshold has been reached, the development of trade unionism and collective bargaining can also contribute, through the introduction of a statutory minimum wage, to a levelling of the disparities of earnings among industries and occupations. All these factors tend to lead to a reduction of the general inequality of incomes.

UNDERUTILISATION OF THE LABOUR FORCE

In the developing countries a permanent surplus supply of labour will be reflected in the unemployment or underemployment of a relatively large proportion of the labour force. A study of the dispersion of incomes by sector or subsector of economic activity, by occupation or by employment status is thus insufficient because it leaves out of account people who are excluded from economic activity. It may be, moreover, that the dispersion of incomes is less in each socio-occupational category than in the total population because the latter does include people who are reduced to inactivity. This shows that the level of economic activity has considerable effect on income distribution.

It would be incorrect, however, to draw a clear distinction between persons who have a job and receive a cash income and those who, having no job, receive no income and are a burden to others. In the economies in which the employment market is poorly organised and in which the self-employed are predominant, there is always a category of marginal workers who receive no income, or little income, in cash, or whose income is very small by reason of their low productivity.

The concept of underemployment covers these various situations. The sum of complete unemployment and of underemployment represents underutilisation of the national labour force.[23] Before examining the relationship between the level of employment and the distribution of incomes, some reference must be made in very general terms to the causes of that underutilisation.

In the developing countries, many factors lead to a number of situations intermediate between full employment and complete unemployment. The smaller undertakings, which are numerous and scattered, especially in the rural areas, offer part-time jobs more frequently than full-time employment, as do the large industrial undertakings. It is generally possible for workers who have an interest or whose families have an interest in a small undertaking to work in it without pay or with little pay in exchange for their subsistence. In any case, the worker will submit to total unemployment only if his family is in a position to support him without receiving anything in return. Thus, between the two extreme groups of fully employed persons and wholly unemployed persons, there are various categories of partly unemployed or underemployed persons who are poorly remunerated.

The sectoral dualism of an economy, with rural areas in which traditional activities predominate and urban areas in which modern activities take root, must therefore be the starting point of an examination of unemployment and underemployment in the developing countries. The potential existence of a rural surplus of labour is usually regarded as fundamental to the employment situation.

Rural areas

A salient characteristic of rural areas, and more generally of traditional activities, is that the employment of labour is governed much more by custom and social constraints than by the laws of the market. The situation can be briefly outlined as one in which work is a fixed factor; all persons are entitled to paid employment, at any rate at the minimum level of subsistence, even if their marginal productivity is very low or even nil. In such a situation there is very little visible unemployment in a rural environment. Underutilisation of labour assumes the form of work with low productivity and very low remuneration. The volume of this type of underutilisation, which can be considerable, is particularly difficult to assess.

There can be several reasons for the appearance and growth of visible unemployment: they are connected with the general modernisation of an economy.

Visible unemployment is caused first when customs are abandoned and there is a break with the traditional pattern of life in the course of modernisation and of exposure to a market economy. These changes prompt landowners and farmers to use the services only of workers whose productivity covers their remuneration, and to dismiss surplus labour. Disguised unemployment turns into visible unemployment without necessarily modifying appreciably the total underutilisation of the available labour.

In practice, that transformation does not take place abruptly. As has already been indicated, the economically active population does not consist only of landowning farmers and agricultural workers. There are farms of unequal size, landowning or tenant farmers, a landless peasantry and wage earners, just as there is a whole series of activities that are accessory to agriculture. The small landowners can both till their own land and put in some time on larger farms; the members of the farmers' families can engage in non-agricultural activities (local trading, craftsmanship). Even though nobody enjoys a guaranteed minimum income, family or village solidarity enables everyone to survive after a fashion.

That economic and social equilibrium is progressively upset by rationalisation, technical progress and improvements in transport and communications. The sharper the division between landowners and landless peasants, the more rapidly the change takes place. It is no doubt inevitable if agricultural productivity is to be increased and farming improved. Its counterpart is an increase in visible unemployment either in the rural areas or in the urban as a consequence of migration. That increase in visible unemployment raises specific problems of employment policy.

The increase in unemployment can be due also to the influence of education. Concern for economic independence and for development has prompted many countries to devote large resources to education and to training. Many newly educated young people are reluctant to work under the same conditions as their parents; they try to avoid manual work, especially in agriculture, and display a marked preference for jobs in the service industries. Some of them migrate to towns, where they hope to find better opportunities of employment; others remain without work rather than accept a job that does not suit their aspirations. There can thus be a particularly high proportion of educated young persons among the unemployed of the comparatively underdeveloped countries. Furthermore, in economies in which the employment market is not very active and where the services of newcomers to that market are not much in demand, there is a preference in many cases for older workers. The latter have more experience and have acquired certain habits of work; they generally have family responsibilities which restrain employers from terminating their employment. There is thus formed a reserve of young jobseekers awaiting offers of employment. That situation, which is to be found in industrialised countries during periods of recession, assumes a character of permanence in the organised sector of developing economies.

Yet the existence of relatively widespread unemployment among educated young persons does not mean that the total amount of unemployment is itself any the greater. The number of jobs available and the number of unemployed persons can be independent variables. The presence of a comparatively large proportion of unemployed young persons could signify only that the composition of the unemployed population was biased in that direction. Where that was the case, the unemployment of young people should diminish in the event of an adequate increase in employment opportunities. Nevertheless, in so far as that unemployment was due to the refusal of those concerned to accept work that did not correspond to their aspirations, the proportion of the unemployed in that category could remain permanently a relatively large one.

Urban areas

Although average rates of unemployment in all parts of the world are distinctly higher in urban areas than in rural, the most commonly accepted view is that the primary cause of urban unemployment lies in the rural areas, especially in agriculture. In a situation of strong demographic pressure, the underemployed agricultural population represents an almost inexhaustible reserve of labour not only for rural but also for urban activities. The labour surplus theories of Lewis and others are based on this fact.[24] High rates of urban unemployment result from a transformation of underemployment in relatively unproductive and poorly paid agricultural work into visible unemployment. That transformation takes place through the rural-urban migration that was examined above. In general the migrants are not at the outset completely unemployed, but family workers with low incomes. If they have no other means of subsistence, they manage to find poorly paid employment in the informal sector of the urban economy. In such cases the reserve of underemployed rural workers spills over directly into an equally underemployed urban labour reserve. To a large extent, relatively unproductive and poorly paid work, on the one hand, and total unemployment, on the other, are thus interchangeable categories, and it is in urban areas that the substitution takes place.

While the underutilised rural population provides an almost unlimited supply of labour for the urban employment market, the actual volume of unemployment depends also on the behaviour of demand for labour, which is governed mainly by the rate of economic growth and the choice of production techniques.

In a developing economy with a large surplus supply of labour from the agricultural sector the absorption of unemployment depends, in the first place, on the rate of growth of non-agricultural activities, especially in the modern urban sector because it is there that new jobs can be created. Hence increases in visible unemployment have often been held to be due to slowness in the expansion of modern activities, insufficient investment and underutilisation of existing production capacity.

Nevertheless, a fast rate of growth in non-agricultural, especially industrial, activity can be insufficient to meet an increase in population as long as that activity accounts for only a small proportion of total employment. For example, if the total labour force increases by 2 per cent a year while non-agricultural activities account for 20 per cent of the jobs, several years will be needed for the number of non-agricultural jobs to rise by 10 per cent a year, which implies an at least equal rate of growth of production (on the extreme assumption that production and employment develop proportionately); such a rate may be unattainable in many branches of production.

The effect of changes in production on employment depends, moreover, on the nature of the activities in which the process starts and on the indirect effect of their growth on the growth of other activities. The process of industrialisation thus not only creates employment in manufacturing: it contributes to the diversification and modification of national activities and strengthens the international position of the country concerned. The expansion of industrial production has favourable effects on employment in all activities that supply goods or services to the industrial sector (raw materials, trade, transport, financial services) and in those that provide consumer goods to entrepreneurs and to industrial workers, as well as in those that provide products that can be sold abroad. Other things being equal, the role played by industrialisation as a source of job creation cannot be underestimated.[25]

However, this argument must be qualified in so far as the choice of techniques of production exercises an influence on the volume of non-agricultural employment. Experience in many countries has shown that while the creation of jobs was linked to the development of production, the growth of employment was slower than that of production, especially in the modern industrial sector. One of the reasons for that fact lies in the growth of capital-intensive production, or, in other words, in the adoption of less labour-intensive techniques and in a rise in the ratio of capital to labour. The developing countries have recourse to the techniques used in the industrialised countries, where capital resources are more plentiful. Such techniques are incapable of generating the employment opportunities required by the increase in the size of the labour force. That practice is characteristic especially of large modern undertakings; where small establishments retain a role of importance, the techniques adopted are generally labour-intensive and the employment problems less acute.[26]

In view of this situation, it is desirable to consider whether there is a genuine freedom of choice with regard to the techniques of production to be used in the modern industries of developing countries; whether it is possible to define an optimum degree of capital-intensiveness; and how investment decisions can be influenced in order to direct them into the right channels. From studies that have been made it appears that in most activities more labour-intensive methods could be used but that the degree of flexibility of techniques and the "normal" intensiveness of labour vary widely from one type of activity to another. Consequently a policy of economic development aiming at employment creation should prompt the countries concerned to specialise in labour-intensive forms of production.[27]

Relationship between employment and income distribution

It is generally accepted that there is a relationship between the level of employment and the distribution of incomes. However, the direction of this relationship is not easy to determine. In a study of income distribution the first point that needs to be brought out is the influence of underemployment on the degree of inequality. In so far as unemployment, whether total or partial, increases the dispersion of incomes, action to reduce the inequality must be taken at the level of employment policy. However, it should be noted that while a reduction of unemployment reduces the dispersion of earnings, it does not necessarily diminish the general inequality of incomes: everything depends on the effect of the increased volume of employment on the share of the national income devoted to the remuneration of capital.

Modifications, whether self-generated or induced, of the distribution of incomes can, in turn, exercise an influence on employment, and it is the nature of that influence that raises difficulties. If a reduction of income inequality promotes an expansion of employment, that may lead to a new narrowing of the dispersion; there will be a cumulative process that may result in a new equilibrium of income distribution and employment. If, on the other hand, a reduction in the inequality of incomes generates more unemployment, any policy of equalisation will rapidly come up against serious difficulties.

Consideration will now be given to the two aspects of the relationship, it being understood that there can be cause and effect both ways and that there can ensue a series of chain reactions the extent of which it is not yet possible to assess.

Influence of the level of employment on income distribution

So far as the influence of the level of employment on the dispersion of incomes is concerned, the point can be made that in any economy, whatever may be the stage of its development, an increase in unemployment or in underemployment contributes to an aggravation of inequalities of remuneration and of standards of living by increasing the number of low incomes. That tendency, which has been found to occur in industrial economies during phases of economic depression, assumes a character of permanence during the first stages of economic development, underemployment then becoming one of the main features of the problem of poverty.[28]

In a general way, most of the theories of underdevelopment lay stress on the dual character of the less developed economies, that is, on the coexistence of a traditional and mainly agricultural sector and a modern, industrial and urban sector. The high productivity of workers in modern undertakings by comparison with traditional activities enables relatively high wages and salaries to be paid and large profits to be obtained. Since modern undertakings are located mainly in urban areas, the disparity between urban and rural incomes tends to increase, thereby contributing to an increase in the general dispersion of incomes.[29]

As has been shown, one of the effects of that disparity is that it attracts to the towns workers inadequately employed in rural areas and transforms rural underemployment into total urban unemployment. As long as there subsists a reserve of underutilised labour in rural areas, the unemployed cannot be absorbed and the dispersion of incomes will remain wide and even increase. Only the disappearance of the surplus labour force and the transformation of labour into as scarce a factor as capital will make it possible for the forces of equalisation to make themselves felt.[30]

Viewed from that angle, the degree of inequality of incomes depends closely on the volume of employment which the economy is capable of generating. The disappearance of permanent unemployment is regarded as indicating that the structure of the economy has changed and as a prerequisite for a reduction or inequality. The aim of a more equitable distribution of incomes is thus closely associated with a policy of full employment.

Influence of changes in income distribution on employment

The influence of changes in income distribution on employment is not as clear as the influence of the level of employment on income distribution. If the hypothesis of a progressive redistribution effecting a transfer of incomes from the rich to the poor is taken as a starting point, Keynesian theory would suggest that such a transfer will reduce savings and stimulate consumption. The accumulation of capital needed for economic growth will be slowed up and the creation of jobs will be reduced. An equalisation of incomes would thus contribute to an increase in unemployment.

Account must be taken, however, of effects on the structure of consumption. If it is accepted that the basic products (food and clothing) for which there is a demand on the part of the poor are produced by methods that are less capital-intensive than those used for the production of luxury goods for which there is a demand from the rich, an equalising redistribution will create jobs; but, conversely, it has to be considered that there is a demand among the rich not only for personal and domestic services but also for craft products made by traditional methods requiring much labour.

Moreover, if it is accepted that the propensity to consume imported products is stronger among the richer sections of the population than among the poorer, then the greater the dispersion of income the greater will be the demand for foreign products, thereby diminishing the possibilities of importing the capital goods and intermediate products needed for the creation of new jobs. In that case, a progressive redistribution of incomes will promote an expansion of employment.[31]

What would be the net result of these different reactions? A first answer to that question has come, in the framework of the World Employment Programme, from the preparation of a model designed to measure the effect of a modification of income distribution on the structure of consumption, on savings and on production, and hence on the level of employment. Applied first to the Philippines, that model has subsequently been applied to other countries as well.[32]

In broad outline, the method consists in dividing the population of households into deciles, each decile being characterised by a specific pattern of consumption and a specific propensity to save. Prices being assumed to be fixed, the consequences of a modification of the distribution of incomes are examined for a distribution differing from the actual distribution, and the effects of that change on private consumption, on imports of consumer goods and on savings are determined. The volume of production and of income corresponding to the new patterns of consumption are also calculated. The final effect on employment is determined by means of a semi-closed input-output model, which describes the type of economic equilibrium that would correspond, on the assumptions made, to different distributions of personal incomes, particular stress being placed on the level of employment. The exercise is thus a static comparative simulation.

Use of that model indicates that in certain cases a reduction of inequality of incomes would have beneficial effects on employment.

In the Philippines, a drastic diminution of inequality that brought the

Gini coefficient down from 0.47 to 0.25 would result in an increase in employment by some 10 per cent. In Iran, a reduction that brought the Gini coefficient down from 0.52 to 0.4 would be accompanied by an increase in employment by over 5 per cent, while a transfer to the poorer groups of 10 per cent of total income would raise employment by some 4 to 5 per cent. In Malaysia, a moderate redistribution of incomes would have a modest effect (plus 1 per cent) on employment; drastic redistributions would lead to an increase of 3 to 4 per cent. The effect would vary considerably from one sector to another: it would be appreciable in the case of agricultural activities, small in the case of commercial activities and neutral in the case of production for export and of industry, construction and public works and financial services; on the other hand employment would diminish in transport and communications as well as in personal and domestic services. The diversity of effects results from the modifications of the pattern of consumption that would follow the redistribution of incomes.

In those three countries the positive effect on overall employment is due to the shift of consumption towards products manufactured by less capital-intensive means. As a result, the increase in employment is for the least skilled and least productive labour; it is accompanied by a fall in productivity and in income per employed person; in other words, the overall product and personal income increase less than employment. An egalitarian redistribution of incomes causes also a slight deterioration in the balance of payments and especially an appreciable reduction of private savings, with, consequentially, a fall in the rate of growth of the overall product and of employment (by about 0.5 per cent in the Philippines).

In the Republic of Korea, the economy appears to be much less sensitive than in most of the other developing countries to modifications of the distribution of incomes, which in any case is more equal than in the other countries (the Gini coefficient is about 0.4 as against more than 0.5 elsewhere). The disparity between urban and rural incomes is not very wide, the differences in productivity and in incomes between sectors of industry are small, and the structure of consumption does not differ between one group and another. The advantages that might be expected elsewhere from a policy of redistribution are therefore much less considerable in the Republic of Korea.

A study carried out by a similar method for Colombia, which is a country in which the distribution of income is relatively unequal, shows that the analysis must be qualified. In that country a fairly pronounced redistribution of the incomes of the rich among the poor would have a negligible negative effect on the volume of production and a small positive effect on the level of employment.[33] The initial importance of the concentration of incomes cannot suffice, therefore, to explain the difference in effectiveness between measures of redistribution. In practice, a relatively equal distribution of incomes cannot be imposed by simple measures of transfer; it has to be integrated into the whole organisation of the economy, which implies co-ordination of all the instruments of economic policy.[34]

INTER-RELATIONSHIP OF THE VARIOUS ELEMENTS OF INEQUALITY

At the close of this examination of the factors accounting for inequality of incomes, it should be stressed that the foregoing analysis, however comprehensive it may have been, has barely touched on the question of their interconnections. In that sense the approach has been limited to partial analysis: it excludes general equilibrium models, the preparation of which will constitute a new stage of research. There are nevertheless some points that can already be brought out at this stage concerning the inter-relationship between the various factors.

In the least developed countries where the great majority of the economically active population is engaged in agriculture and in traditional activities, the intersectoral disparity in average incomes is very large because the share of agriculture in total income is not markedly greater than in more advanced economies. In other words, the difference in productivity and in average income between the agricultural sector and the non-agricultural sector accounts for about half of the general inequality of incomes. That simple fact justifies the dualistic theories that have appeared among the first attempts at an overall interpretation of inequalities.

A reduction of the intersectoral disparity of incomes implies both an increase of agricultural income and the absorption of a part of the rural population by non-agricultural and mainly urban activities. There can be no increase of agricultural income without a development of cash crops, with an expansion of commercial agriculture and a progressive integration of the traditional sector in the market economy. That development can lead, however, at any rate during the period of adjustment, to an increase in inequality of incomes in the rural areas by increasing inter-regional disparities in the level of living. The dispersion of incomes in the agricultural sector and in rural areas thus has its origin not solely in the distribution of landed property but in the general effect of commercial, technical and structural changes which accompany development.

The shift of population that takes place spontaneously from the countryside to the towns contributes to an increase of income inequality in urban areas. In a general way, rural-urban migration tends to transform the underemployment of the relatively unproductive rural labour force into visible unemployment.

In so far as that unemployment lies heavy on the urban employment

111

market and contributes to an increase of income inequality, any action designed to reduce inequality becomes inseparably associated with employment policy. The relationship between employment and distribution of incomes is, moreover, reciprocal: while a reduction of unemployment can reduce the dispersion of incomes, conversely a diminution of the dispersion can, in certain circumstances, promote an expansion of employment.

There are nevertheless specific causes of the increase of income inequality in urban areas. It is in the towns, where the main development of modern activities takes place, that the largest incomes from entrepreneurship are distributed and that the diversification of labour gives rise to the widest disparities of wages and salaries. Experience shows, moreover, that an increase in average incomes is accompanied by an increase in their dispersion. All these facts have their origin both in the specific characteristics of occupations and jobs and in the individual characteristics of economically active persons (sex, age, ethnic origin, state of health, education).

It is clear that all these factors are closely interconnected. For example, the heads of households in the rural areas have incomes that are, on the average, lower than those in urban areas; but they also have a much lower level of education: they are more frequently self-employed than remunerated employees and they use a smaller amount of capital per worker. There is obviously interaction between the various factors (location in country or town, agricultural or non-agricultural sector, employment status (self-employed or employee), level of education, as well as, in many cases, size of household, age of family head, etc.).

Distinct socio-economic groups can be defined in terms of that interaction. In the developing countries the disparities in average incomes between these groups that are directly imputable to causes such as the structure of the gross product, the sectoral distribution of the economically active population and differences in productivity and in capital-intensiveness account for 60 to 80 per cent of income inequality, which is a much higher proportion than in the developed countries. Estimations of income distribution by groups thus provide one of the most fruitful ways of analysing the general distribution of incomes.

If there is to be a change in the distribution of incomes, there has to be a modification of the combined effect of the various factors of inequality. The formulation of a real policy of income distribution is not conceivable, therefore, independently of an overall change in the economic and social structure. Such a policy has to be a constituent element of a general policy of economic development.

Notes

[1] See Lecaillon and Germidis: *Inégalité des revenus et développement économique* (1977), pp. 172–173.

[2] On these questions see Pang: "Growth, inequality and race in Singapore" (1975), pp. 15–28, especially pp. 17–18 and 24–25; and Lean: *Employment and income distribution in West Malaysia* (1975), pp. 48–49.

[3] Lecaillon and Germidis, op. cit., pp. 70, 201.

[4] Mach: "Selected issues on health and employment" (1979), p. 142.

[5] Stevens: *Health, employment and income distribution* (1975).

[6] Richards: *Some distributional issues in planning for basic needs health care* (1979), especially pp. 4–7, 31–33; see also Mach, op. cit., pp. 140 et seq.

[7] Carter: "The genetic basis of inequality" (1976).

[8] See van Ginneken: *Rural and urban income inequalities in Indonesia, Mexico, Pakistan, Tanzania and Tunisia* (1976), pp. 44–45; idem: *Socio-economic groups and income distribution in Mexico* (1980), p. 54; Skolka and Garzuel: *Changes in income distribution, employment and structure of the economy* (1976), pp. 8–9; Encarnación: *Income distribution in the Philippines* (1974), pp. 21–22.

[9] Richards and Leonor: *Education and income distribution in Asia* (1981), pp. 25–26.

[10] See Blaug: *Education and the unemployment problem in developing countries*, pp. 27 et seq.

[11] Hsia and Chau: *Industrialisation, employment and income distribution* (1978), pp. 61–63, 70, 72; Lean: *The pattern of income distribution in West Malaysia, 1957–1970* (1974), pp. 53–55; idem: *Employment and income distribution in West Malaysia* (1975), pp. 43–46.

[12] See Carnoy et al.: *Can educational policy equalise income distribution in Latin America?* (1979), pp. 7–18; van Ginneken: *Socio-economic groups and income distribution in Mexico* (1980), pp. 26–32; Richards and Leonor, op. cit., pp. 27–33.

[13] Carnoy et al., op. cit., pp. 35 et seq.

[14] Bourguignon: *The role of education in the urban labour market during the process of development* (1979), pp. 32–35.

[15] Richards and Leonor, op. cit., Chaps. 2, 3 and 9.

[16] See Lean: *Employment and income distribution . . . op. cit.*, pp. 27–29; Hsia and Chau: op. cit., p. 47; Lecaillon and Germidis, op. cit., pp. 58 et seq.

[17] The Theil index is equal to the following sum:

$$T = \sum Y_i \; T_i + T_b$$

where Y_i = percentage of group i in total income;
  T_i = value of Theil index for the dispersion of incomes within group i;
  T_b = value of Theil index for the groups as a whole, assuming income equality within each group.

[18] The Theil index for the overall distribution has been calculated for a distribution by deciles, the last one being broken down into twentieths. Consequently, the value given in the table is lower by 15 to 20 per cent than the exact value of T obtained for a breakdown by individuals, not by deciles or twentieths. If the exact value of T for N to infinity is estimated by assuming that the distribution of incomes in the tenth decile follows the Pareto law with a coefficient of 1.7, what is obtained is a value for T that is higher by 18 to 25 per cent than the value calculated according to the distribution by deciles. Verifications of the Pareto law have shown that it gives satisfactory results for the distribution of incomes in the tenth decile (though not for the overall distribution of incomes) and that the estimated values of α are close to 1.7.

[19] Miller: *Aspects of income distribution in Turkey* (1975), p. 26.

[20] Skolka and Garzuel: *Income distribution by size, employment and the structure of the economy* (1978), p. 93.

[21] In the Republic of Korea, the rate of school enrolment in primary education reaches 100 per cent. In 1967 there were over 1.3 million pupils in secondary education and over 160,000 students in higher education, out of a population of 30 million. ibid., pp. 5, 97.

[22] Lecaillon and Germidis, op. cit., pp. 19, 32.

[23] See Richards: *Underemployment and basic needs satisfaction* (1977), pp. 4 et seq. See also, for the discussion that follows, Lydall: *Unemployment in developing countries* (1977).

[24] Lewis: "Economic development with unlimited supplies of labour" (1954).

[25] Lydall: *Unemployment in developing countries* (1977), pp. 23–24.

[26] On the development of industrial production, the expansion of employment and the choice of techniques, see for example Ewusi: *Employment performance of Ghanaian manufacturing industries* (1977); Solis: *A monetary will-o'-the-wisp* (1977), Part I, pp. 43–45; Wada: *Impact of economic growth on the size distribution of income* (1975), pp. 154–155; Gupta: *Solving India's employment problem* (1975), pp. 6–9.

[27] Lydall, op. cit., p. 28.

[28] Richards, op. cit., pp. 4 et seq.

[29] Lydall, op. cit., p. 25.

[30] Wada, op. cit., pp. 153–154.

[31] See the report of the mission that went to Colombia in 1970 under the auspices of the ILO and with the participation of a number of other international organisations for the purpose of formulating a strategy for the development of employment: ILO: *Towards full employment* (1970), pp. 145–148.

[32] See Paukert, Skolka and Maton: *Redistribution of income, patterns of consumption and employment* (1974); Skolka and Garzuel: *Changes in income distribution, . . .,* op. cit., idem: *Income distribution by size, . . . op. cit.,* Maton and Garzuel: *Redistribution of income, patterns of consumption and employment* (1978).

[33] Bourguignon: *General equilibrium analysis of the Colombian income distribution* (1978).

[34] Paukert, Skolka and Maton: *Income distribution, structure of economy and employment* (1981).

INCIDENCE OF TAXATION AND GOVERNMENT EXPENDITURE ON HOUSEHOLD INCOME 5

Changes in the distribution of household incomes can be brought about by governments indirectly and in the long run by such measures as a reform of the system of land tenure, the application of an employment policy or of an incomes and prices policy, guidance in the choice of particular technologies or action in the fields of public health and education. Changes in income distribution can also be brought about directly and immediately (in the following financial year) through taxation and government expenditure.

The effects of taxation and public expenditure on household incomes can be studied by the methods employed in developed countries.[1] When applied to the less developed countries, however, these methods raise a number of problems. In most cases the rate of direct taxation can be meaningless because the incomes declared are understated to a much greater extent in developing countries than in developed countries. It is most desirable, therefore, to calculate the rate from two independent sources: the tax on income and the incomes estimated on the basis of surveys and corrected by reference to the national accounts. The most usual method of imputing tax on companies (half imputed to the shareholders and the other half to consumers) may not be applicable in countries where, thanks to tariff barriers and by reason of the size of the national market, many if not all companies are in a monopoly situation enabling them to shift the whole burden of the tax on to the consumer. In many cases, too, a large proportion of the factor incomes accrues to foreigners (remittances of dividends and interest payments, as well as transfers of parts of the salaries payable for technical co-operation); these incomes, moreover, may be partly exempt from taxation. In addition, under some national budgets much of the revenue is raised by export duties for which imputation raises special problems: a reduction of these duties would alter the volume of exports, and consequently the distribution of incomes; it would be necessary to use a macro-economic model in order to assess the ultimate effect of such a change. Lastly, in some countries there is considerable deficit budgeting, which is financed by the issue of money. It would be necessary to carry out an analysis of the effects of inflation on the factorial distribution of incomes in order to ascertain how the burden of the deficit financing is distributed among households.

A study of the incidence of public expenditure also raises difficulties that are specific to the comparatively undeveloped countries. In the first place, even in countries where there is comparatively little intervention by the State in economic affairs, governments will seek to promote certain activities through the allocation of a substantial proportion of public expenditure under a wide variety of headings. It is difficult to impute expenditure of that kind. For example, if assistance to agriculture is given in a score of different ways, it will be necessary, on the one hand, to estimate the distribution of the expenditure among the farmers according to their respective income brackets (a calculation for which the requisite information is usually unavailable) and, on the other hand, to determine the beneficiaries of the assistance (do the farmers alone derive from it an increase in their incomes or is it of some advantage also to consumers?). It is clear that any assessment of the distribution of that expenditure elsewhere than in a country where the necessary surveys and studies have taken place can be no more than a rough approximation.

For all these reasons, the estimates to be given below of the incidence of taxation and government expenditure must be treated with prudence: they refer to likely orders of magnitude rather than to precise and exact values.

INCIDENCE OF TAXATION

Hong Kong

A distinguishing feature of the Hong Kong Government's budget is that certain special resources (land sales, interest income from reserves held overseas, etc.), together with revenue from postal services, account for 21 per cent of total revenue. R. Hsia and L. Chau examined the usual taxes and duties, excluding small parts of them (tax on interest, stamp duties, estate duty) which do not affect low-income families and which, had they been taken into account, would not have modified the conclusions on the progressive character of the fiscal system. The tax on corporate profits has been imputed to the shareholders, while indirect taxes and rates have been allocated according to the results of a household budget survey which distribute them under various headings, including that of housing.[2]

Table 24 summarises the findings. The direct taxes really affect only the tenth decile: they reach a rate of 10 per cent in the case of the group of the richest 5 per cent of the population. Indirect taxes represent a small

Table 24. Direct and indirect taxes as percentage of household primary income by incomes class in Hong Kong, 1971

Income class	% of population	% of total primary income	Direct taxes	Indirect taxes[1]	Rates	Totals	
						Indirect taxes plus rates	All taxes considered
1	4.8	0.7	—	3.70	1.60	5.30	5.30
2	10.5	3.1	—	3.69	1.14	4.83	4.83
3	24.1	11.7	—	3.04	1.19	4.23	4.23
4	19.8	13.5	—	2.82	1.29	4.11	4.11
5	11.4	9.9	—	2.46	1.96	4.42	4.42
6	9.5	10.1	—	2.64	1.59	4.23	4.22
7	7.3	9.6	0.2	2.27	2.58	4.85	5.05
8	4.7	8.0	0.5	1.87	1.90	3.77	4.22
9	3.2	7.1	1.6	2.04	1.84	3.88	5.45
10	3.1	10.7	6.4	2.15	1.76	3.91	10.27
11	1.6	15.7	16.3	1.53	1.37	2.87	19.21

[1] On alcoholic drinks, tobacco, transport and entertainment.
Source: Hsia and Chau, *Industrialisation, employment and income distribution* (1978), p. 154.

proportion, decreasing as one rises in the income scale (between about 3 and 3.7 per cent in the case of the poorest groups and between about 1.5 and 2 per cent in the case of the richest). The property tax is neutral in its effect. It follows that the fiscal system as a whole (direct and indirect taxes) is progressive: the overall rate of levy varies between 4.4 and 5.3 per cent for the first nine income brackets (with a minimum for the intermediate brackets) and then rises to, respectively, 10.3 and 19.2 per cent for the last two income brackets.

India

An analysis of taxes in India has been carried out by A. Gupta by methods differing somewhat from those followed for the other countries.[3] A few taxes are omitted but the ones examined (taxes on income and on corporate profits, indirect taxes, customs duties) account for more than 98 per cent of the Central Government's revenue. The analysis is of further interest in that it covers three years (1953–54, 1963–64, 1973–74) that are sufficiently far apart to reveal changes that have taken place.

For the purpose of ascertaining the incidence of indirect taxation, consumption patterns were estimated from household surveys. These sources are fairly reliable though they underestimate the incomes of rich households, which are less accessible to investigators. For the calculation

Table 25. Percentage distribution of cash consumption expenditure and indirect taxes, by groups of income deciles, in India, 1953–54, 1963–64, 1973–74

Deciles	1953–54			1963–64			1973–74		
	Expen-diture	Taxes		Expen-diture	Taxes		Expen-diture	Taxes (estimates)	
		A	B		A	B		A	B
1 to 5	29.1	20.8	21.6	34.4	25.5	25.5	26.8	19	19
6 to 9	46.5	41.3	42.0	42.4	40.2	40.1	46.7	41	41
10	24.4	37.9	36.4	23.2	34.3	34.4	26.5	40	40

Key: A: Corporation tax imputed to shareholders; export duties imputed to exporters. B: Corporation tax and export duties passed on to the consumer.
Source: Gupta, *The rich, the poor and the taxes they pay in India* (1975), p. 47.

of the incidence of direct taxation, recourse was had not to tax returns, which are unusable,[4] but to the best estimates of income distribution.

It was assumed that income taxes and property taxes, as well as estate duty and taxes on expenditure and on gifts, were borne in their entirety by the tenth decile; only a very small minority is liable to payment of those taxes and under 2 per cent of the economically active population pay income tax. As for corporation tax and duties on exports, it was assumed either (Variant A) that corporation tax is imputable to the shareholders and that export duties are imputable to the exporters (direct taxation) or (Variant B) that both forms of taxation are passed on to the consumer (indirect taxation).

In the case of direct taxation, it was found, under Variant A, that the rate levied on the tenth decile increased from 5.5 per cent in 1953–54 to 8.4 per cent in 1963–64 and then fell to 7.4 per cent in 1973–74; while this latter figure was still above the 1953–54 level, the share of the tenth decile in the distribution of income had risen in the meantime from 35 to 40 per cent. Under Variant B, the rate of direct taxation rose from 3.4 per cent to 4.2 per cent, and then declined to 3.8 per cent.

Table 25 shows the distribution of cash expenditure on consumption and the distribution of indirect taxation. The poorer households (first five deciles) paid from about 20 to about 25 per cent of the indirect taxes whereas their share of expenditure ranged from 27 to 35 per cent. The richest households (tenth decile) paid from 35 to 40 per cent of those taxes while their share of consumption fluctuated around 25 per cent. In that sense, the indirect taxation on consumption is progressive, but the distribution of cash consumption expenditure is less concentrated than the distribution of incomes, which is closely similar to the distribution of indirect taxation. For the year 1973–74, the shares of deciles 1 to 5, 6 to 9

Table 26. Percentage distribution of national income and of taxation, by income deciles, in India, 1973–74

Deciles	Share of national income	Share of taxation (direct and indirect)	
		A	B
1 to 5	22.0	13.5	16.1
6 to 9	40.9	29.1	34.8
10	37.1	57.4	49.1
	100.0	100.0	100.0

Key: Same as for table 25.
Source: Gupta, *The rich, the poor and the taxes they pay in India* (1975), p. 49. Authors' estimates of the national income distribution.

and 10 are, respectively, 19, 41 and 40 per cent of the indirect taxes and, respectively, 21, 39.5 and 39.5 per cent of the national income. Seen from that angle, indirect taxation has no equalising effect.

Since direct taxation bears solely on the tenth decile, the incidence of the whole of the taxes collected by the Central Government is progressive. The contribution made by the richer categories represents a share in taxation that is proportionately larger than their share in the national income, as may be seen from the figures in table 26. It may be noted, however, that in 1953–54 the tenth decile's share in taxation was equal to its share in 1973–74 and that in 1963–64 its share was higher, whereas its share in the national income was lower in both of those earlier financial years.

Iran

Iran's taxation system is the subject of a study by F. Mehran.[5] The study refers to the year 1971. Taxation, which was proportional to income, was levied at a comparatively low rate in view of the large revenues from oil. The duties on exported oil constituted the Government's main source of revenue: in 1971–73 they amounted to more than twice the Government's revenues from other taxes. The study covers all these other revenues, including duties on oil sold in Iran itself and the taxes on the profits of the National Iranian Oil Company. The only taxes not covered are those levied by the municipalities, which were equivalent in 1973 to no more than 4 per cent of the Government's revenues. For the distribution of primary incomes, Mehran refers to some research work of his own[6] and makes use of documents published by the Ministry of Finance on tax revenue, as well as of several household budget surveys for the distribution of indirect taxes.

The methods of imputation follow the usual principles except that in the case of four types of tax the author uses a variety of assumptions. For the direct taxation of the income of individual entrepreneurs and other self-employed persons, of members of the professions and of farmers, he chooses four methods of distribution: (a) according to the tax returns of these economically active persons; (b) half as under (a) and half according to consumption expenditure; (c) entirely according to consumption expenditure; (d) half as under (a), a quarter according to consumption expenditure and a quarter according to urban wages and salaries. The same four methods of imputation are used in the case of corporate profits tax, the distribution among shareholders or owners of capital being made according to the income from urban property. In the case of rental income, the tax is imputed to income from urban property or to expenditure on housing or, again, equally between the two. Lastly, duties on imported products are imputed either entirely to consumption expenditure or half to consumption expenditure and half to urban wages and salaries.

While the choice between the two methods of imputing the duties on imports does not affect the incidence of those duties, and while the methods of distribution proposed for the corporate profits tax and for the rental income tax are usual, method (c) and even methods (b) and (d) for the distribution of the tax on the income of self-employed persons are somewhat questionable and rarely used. Method (c) could mean that, in each profession, there was an understanding between its members enabling them to behave monopolistically towards the buyers—a hypothesis that does not appear to tally with the practice of the majority of self-employed persons.

Table 27 shows the results obtained on the most favourable assumption from the point of view of redistribution and on the least favourable assumption. It is probable that the most plausible imputations for the corporate profits tax and for the rental income tax are situated somewhere between assumptions (a) and (c). Under assumption (a), there is a moderate progressivity in direct taxation, the rate rising from 1.5 per cent for the first two deciles to 4.4 per cent for the tenth decile; the indirect taxes amount to an almost constant percentage of primary income, except for the first decile (an average of 6.4 per cent instead of 5.1 per cent). As for assumption (c), it makes direct taxation proportional to income, with deciles 6 and 7 being a little less affected than the average (3.2 per cent) and the first decile (3.5 per cent), as well as the ninth and tenth deciles (3.4 per cent, 3.3 per cent), being slightly more affected than the average. It makes indirect taxes regressive: the percentages drop from 7.1 and 5.9 for the first and second deciles to 4.8 and 5.1 for the last two deciles.

Since the most acceptable method of imputation seems to lie between assumption (a) and (c), the averages of the two rates of overall taxation corresponding to those assumptions have been calculated. They

Table 27. Direct and indirect taxes as percentages of household primary income, by deciles, in Iran, 1971

Decile	Direct taxes		Indirect taxes		Total (direct and indirect taxes together)		
	a2	c1	a2	c1	a2	c1	Average
1	1.6	3.5	6.4	7.1	8.0	10.6	9.3
2	1.4	3.2	5.4	5.9	6.8	9.1	8.0
3	1.4	3.1	5.0	5.5	6.4	8.6	7.5
4	1.3	3.0	4.9	5.4	6.2	8.4	7.3
5	1.4	3.0	5.0	5.2	6.4	8.2	7.3
6	1.6	2.7	5.1	5.4	6.7	8.1	7.4
7	1.6	2.7	5.1	5.3	6.7	8.0	7.4
8	2.0	2.9	5.2	5.0	7.2	7.9	7.5
9	3.2	3.4	5.0	4.8	8.2	8.2	8.2
10	4.4	3.3	5.2	5.1	9.6	8.4	9.0

Tax on income of individual entrepreneurs and other self-employed persons, on members of professions and on farmers:
Assumption *a*: imputed to these economically active persons;
Assumption *c*: imputed wholly to the consumers.

Corporate profits tax:
Assumption *a*: distributed as in the case of revenue from urban property;
Assumption *c*: distributed as in the case of consumption expenditure.

Tax on rental income:
Assumption *a*: distributed as in the case of revenue from urban property;
Assumption *c*: distributed as in the case of housing expenses.

Import duties:
Assumption 1: distributed as in the case of consumption expenditure;
Assumption 2: distributed partly (half) as in the case of consumption expenditure and partly (half) as in the case of urban wages and salaries.

Source: Mehran, *Taxes and incomes* (1975), p. 60.

show that taxation had virtually no equalising effects. With an average of 8.3 per cent, all the rates are situated between 7.3 and 9.3 per cent. There is barely a trace of a U-curve, since the maximum rates are reached for deciles 1 and 2, on the one hand, and deciles 9 and 10, on the other, while the lowest rates are for deciles 4 to 7.

Philippines

The incidence of the taxation system in the Philippines has been studied in depth for the years 1961 and 1971 by the National Tax Research Center. E. A. Tan has described the methods followed and the results obtained.[7] Only those features of the methods that are specific to them will be indicated here, leaving aside instances of application by the usual methods.

The Center assumed that a third of the income tax collections from self-employed persons was shifted forward to the consumers and that a third of the tax collections from corporations was likewise shifted

Table 28. Taxes on income and property and indirect taxes as percentages of household primary incomes, by income bracket, in the Philippines, 1971

Income bracket	% of population	% of total primary income	Income and property taxes	Indirect taxes	Total
1	5.2	0.5	6.7	54.5	61.2
2	12.1	2.4	3.3	29.4	32.7
3	12.1	4.1	2.5	22.3	24.8
4	11.9	5.5	2.4	19.8	22.2
5	9.6	5.8	2.5	17.5	20.0
6	8.1	6.0	2.5	16.2	18.7
7	12.5	11.6	3.2	14.7	17.9
8	7.5	8.9	3.6	13.9	17.5
9	5.0	7.3	5.6	14.0	19.6
10	6.3	11.7	5.8	13.6	19.4
11	3.6	8.5	5.6	13.1	18.7
12	3.7	11.9	17.3	12.5	29.8
13	1.1	5.1	22.6	12.5	35.1
14	1.3	10.7	15.9	8.3	24.2

Source: Tan, *Taxation, government spending and income distribution in the Philippines* (1975), p. 29.

forward. In the case of import duties, 90 per cent was imputed to the consumers and 10 per cent to the importers. The employers' contributions to social security were taken into account and were distributed among the consumers, the employers and the wage or salary earners in the proportions of half, a quarter and a quarter respectively. A survey of 7,000 households carried out in 1971 provided the necessary data on consumption expenditure by items.

As table 28 shows, the taxes on income and on property are distinctly progressive inasmuch as the rate reaches about 19 per cent for the last three income brackets (5.9 per cent of the population) but only from 2.5 to 6 per cent for the other income brackets. The indirect taxes, on the other hand, are sharply regressive, the rate diminishing consistently from the first income bracket (54.5 per cent) to the last (8.3 per cent). As a result, the overall rate of taxation follows a U-curve: it falls from a maximum of 61.2 per cent for the first income bracket to 17.9 and 17.5 per cent for the seventh and eighth income brackets, and then rises to 35.1 and 24.2 per cent for the last two income brackets. The two deciles liable to the minimum rates of tax are the seventh and eighth; those bearing the maximum rates are situated at the two extremities (the first and second deciles at one end and the tenth decile at the other). The estimate of the share of the first income bracket (5.2 per cent of the population) in the distribution of incomes is highly uncertain, as is any estimate of the lowest incomes. As a result, the figure of 61.2 per cent for the overall rate of

Table 29. Direct and indirect taxes as percentages of household primary incomes, by income bracket, in Sri Lanka, 1973

Income bracket	% of population	% of total primary income	Direct taxes	Indirect taxes	Total
1	2.8	1.6	1.5	8.8	10.3
2	21.7	13.2	1.2	11.4	12.6
3	49.5	40.7	1.7	13.7	15.4
4	21.4	28.6	2.8	15.8	18.6
5	2.1	4.8	5.3	17.3	22.6
6	2.5	11.1	12.4	22.0	34.4

Source: Alailima, *Fiscal incidence in Sri Lanka* (1978), pp. 34–36.

taxation is of little significance. It would be better to combine the first two income brackets (17.3 per cent of the population), for which the corresponding rate of taxation would amount to 37 per cent.

Sri Lanka

The case of Sri Lanka is of particular interest: it shows how indirect taxation, like direct taxation, can have a progressive incidence in a developing country with a large rural sector. As a result the overall incidence of taxation, both direct and indirect, is distinctly progressive, rising from about 12 per cent for the first two deciles to 34.4 per cent for the richest income group (2.5 per cent of the population).

In the study by P. J. Alailima,[8] the various taxes are imputed according to the usual rules, except that the corporate income tax is distributed in its entirety in the same way as the dividends. Since that tax is a light one, the results would be almost the same if half of it were imputed to consumers and the other half to the share-holders.

Table 29 shows the progressive nature of each category of revenue. The direct taxes rise from 1.5 per cent of the primary income for income brackets 1 to 5 to 12.4 per cent for the last income bracket (2.5 per cent of the population). The progressivity of the indirect taxes, although more moderate, is just as clear: the rate rises from 11 per cent for the first two groups to 20 per cent for the last two (one-twentieth of the population), with a regular progression from the first to the last income group.

A more detailed analysis of indirect taxes explains how progressiveness results from, on the one hand, a business turnover tax and, on the other, a system of levies and premiums under a scheme of foreign exchange entitlement certificates. The business turnover tax varies from 1 per cent for labour-intensive ventures and those making use of local raw

Table 30. Direct and indirect taxes as percentages of household primary incomes, by income bracket, in Chile, 1969

Income bracket	% of population	% of total primary income	Direct taxes	Indirect taxes	Total
1	29.8	7.6	1.5	17.0	18.5
2	31.6	20.1	3.5	13.1	16.6
3	17.6	18.9	4.1	12.7	16.8
4	7.4	11.2	4.4	11.4	15.8
5	4.5	8.7	5.6	10.8	16.4
6	2.9	7.1	7.0	11.2	18.2
7	2.7	8.0	7.6	10.4	18.0
8	1.5	5.9	7.5	12.7	20.2
9	2.0	12.5	15.5	11.2	26.7

Source: Foxley et al., *Redistributive effects of government programmes* (1979), pp. 43, 46.

materials, to 48 per cent for petroleum. The amount of tax collected in 1973 from the petroleum products and motor vehicles sectors accounted for 38 per cent of the total revenue obtained from that business turnover tax. Since the most heavily taxed goods are purchased especially by the richer households, the incidence of the tax increases with the income, from 2.7 per cent for the first two deciles to 6.5 per cent for the last income group. The scheme of foreign exchange entitlement certificates was introduced by the Government of Sri Lanka in 1967 in order to correct an imbalance in external payments. The scheme provided for the imposition of a 65 per cent levy on the value of almost all imports (not including rice, flour, pharmaceutical products, fertilisers and some other goods) and for the payment of a bonus of 65 per cent on exports (excluding traditional products such as tea and rubber). The scheme results in a net gain for the poorest households, and at the same time bears heavily on urban households owing to their propensity to consume imported goods.

Chile

An analysis of taxation in Chile has been carried out by A. Foxley and others: it is detailed and complete, taking all tax revenue into account.[9]

For direct taxation, the selected methods of imputation in the benchmark case shown in table 30 are among the least questionable. The tax on corporate profits is distributed equally between owners and consumers. In the case of unincorporated enterprises, three-quarters of the tax is imputed to the owners and one-quarter to consumers. The whole of the taxes on capital are distributed among the owners of each category of assets. For the sales tax, the commodities liable to the same rate of tax were grouped together and the data on consumption were then classified in a corresponding way to determine the distribution of these taxes. The results of the analysis relating to indirect taxation have been checked and confirmed by reference to another study on the incidence of indirect taxation based on a family budget survey carried out in the Santiago metropolitan area.

Table 30 shows the progressivity of the direct taxes and the regressivity of the indirect taxes. In the case of the former the rate rises from 1.5 per cent for the first income bracket (deciles 1 to 3) to 15.5 per cent for the last income bracket, with an average of 9 per cent for the last four income brackets (tenth decile). On the other hand the indirect taxes bear much more heavily on the first income bracket (17 per cent) than on the following ones (deciles 4 to 10: from 10.4 to 13.1 per cent). Among the latter, the incidence tends to lessen as income increases; the average rate for the last four income brackets is 11.3 per cent, as against 13.1 per cent for the second income bracket.

The taxation system taken as a whole has hardly any effect on income inequality. The rate of taxation does follow, it is true, a U-curve inasmuch as its incidence falls from 18.5 per cent for the first income bracket to 15.8 per cent for the fourth bracket and then rises to 26.7 per cent for the last income bracket. The variations are, however, slight; excluding the last income bracket (2 per cent of the population), the rate oscillates between 15.8 and 20.2 per cent as against an average of 18.4 per cent. Moreover the rates for the last income brackets, especially the ninth, may be over-estimated: the primary distribution was based on a survey, the figures being adjusted proportionately so as to make the sum of the household incomes tally with the same aggregate in the national accounts. There is, however, a strong likelihood that the adjustments for the upper income brackets were insufficient. If that was the case, the real rates for income brackets 8 and 9 would be close to the average, with the result that the overall rate of taxation would be almost constant for all the deciles and a little below the average for the ninth decile on its own.

Incidence in developed and developing countries: A general conspectus

It will be useful to pull together the strands that emerged above. Since there are differences between the countries in the decile composition of income brackets, any comparison of the incidence of taxation by income brackets would be devoid of significance. It is the rates of taxation for households similarly situated in the distribution of incomes, that is, in the same centile or decile, that have to be compared. Where the available estimates refer to incidence by income brackets, the incidence by deciles must be calculated through extrapolation. The yields from that method are, however, approximate so that the results, as set out in table 31, are

Table 31. Taxes as percentages of household primary income, by deciles, and incidence of taxation on income distribution, in 12 countries or territories

Deciles	Chile 1969	Colombia 1966	Panama 1970	Peru 1969	Puerto Rico 1963	Hong Kong 1971	Iran 1971	Malaysia 1958	Philippines 1971	Sri Lanka 1973	United States 1970	United Kingdom 1975	Deciles
1	18.5	15	9	5	14	5.0	9.3	20	42	12	59	180	1
2						4.6	8.0		32		46	45	2
3		10	13	6.5	16	4.2	7.5		25	15.4	47	41	3
4	16.5		14	9		4.2	7.3		22		37	39	4
5		10	15	9.5	17.5	4.1	7.3	18	20		34	39	5
6		10	15	15		4.1	7.4		19		34	39	6
7	17	11	15	16	18.5	4.4	7.4		18	18.6	31	38	7
8	17	11	16	18	18	4.3	7.5	14	17.5		31	38	8
9	16	11.5	17	20	18.5	4.8	8.2		19.5		29	38	9
10 { 5%	18	12	23	24	18	5.0	9.0	18	22	29	29	40	10 { 5%
10 { 5%	24	25				15.0	9.0		29		38	41	10 { 5%

Gini coefficients[1]	Chile	Colombia	Panama	Peru	Puerto Rico	Hong Kong	Iran	Malaysia	Philippines	Sri Lanka	United States	United Kingdom
Before tax	0.456	0.555	0.590	0.605	0.502	0.439	0.578	0.421	0.479	0.234	0.444	0.423
After tax	0.448	0.540	0.571	0.578	0.498	0.420	0.577	0.420	0.477	0.202	0.456	0.442

[1] The Gini coefficients are calculated directly from the income groups; they are not comparable as between one country and another.

Sources: Hong Kong, Iran, Philippines, Sri Lanka, Chile: tables 24 and 27–30. Colombia: Berry and Urrutia, *Income distribution in Colombia* (1976); Panama: Sahota, "The distribution of the benefits of public expenditure in Panama" (1977); Peru: Webb, *Government policy and the distribution of income in Peru 1963–73* (1972); Puerto Rico: Mann, "Net fiscal incidence in Puerto Rico" (1973); Malaysia: McLure, "Incidence of taxation in West Malaysia" (1972); United States: Reynolds and Smolensky, *Public expenditures, taxes, and the distribution of income* (1977), Appendix D-E, pp. 115–132; United Kingdom: Central Statistical Office, "Effects of taxes and benefits on household income, 1975" (1976), p. 111.

subject to a certain margin of error. The table covers five of the countries that were examined above as well as five others that have been the subject of similar studies; two developed countries are included in the table for purposes of comparison.

In six out of the ten developing countries or territories the rate of incidence follows a U-curve, whereas in the four others (Panama, Peru, Puerto Rico and Sri Lanka) it increases continuously with income. It is necessary, however, to treat with prudence the shape of the curve for the low incomes, which are not known with any precision so that a variation of less than one percentage point (for example, between 5 and 4.2 for deciles 1 and 3 at Hong Kong) may not be significant. In the former six cases, the maximum rate of taxation occurs either in the first deciles (Malaysia, Philippines) or in the last decile or last twentieth (Chile, Colombia, Hong Kong). The minimum rates of taxation apply to deciles 5 to 9 rather than to the first deciles, and the households whose incomes place them above the median seem relatively favoured by comparison with the others.

Taken as a whole, taxation has no effect or only a slight effect on the inequality of incomes by reason either of the U-curve for the rate of taxation or of the very slow rise in the rate, which, for example, rises from 14 to 18 per cent in Puerto Rico from the first decile to the last. In three countries (Iran, Malaysia, Philippines), the Gini coefficient is the same after tax as before tax. Elsewhere (Chile, Colombia, Puerto Rico), the drop in the coefficient due to taxation is negligible (less than 3 per cent). The drop is significant only in Panama (0.571 instead of 0.591), in Peru (0.578 instead of 0.605), in Hong Kong (0.414 instead of 0.439) and in Sri Lanka (0.201 instead of 0.234), which are countries where the rate of taxation for the last twentieth reaches figures well above the average.

The comparison with the United States and the United Kingdom leads to results that are surprising at first sight. In those two countries, where the rate of taxation diminishes as income increases, taxation causes a rise in the Gini coefficient. For the United States there is a U-curve with a minimum for the well-to-do households of the ninth decile and the penultimate twentieth. The explanation of that paradox lies in the scale of transfer payments in those countries. The households in the first two deciles pay practically no direct tax, but the indirect taxes which they pay are important in relation to primary incomes, since their consumption is paid for, to a high degree, from transfer payments. Thus, as the comparison between the United States and the United Kingdom shows, the more the poorer households are aided by the State, the more indirect taxes do they pay and the more does the ratio of indirect taxes to primary income rise. That ratio is much lower in the developing countries, where the poorest households receive much less state aid. The estimate of the incidence of taxation would be a very different one for the developed countries if reference were made to an adjusted income (primary income increased by public transfers and diminished by direct and indirect taxes) instead of to the primary income. In that case, the rate of taxation would rise with the income. On the other hand, for the developing countries the estimate would not be modified by reason of the smallness of the monetary transfers. Thus, in the United States and more especially in the United Kingdom, taxation on adjusted income is distinctly progressive, whereas among the developing countries under consideration that situation appears in only four cases.[10]

Since the expenditure with a progressive incidence accounts for about two-thirds of the specific expenditure, the effect of specific expenditure is advantageous to the poorer households: as incomes rise, the percentages fall from 17.7 to 11.4 per cent for income brackets 1 and 2 (one-quarter of the population) and from 4.3 to 3.1 per cent for income brackets 10 and 11 (one-twentieth of the population).

Progressivity becomes markedly reduced, however, when account is taken also of the general expenditure on the assumption that it is distributed according to income (distribution *(b)*): this reduction is due to the large share of the budget (65 per cent) taken up by general expenditure. The incidence becomes barely twice higher for the first quarter of the population (income brackets 1 and 2: 28.5 and 22.2 per cent) than for the last twentieth (15.1 and 13.9 per cent). Since the average income of the rich households is about 36 times larger than that of households in the poorest quarter of the population, under distribution *(b)* the rich families receive transfers that are 18 times greater in absolute value.

INCIDENCE OF PUBLIC EXPENDITURE

In order to determine the incidence of public expenditure, a distinction must be drawn in the developing countries, as in the developed, between general expenditure (administration, justice, diplomacy, defence), which concerns the whole population, and specific expenditure that can be imputed to certain individual persons or, rather, to certain households (since many transfers are made to families, the individual is not a suitable unit for this kind of analysis). Since there are almost insurmountable and well known difficulties in imputing general expenditure, some economists claim that such imputation is a sterile exercise which should not be attempted.[11] Under the usual methods of imputation, distribution among groups is made according to their weight in the total population, their share of primary incomes, or their wealth.[12] The principle of equal distribution in line with the distribution of the population may be justified in the case of developed countries where the socio-political conditions make it possible for choices of general expenditure to result from a collective decision and where all population groups benefit from the expenditure to a similar extent. In the developing countries, on the other hand, the population is generally less closely associated with decision-making. The public services are usually located in the towns while the rural areas, where most of the poorer households live, are inadequately catered for. It cannot be said, therefore, that the whole population benefits equally from general expenditure. Imputation according to wealth is not practicable in most cases because of the lack of the necessary statistical information. The most satisfactory solution consists, therefore, in imputation of general expenditure according to primary incomes. This hypothesis implies that the incidence is neutral, and does not change the distribution of primary income. As a result the distribution of general expenditure is less equal in developing than in developed countries. The point can be made in that regard that the poorest families, who live in rural areas, are generally more neglected by the public services in the developing countries than in developed countries. However, in view of the objections that can be made to any attempt to impute general expenditure, it is perhaps imputation according to primary income, which makes general expenditure play a neutral role in the equalisation of incomes, that offers the best solution.

For some countries, areas or territories (Hong Kong, India, Sri Lanka, Botswana), only certain specific items of expenditure have been taken into account in the analyses that follow; for the others (Iran, Philippines, Chile), all expenditure, including general expenditure, is taken into account and imputed to households.

Hong Kong

There are several special features in the structure of public expenditure in Hong Kong: military expenditure is insignificant; social expenditure in the broad sense (education, public health, housing, public assistance and social services) plays a very important role: it amounted in 1971–72 to 44 per cent of the total. It is the distribution of social expenditure among households that has been studied by Hsia and Chau.[13] They thus analyse nearly all the expenditure on specific items, some expenditure on economic services having accounted for only 9 per cent of the budget. The incidence of the various categories of social expenditure, as percentages of household primary income, is shown in table 32.

For primary education, it was assumed that all households received the same transfer if they had the same number of children, since the school attendance rate of children of primary school age is very high (86.5 per cent) and families with low incomes are exempted from payment of fees in most of the aided private schools. As a result, there was a practically equal distribution of expenditure on primary education. Expenditure on

Table 32. Social expenditure in percentages of household primary income, by income groups, in Hong Kong, 1971

Income groups	% of population	% of total primary income	Housing	Education				Health	All expenditure covered
				Primary	Secondary	Higher	Total		
1	4.8	0.7	9.9	9.0	1.7	0.9	11.6	10.3	31.8
2	10.5	3.1	6.5	7.8	1.5	1.0	10.3	7.1	24.2
3	24.1	11.7	8.0	7.8	1.5	1.0	10.3	5.9	24.2
4	19.8	13.5	7.2	6.8	1.3	1.0	9.1	5.0	21.3
5	11.4	9.9	5.9	2.2	1.0	0.7	3.9	4.0	13.8
6	9.5	10.1	4.7	2.0	0.9	0.3	3.2	3.6	11.5
7	7.3	9.6	3.0	1.5	0.7	0.3	2.5	2.8	8.3
8	4.7	8.0	2.1	1.2	0.5	0.4	2.1	2.2	6.4
9	3.2	7.1	1.0	0.9	0.4	2.2	3.5	0.6	5.1
10	3.1	10.7	0.3	0.5	0.3	1.3	2.1	0.4	2.8
11	1.6	15.7	0.04	0.2	0.1	0.4	0.7	0.1	0.8

Source: Hsia and Chau, *Industrialisation, employment and income distribution* (1978), p. 165.

education thus represented a proportion of primary income which decreased rapidly as income increased. Secondary education was also, though to a lesser degree, a progressive transfer. Since the census of 1971 showed the number of young persons who were already economically active, it was assumed that the others were at school. That method may have overestimated the redistributive character of secondary education; it is probable that the young people who were not economically active but were the children of richer families had all completed their secondary education whereas some of those in the poorer families may not have done so. Since candidates for a university grant have to submit declarations of their families' resources, that information provides a criterion for estimating the distribution of students by size of family income. The applicants for grants belong to the first eight income groups and the transfer is progressive (moving from 1 per cent of primary income to 0.4 per cent). The probability of entering a university increases less rapidly than income after passing from the lower income groups to the eighth group owing to the strict system of selection. (Children of the richer families—income groups 9, 10 and 11—can cross that obstacle more easily thanks to the family environment.) Taken as a whole, the expenditure on education has a distinctly progressive incidence inasmuch as the transfer drops from over 10 per cent of primary income for the poorer families to 2 per cent for the richer ones (income groups 9 to 11, or 8 per cent of the households). This incidence results from the very high rate of enrolment in primary schools and from the public assistance granted to pupils and students in secondary and higher education. The example of Hong Kong shows that, under certain conditions, expenditure on education can have a more redistributive incidence so far as the distribution of human capital is concerned than is sometimes thought (see the section on education in chapter 4).

The division of patients between the public and the private sector explains the very progressive incidence of expenditure on medical and health services. In the government hospitals and clinics, which account for most of the public-sector health expenditure, medical care is virtually free. The private sector provides medical care for the richer families, government hospitals being overcrowded. The expenditure on medical care has been distributed by size of income. The other expenditure on public health relating to preventive measures such as vaccination and health education has been distributed equally among all the households.

In the field of housing, government action takes three forms: resettlement, low-cost housing and the financing of two semi-official building societies. The resettlement estates take in the poorest families: rents are charged at a quarter of the market price. These subsidies benefit some 1.5 million persons. The transfer has a rather marked incidence for the first six deciles (income groups 1 to 4), amounting to 7 to 10 per cent of the primary income. It then diminishes rapidly as income increases, thereby becoming very progressive.

The policy of direct aid to poor families (assistance in kind or in cash) plays a negligible role: such aid accounted for only 1.6 per cent of public expenditure in 1970–71.

By thus providing the poorer families with free, or very low-cost, primary education, medical care and housing, albeit for an expenditure that absorbed nearly half of its budget, the Government of Hong Kong succeeded in raising the standard of living of families with low incomes. As table 32 shows, the total expenditure relatively to primary income ranged from 24.2 to 31.8 per cent for the first four deciles.

India

Gupta has estimated approximately the expenditure of India's Central Government on education, public health, housing, transport and communications and agriculture, and has allocated it among two broad categories of people: the poor (two-thirds of the population in 1973–74 according to the definition used) and the non-poor.[14] He divides government expenditure on education between primary and secondary education (about 30 per cent of total expenditure) and university and other higher education (70 per cent). According to a study relating to West Bengal 61 per cent of the expenditure on primary and secondary education is allocated to poor families, while according to a study relating to Gujarat, in which poverty is defined more widely, 39 per cent of the expenditure on higher education is allocated to the lowest income families,

131

whose share might be smaller under a narrower definition of poverty.

That poor families have benefited from the expenditure on public health is attested by an increase in the average expectancy of life at birth from 32 years in 1951 to 53 years in 1971. Even though wide inequalities may still subsist, that fact is confirmed by a survey of visits to outdoor departments of hospitals, bed-days stayed in indoor departments and vaccinations taken which was carried out in West Bengal. It has been estimated that at least 45 per cent of the expenditure on medical services goes to poor families.

On the other hand the Central Government's expenditure on transport and communications and on housing does nothing to improve the standard of living of poor families. Few of the direct users of transport belong to the poorer groups and, as for the sellers of transported agricultural produce, they generally have large or medium-sized farms. The Government has built and rented housing at below the market price. A survey has revealed, however, that the rents payable by the poorer families gave twice the rate of return of rents paid by the top wage earners. It has been estimated that the poor families' share of the expenditure on housing amounts to only a quarter.

Over 80 per cent of the Central Government's budgeted expenditure for agriculture in 1973–74 was intended to benefit the vulnerable sections of the population (subsidised sales of food grains and milk, assistance to small farmers holding not more than 3 hectares of land and to agricultural labourers, crash scheme for rural employment and nutrition programmes). In practice the selective incidence that was intended has not been achieved. Thus the poor have not been the only beneficiaries of the system of distribution of food grains, while the assistance intended for small cultivators has in many cases been given to relatively prosperous farmers. Only the nutrition programmes have been for the exclusive benefit of poor families. As for the other expenditure for agriculture (under 20 per cent of the total), it is concerned with such matters as agricultural research, animal husbandry, forestry and training, and is of little direct benefit to poor families, technological innovations tending "to be exploited most by those who have the required financial and other resources".

As is clear from the foregoing particulars, there is a divorce between the intentions of the Central Government, which are to finance numerous schemes solely or primarily in the interest of the poor families, and the results obtained, since the share of the poor in the resources appropriated for the various activities referred to above amounts to less than half.

Iran

There is a comprehensive study of the incidence of public expenditure in Iran by Mehran, who takes into account all forms of public consumption expenditure, excluding municipalities' expenditure and non-budgetary programmes such as the workers' profit-sharing scheme, land reform and commercial licensing, and omitting capital expenditure and deficit financing. The urban and rural family budget surveys carried out in 1971 are the principal sources used for allocating the expenditure.[15]

For education, account is taken of assistance to private schools. The amount of that assistance per pupil is less than the unit cost in the public sector, so that the richer families who sent their children to private schools benefit from a transfer falling below the average. The same applies to the poorer families but for an entirely different reason: they do not send all their children to primary school although primary education is supposed to be compulsory.

In the expenditure on health, that relating to prevention has been distributed equally among all the households. It has been possible to allocate the expenditure on hospitals on the basis of a survey which classified patients by occupational group. Expenditure in rural areas, the first purpose of which is to eradicate malaria, has been distributed according to the number of rooms available to households. For the expenditure relating to the Rural Health Corps, use has been made of the number of visits paid to a Health Corps centre.

Of the expenditure on social welfare, 87 per cent went to the pension fund for civil servants, who are almost never to be found in the first deciles; this expenditure has been distributed according to a budget survey which indicated the source of income. Part of the other expenditure on welfare (8 per cent) was appropriated for the benefit of poor households (contributions to rural social insurance, and especially subsidies to various institutions); it has been allocated to the first four deciles according to the number of unemployed persons in each income bracket.

Expenditure of an economic nature was devoted chiefly to agriculture on the one hand and to transport and communications on the other. Expenditure on maintenance and exploitation of natural resources has been distributed according to the number of households in each income bracket. The expenditure on programmes such as extension services, veterinary and animal husbandry services and improvement and increase of farm and livestock products has been allocated to rural households according to their income. Subsidies granted for cereals and for meat have been distributed by income bracket according to the households' expenditures on those products. With regard to roads, the allocation of expenditure follows the usual method but taking into account the higher cost of maintenance in respect of motorised goods transport vehicles. For the other means of transport and for telecommunications, the expenditure has been distributed according to household consumption. The other expenditure is concerned mainly with manpower, mining, industry,

Table 33. Public expenditure as a percentage of household primary income, by income class,

Income class	% of population	% of total primary income	Specific expenditure					
			Education			Health	Social welfare	Agriculture
			Primary	Secondary	Higher			
1	11.0	1.4	5.7	1.5	—	6.4	1.0	2.2
2	13.7	3.3	4.2	1.4	—	2.7	0.6	1.6
3	14.5	5.0	3.1	0.7	—	1.7	0.4	1.3
4	11.7	5.3	2.4	0.9	—	1.3	0.4	1.1
5	19.6	12.7	2.1	1.1	—	0.9	0.5	0.8
6	10.2	10.3	1.6	0.5	0.1	0.6	0.4	0.6
7	8.0	8.5	1.5	0.5	0.2	0.5	0.5	0.4
8	3.9	7.2	0.9	0.5	0.1	0.3	0.5	0.3
9	4.4	11.1	0.4	0.8	0.7	0.2	0.5	0.3
10	2.9	11.7	0.24	0.16	1.5	0.1	0.5	0.2
11	2.1	23.5	0.2	0.1	0.8	—	0.5	0.2

Key: a = equal distribution among households; b = distribution according to incomes.
Source: Mehran, *Distribution of benefits from public consumption expenditures among households in Iran* (1977), pp. 39–40 and Appendix A to H.

commerce, rural and urban development, housing and tourism, for which the allocations are based on household income or consumption. Lastly, interest payments on the national debt have been distributed among households in the same way as other payments of interest.

For general expenditure, Mehran proposes five distributions: *(a)* equal distribution among all households; *(b)* distribution according to income; *(c)* half distribution as under *(a)* and half as under *(b)*; *(d)* distribution according to a logarithmic utility function; and *(e)* distribution according to a hyperbolic utility function.[12] The figures given in table 33, which indicate the incidence of the various categories of expenditure as a percentage of household primary income, refer, in the case of general expenditure, to distributions *(a)* and *(b)*.

The figures reveal the progressivity of the expenditure on education (primary education, and to a lesser extent secondary education), public health and agriculture. On the other hand the expenditure relating to higher education, transport and communications and interest payments is regressive. (In the case of interest payments, there may be a bias in the method of allocation, the richer families lending relatively more than other families to the private sector.) The expenditure on social welfare and the miscellaneous expenditure have no effect on income inequalities owing, in the first case, to the large amount paid out in pensions to civil servants and, in the second case, to the constant effects of various aids to the economy on expenditure or on incomes.

in Iran, 1971

Transport, communications	Miscellaneous	Interest payments	Total	General expenditure		Total expenditure	
				a	b	a	b
0.2	0.5	0.2	17.7	66.4	10.8	84.1	28.5
0.2	0.6	0.1	11.4	38.1	10.8	49.5	22.2
0.2	0.7	—	8.1	26.9	10.8	35.0	18.9
0.3	0.9	0.1	7.4	21.1	10.8	28.5	18.2
0.3	1.1	0.2	7.0	14.9	10.8	21.9	17.8
0.3	1.2	0.1	5.4	9.7	10.8	15.1	16.2
0.4	1.3	0.2	5.5	7.0	10.8	12.5	16.3
0.5	1.1	0.2	4.4	5.5	10.8	9.9	15.2
0.6	1.2	0.2	4.9	4.0	10.8	8.9	15.7
0.6	0.7	0.3	4.3	2.6	10.8	6.9	15.1
0.6	0.3	0.4	3.1	1.0	10.8	4.1	13.9

Philippines

For the allocation of public expenditure in the Philippines, the most appropriate source is available: it is a survey of 1,345 households which was carried out in 1974 for the purpose of establishing exactly who were the beneficiaries of public services. The results of the survey have been described by E. Tan.[7] It is to be noted, however, that the upper incomes are likely to have been underestimated, with a resulting overestimate of the incidence of expenditure for the last decile.

The expenditure on education has been distributed as follows: in the case of primary and secondary education, according to the number of children in each family who had been to school; in the case of higher education, according to the number of students in each income class. The expenditure on health has been distributed according to the number of times each family obtained consultations and treatment in hospital during the year, but no account being taken of qualitative differences between the services. The social welfare expenditure consists in assistance in kind to the poorest families, the cash value of the assistance being estimated from the survey. It was assumed that the expenditure on land reform was intended to benefit agricultural labourers, and it has been distributed like their wages. Expenditure on rural development was covered by the survey. For transport, the usual methods of allocation to owners of motor vehicles and to consumers have been followed. The "other" expenditure is highly diversified. Payments of interest on the national debt have been allocated in their entirety to the tenth decile, as

Table 34. Public expenditure as a percentage of household primary income, by income class, in the Philippines, 1971

Income class	% of population	% of total primary income	Specific expenditure								General expenditure		Total expenditure	
			Education		Health	Social welfare	Land reform, rural development	Transport	Other	Total	a	b	a	b
			Primary, secondary	Higher										
1	17.3	2.9	17.8	—	5.4	0.5	1.7	6.0	0.2	31.6	53.3	8.9	84.9	40.5
2	24.0	9.6	7.9	—	1.0	0.1	1.0	4.2	0.2	14.4	22.4	8.9	36.8	23.3
3	17.7	11.8	5.4	—	0.8	—	0.9	3.6	0.2	10.9	13.4	8.9	24.3	19.8
4	12.5	11.6	5.9	—	0.9	0.1	0.5	1.6	0.2	9.2	9.7	8.9	10.9	18.1
5	12.5	16.2	4.7	—	0.7	—	0.8	3.4	0.3	9.9	6.9	8.9	16.8	18.8
6	9.9	20.2	3.1	—	0.6	—	0.3	3.4	0.3	7.7	4.5	8.9	12.2	16.6
7	6.1	27.7	1.7	0.5	0.6	—	0.2	1.5	0.4	4.9	2.0	8.9	6.9	13.8

Key: a = equal distribution among the households; b = distribution according to the incomes.
Source: Tan, Taxation, government spending and income distribution in the Philippines (1975), pp. 49–54.

has the expenditure on the services of the Bureaus of Mines and of Forestry. The budget of the Department of Labor has been distributed like the wages and salaries of non-agricultural workers, while the budget of the Department of Commerce and Industry has been distributed like the primary incomes of households.

Table 34 indicates the incidence of the various categories of expenditure, the general expenditure being distributed either equally among the households (assumption *(a)*) or like the incomes (assumption *(b)*).

Several categories of expenditure are highly progressive (that on education at the primary and secondary levels, on public health and on social welfare, on land reform and on rural development). In this case the expenditure on education plays a decisive role by reason of its level: 17.8 per cent of the incomes for income class 1 and 7.9 per cent for class 2, as against 3.1 and 1.7 per cent for the last two income classes. There is little progressivity in the expenditure on transport, the percentage being almost constant from the second to the sixth income classes. Lastly, the miscellaneous expenditure and that relating to higher education are more advantageous to the families in the last income bracket than to the others. The incidence of the specific expenditure as a whole nevertheless remains distinctly progressive to the benefit of the first two income brackets (40 per cent of the population).

If account is taken also of the general expenditure, on the assumption that it is distributed like the incomes (assumption *(b)*), the progressiveness subsists, though less strongly. The rates for the first two income classes reach 40.5 and 23.3 per cent respectively, as against an average of 19 per cent for income classes 3, 4 and 5 and then 16.6 and 13.8 per cent for the well-off and the rich (16 per cent of the population). It must not be overlooked, however, that the figures are percentages: in absolute value, the transfers benefiting the households in the last two income classes represent, respectively, four and eight times the benefits accruing, on the average, to the households in the first two income classes.

Sri Lanka

As in Hong Kong and in the Philippines, specific expenditure in Sri Lanka is highly progressive, its overall incidence ranging from 31.1 and 19.2 per cent for the first two income groups down to 6.5 and 4.1 per cent for the last two (see table 35). The food subsidies, especially for rice and flour, play an important role: they exceed 6 per cent of the primary income for income groups 2 and 3 (70 per cent of the population). The case of Sri Lanka is of particular interest in this regard in that there is systematic application of a policy of subsidisation. The food is purchased centrally by the Food Commissioner's Department and distributed through a network of co-operative societies and retail outlets. Every person who

Table 35. Public expenditure as a percentage of household primary income, by income group, in Sri Lanka, 1973

Income group	% of popu-lation	% of total primary income	Food subsidies	Health	Education Primary	Secondary	Higher	Social welfare	Housing	Agriculture	Transport	Total
1	2.8	1.6	3.2	4.4	3.8	1.6	0.4	14.4	0.1	3.0	0.2	31.1
2	21.7	13.2	6.2	3.6	4.6	1.6	0.2	0.1	0.8	1.8	0.3	19.2
3	49.5	40.7	6.5	2.1	3.6	1.9	0.4	0.1	0.1	1.6	0.6	16.9
4	21.4	28.6	4.0	1.0	2.2	1.8	0.5	0.03	0.1	1.0	1.0	11.6
5	2.1	4.8	1.0	0.4	1.1	1.1	0.5	0.01	0.1	1.1	1.2	6.5
6	2.5	11.1	-0.02	0.1	0.6	0.7	0.4	—	—	1.4	0.9	4.1

Source: Alailima, *Fiscal Incidence in Sri Lanka* (1978), pp. 71–75.

does not pay any direct taxes is entitled to draw a free ration (1 lb of rice per week in 1974), while taxpayers and persons needing a larger quantity than the free ration pay at a price above the producer's selling price.

Primary education, too, has a significant redistributive effect, its absolute value being constant at whatever level of income. The same applies, though in a lesser degree, to secondary education. The measures of assistance to the sick, to old people and to orphans apply only to the poorest. The expenditure on public health finances free medical and other care, thereby meeting over half of the demand for care. Because the middle and high income groups turn mainly to the private sector, health expenditure has a highly redistributive incidence, ranging from 4.4 per cent of primary income for income group 1 down to 0.1 per cent for the richest people. Other expenditure (higher education, transport), which concerns mainly urban households, has no redistributive incidence. Since the expenditure as a whole amounts to a constant sum at whatever level of primary income, it contributes significantly to a reduction of inequalities.

Chile

Like the study on Iran, the study by Foxley and others on redistribution in Chile in 1969 is one of the most complete studies that are available.[16] Based on a wide definition of the public sector that includes all the autonomous public agencies and the social insurance funds, it takes into account all the programmes having specific objectives such as land reform and training of small farmers. The corresponding expenditure is then related to that of the government departments concerned with the same sectors, as for the expenditure of the agricultural services in the case of the programmes just mentioned. Clear distinctions are drawn between the various categories of expenditure. Thus expenditure for agriculture is shown under nine headings (e.g. land reform, support for small farmers, agricultural development, conservation of natural resources, irrigation), while expenditure for industry and mining is shown under seven. That breakdown enables detailed allocations to be made. In the case of agriculture, for example, there are allocations to agricultural workers, to small agricultural producers, to medium-scale and large-scale agricultural producers, to the agricultural population as a whole and to the total population, as well as to consumers. The analysis is similarly detailed in the case of the other fields of state intervention: transport and communications, energy, education, public health, social welfare, housing. The methods of allocation follow the usual rules. In the case of the general expenditure, the two forms of allocation that have previously been noted are used: equal distribution among all households *(a)* and distribution according to the distribution of incomes *(b)*.

The methodology employed and the taking into account of the

autonomous public agencies and the social insurance funds give a particular interest to the results obtained. They are summarised in tables 36 and 37 but are given in greater detail in the study itself; in the case of agriculture, for example, there are details of expenditure relating to land reform and to support for small farmers. Such detailed information is particularly useful for improving the assessment of the redistributive effect of public expenditure.

Total expenditure on education at all levels reaches 14.2 per cent of income for the first income bracket (deciles 1 to 3) and then drops down to 3 per cent for the last income bracket. Owing to the concentration of expenditure on higher education and perhaps also on secondary education to the benefit of the highest income brackets, that fall is much less rapid than the one for public health from 16.5 to 0.4 per cent. In the case of education the richest households thus benefit from transfers that are five times larger in absolute value than the transfers to poor households, whereas in the case of public health the transfers are smaller in absolute value for the richer households than they are for the poorer.

The expenditure on public health has a pronounced redistributive incidence: from the first income bracket (first three deciles) to income brackets 7 to 9 (last twentieth), the rate drops from 16.5 to 0.7 per cent. The share of the first six deciles (income brackets 1 and 2) is greater than their proportion of the population (68.4 per cent as against 61.4 per cent). In absolute value, the transfer received diminishes as income increases. That situation arises out of the organisation of health facilities in Chile, the richer families having recourse to the private sector while the poorer ones turn to the public sector. The principal institution, the National Health Service, received 80 per cent of the credits. Some of the programmes of that Service concerned only the poorer families: sanitary improvement, free distribution of milk for low-income schoolchildren, homes for orphans and the aged. From the results of a national survey of more than 9,000 households carried out in 1968 by the Ministry of Public Health, it appeared that the poorer families benefited more than richer families from the Service's principal activities: out-patient visits to hospitals and in-patient treatment. Even so the basic health needs were not always met at the level regarded by the experts as an acceptable minimum. Thus the net deficit to be covered by the public sector was estimated as roughly equal to two out-patient hospital visits per year for the poverty groups, whereas the richer families were receiving adequate medical attention financed mainly by themselves.

Social welfare schemes concerned mainly the workers, the unemployed, orphans and the children of poor families. Their incidence was thus significant only for the households in the first two income brackets (0.7 and 0.4 per cent of primary income).

The public housing programmes played an important role, account-

Table 36. Specific public expenditure as a percentage of household primary income, by income bracket, in Chile, 1969

Income bracket	% of population	% of total primary income	Education	Health	Social welfare	Housing	Social security	Agriculture	Industry	Transport, communications	Mining, energy	Total Including social security	Total Excluding social security
1	29.8	7.6	14.2	16.5	0.7	5.1	22.3	6.2	0.2	7.4	0.7	73.3	51.0
2	31.6	20.1	8.0	6.5	0.4	5.1	14.9	3.6	0.2	6.1	0.7	45.5	30.6
3	17.6	18.9	6.0	3.1	0.1	3.4	12.4	2.1	0.2	5.6	0.7	33.6	21.2
4	7.4	11.2	5.2	2.0	0.1	3.9	11.6	1.8	0.2	5.8	0.7	31.3	19.7
5	4.5	8.7	4.7	1.6	0.1	2.6	10.6	1.3	0.2	5.7	0.7	27.5	16.9
6	2.9	7.1	3.7	1.1	—	1.8	9.1	1.3	0.2	7.1	0.7	25.0	15.9
7	2.7	8.0	4.4	0.9	—	2.0	8.8	1.1	0.2	7.0	0.7	25.1	16.3
8	1.8	5.9	4.3	0.7	—	1.1	6.3	1.2	0.2	6.3	0.7	20.8	16.5
9	2.0	12.5	3.0	0.4	—	0.9	4.4	1.7	0.2	7.8	0.7	19.1	14.7

Source: Foxley et al., *Redistributive effects of government programmes* (1978).

Table 37. Total public expenditure, specific and general, as a percentage of household primary income, by income bracket, in Chile, 1969

Income bracket	% of population	% of total primary income	Specific expenditure		General expenditure		Totality of expenditure		
			Including social security	Excluding social security	a	b	a Including social security	b Including social security	Excluding social security
1	29.8	7.6	73.3	51.0	44.7	11.4	118.0	84.7	62.4
2	31.6	20.1	45.5	30.6	17.9	11.4	63.4	56.9	42.0
3	17.6	18.9	33.6	21.2	10.6	11.4	44.2	45.0	32.6
4	7.4	11.2	31.3	19.7	7.5	11.4	38.8	42.7	31.1
5	4.5	8.7	27.5	16.9	5.9	11.4	33.4	38.9	28.3
6	2.9	7.1	25.0	15.9	4.7	11.4	29.7	36.4	27.3
7	2.7	8.0	25.1	16.3	3.8	11.4	28.9	36.5	27.7
8	1.8	5.9	20.8	14.5	2.9	11.4	23.7	32.2	25.9
9	2.0	12.5	19.1	14.7	1.8	11.4	20.9	30.5	26.1

Key: a = assuming equal distribution of government expenditure among all households; b = assuming distribution of government expenditure according to incomes.
Source: Foxley et al., *Redistributive effects of government programmes* (1978).

ing for nearly 4 per cent of the gross national product in 1969. About 80 per cent of the housing units built between 1960 and 1972 benefited from those programmes. The main other public activity was the provision of credit for house building: very low interest rates (0.5 to 2 per cent for most of the projects), with partial re-adjustment of debts outstanding with respect to inflation. These forms of subsidisation have been estimated on the assumption that the rate of interest amounted to 10 per cent in real terms. It was found that the share of subsidies in the loans diminished but that the amount of the loan grew rapidly as the borrower's income rose. The incidence of these forms of aid was progressive, the rate falling from 5.1 per cent for the first income bracket to 0.9 per cent for the last bracket. In absolute terms, however, the benefits were in fact four times larger for the richest families than for the poorest. Thus, despite the large amount of public resources devoted to housing the needs of the low-income families were left unsatisfied in most cases; the reason was that those families did not have enough savings to obtain loans.

In the economic sector, it was agricultural expenditure that had the most progressive incidence, the rate decreasing from 6.2 and 3.6 per cent for the first two income brackets to 1.4 per cent for the last three. The share of the poorer families (income brackets 1 and 2) in that expenditure was of almost the same order as their proportion of the population: 50 per cent instead of 61 per cent. The expenditure most favourable for poor families related to land reform, loans and assistance to small farmers and marketing of agricultural produce. On the other hand, about half of the loans to medium-scale and big farmers and of the expenditure on irrigation benefited the richest families (last twentieth). Thus it was the measures required for modifying the distribution of material assets in the long run that had the more important redistributive effect in the short run.

The expenditure for industry was proportional to household income. It consisted partly of credit and technical assistance to small industry and handicrafts and of loans to medium-scale and large industrial enterprises, and partly of subsidisation of sugar refining (with half of the benefit allocated to the producers and half to consumers). It was the subsidies which, owing to the method of allocation, gave poor families the relatively smallest benefit. The expenditure on transport and communications, as well as on mining and on energy, likewise had no effect on income inequality. Much of it was distributed according to primary income. The distribution of other items was more concentrated, as in the case of expenditure on air transport, one part of which was allocated to air travellers, or expenditure on highways, one part of which was allocated to vehicle owners. Lastly, there were the less concentrated items of expenditure, such as that on transport, part of which was allocated to consumers according to their purchases.

The foregoing analysis brings out the importance of the transfers to the poorer households; they reach 51 per cent of the primary income for the first three deciles, or 73.3 per cent when account is taken of social security payments. Such percentages, which are much higher than those that were noted for the other countries, placed Chile in 1969 in an intermediate position between developing countries having no redistributive policy, such as Iran, and the developed countries, where the percentages for the first decile exceed 100 or even 200. These figures mean that the public and quasi-public transfers modified the living conditions of poor households in a notable degree, and also that they changed considerably the distribution of primary incomes, which decreased (including social security payments) from 73.3 per cent for the first income bracket to 19.1 per cent for the last one.

Botswana

Since Botswana is a country where the level of incomes is still very low and where there is still only a very small industrial sector, it is of interest that there should be available for such a country some first estimates of income distribution, however approximate those estimates may be by reason of the paucity of statistical information. Richard Szal has had recourse both to a regional approach and to the traditional method of income groups for the purpose of assessing the incidence of public expenditure.[17]

At the regional level, it has been possible to record and distribute the principal social and economic expenditure on public health and education, on the one hand, and on water supply, animal health, agricultural extension and community development on the other. Two out of the ten regions (North-East, South-East) are predominantly urban, the urban population accounting for 42 and 60 per cent of the total population respectively. The proportion drops to 3 per cent in the Central Region, and there is no urban population in the seven other regions. As these figures indicate, nearly 90 per cent of the urban population is concentrated in two regions. Since the average income of the urban households in a still traditional economy is much higher than that of rural households, the regional approach, which provides information on the distribution of benefits from expenditure between urban and rural households, provides information also on the distribution among households according to level of income.

With 16.1 per cent of the population, the North-East and South-East Regions are in a privileged situation with respect to education and public health, their share of total expenditure amounting to 24.7 per cent for education and 60.5 per cent for health. While the two regions contain four out of the country's seven hospitals, there can be no doubt that some of their patients come from other regions; precise information on the regional origins of the four hospitals' patients is, however, lacking. On the other hand, the distribution of expenditure on education is more revealing because it is derived from statistics of expenditure by region and from information on the regional origins of the pupils and students at the other levels of education. The urbanised regions are comparatively favoured with respect to secondary education, vocational training and teacher training, their shares of the corresponding expenditure amounting to 26.8, 38.6 and 27.4 per cent respectively. The expenditure on post-primary education is thus about twice higher in those two regions than in the rest of the country.

On the other hand the urbanised regions obtain only a little benefit from the expenditure on water supply, agricultural extension work, animal health and community development, their shares varying between 5.4 and 9 per cent according to the case. The Government subsidises the consumption of water in rural areas but requires water to be paid for at its real cost in towns. As for the expenditure on animal health, technical aid to agriculture and community development, it concerns the farmers almost exclusively. Thus in the two regions in which half the population lives in towns, the transfers received amount to only half of the national average. On the other hand 80 per cent of a programme of assistance to craftsmen and small-scale entrepreneurs goes to beneficiaries in the North-East and the South-East Regions.

From the results of a national household budget survey carried out in 1974–75, it has been possible to allocate public expenditure to households according to their income. Most of the expenditure is distinctly progressive. Such is the case with public health (7.3 per cent of primary income for the first decile, 0.6 per cent for the last decile); education (5.2 per cent for the first quintile, 2.4 per cent for the fifth); the provision of water (3.3 and 1 per cent for the same income groups); and community development (regular diminution from 10 per cent for the first decile to 1 per cent for the last decile). According to the survey the public expenditure on health is of very little benefit to the rich households. So far as education is concerned, the egalitarian nature of the expenditure on primary education outweighs the inegalitarian character of the expenditure on other education. The expenditure on water supply is allocated according to the number of persons per household and of head of cattle owned per household; since the poorest households have no cattle, they benefit less in absolute terms. The expenditure on community development (aid in times of distress, technical assistance, organisation of youth activities) has been distributed like the population, with a resulting pronounced progressiveness. The other expenditure (on animal husbandry and on agriculture) accounts for a constant percentage of primary income, having been allocated according to the number of head of cattle owned or

145

according to agricultural output. The transfers received vary like that income except in the case of the households in the tenth decile, most of them urban, who benefit relatively less.

Taken as a whole, public expenditure is strongly progressive, diminishing as income increases from 31 and 25 per cent for the first and second deciles to 12.7 and 7.1 per cent for deciles 9 and 10. Thus even in an economy in which traditional agriculture predominates, that expenditure can have a significant redistributive effect thanks to the fact that action in the fields of, for example, public health, primary education and community development benefits the poor households as much as the others. Moreover, such action is conducive in the long run to a reduction of the inequality of the primary incomes themselves.

Incidence in developed and developing countries: A general conspectus

The results of the studies that have now been examined make it possible to evaluate the redistributive effect of public expenditure. Adopting the assumption of a distribution of general expenditure according to the primary incomes as being the more acceptable one, account will be taken only of specific expenditure. To the countries that have been considered can be added Colombia, Panama and Puerto Rico, the studies for other developing countries being much too indefinite or incomplete for purposes of international comparisons. To the eight developing countries or territories included in recapitulatory table 38 have been added two developed countries: the United States and the United Kingdom.

As the figures in table 38 show, in all cases, as income grows, public expenditure represents a decreasing percentage of primary income, and the fact is reflected in a fall in the Gini coefficient. However, the redistributive effect varies widely with the country. Very weak in Iran, where the Gini coefficient changes from 0.570 to 0.559, it becomes significant in Chile and in Puerto Rico, especially if account is taken of social security, the Gini coefficient falling from 0.456 to 0.405 in Chile and from 0.502 to 0.431 in Puerto Rico. Colombia and the Philippines are among the countries where the redistributive effect is small (Gini coefficient falls by 0.014 and 0.018), while Panama and Hong Kong are similar to Chile, with falls of 0.031 and 0.040.

Yet even in Chile and in Puerto Rico, the specific public expenditure has a smaller redistributive effect than in the United States and in the United Kingdom, where the Gini coefficient diminishes by 15 and 28 per cent respectively. That effect is due to the large amounts of the transfers in favour of poor households (deciles 1 and 2), which represent 180 and 1,100 per cent of the primary income, as against 112 per cent in Puerto Rico and 73 per cent in Chile. There is likewise a disparity with respect to

Table 38. Public expenditure[1] as a percentage of household primary income, by deciles, and incidence of that expenditure on income distribution, in ten individual countries or territories

Decile	Chile[2] 1969		Colombia 1966	Panama 1970	Puerto Rico[3] 1963	Hong Kong 1971	Iran 1971	Philippines 1971	Sri Lanka 1973	United Kingdom 1975	United States 1970
1	73	51.0	53.5	54.5	112.0	30.0	18.0	32.0	20.0	1100	230
2			26.8			24.0	12.0				130
3			16.9		40.0	24.0	8.5	14.5		95	80
4	46	31.0	17.5	18.0		24.0				46	40
5			15.2		25.0	21.0	7.0	11.0	16.9	29	26
6			11.5	15.0			7.0			25	
7	34	21.0	12.3	11.5	17.0	14.0		9.0		20	19
8	29	18.0	9.7	10.0	13.0	11.5	5.5	10.0	11.6	15	
9	26	16.5	12.7	7.0	10.0	7.0	5.0	9.0		12	
			17.5								
10 { 5%	22	15.0		6.5	6.5	5.5	5.0	6.0	5.3	8	14
5%			8.2	6.5		2.0	3.5	4.0			10

Gini coefficients[4]

	Chile[2] 1969		Colombia 1966	Panama 1970	Puerto Rico[3] 1963	Hong Kong 1971	Iran 1971	Philippines 1971	Sri Lanka 1973	United Kingdom 1975	United States 1970
A	0.456	0.456	0.580	0.590	0.502	0.443	0.570	0.479	0.234	0.423	0.444
B	0.405	0.417	0.566	0.559	0.431	0.403	0.559	0.461	0.210	0.304	0.376

[1] Specific expenditure: general expenditure excluded. [2] First column: including social security; second column: excluding social security. [3] Including social security. [4] The coefficients are calculated directly from the distribution by income classes; they are not comparable as between one country and another. A = before expenditure; B = after expenditure; see table 31.
Sources: Hong Kong, Iran, Philippines, Sri Lanka, Chile: tables 32–37; other countries: see table 31.

households in the third decile, with 80 and 95 per cent for the United States and the United Kingdom respectively as against under 60 per cent for Chile and Puerto Rico.

For the developing countries other than Chile and Puerto Rico the percentages are all much the same in the case of the last decile. The main differences appear in the case of the low-income households. In some countries, the first two deciles receive very little (18 and 12 per cent of primary income in Iran) or little (20 per cent in Sri Lanka, 30 and 24 per cent in Hong Kong, for which economic expenditure has not been taken into account, and 32 per cent in the Philippines). On the other hand the proportion represents over 65 per cent of primary income in Panama (for the first two deciles), 70 per cent in Chile and 110 per cent in Puerto Rico, which, however, is a special case by reason of its political status.

It should also be noted that what is being measured here is the effect of public expenditure on the nominal income of poor households. It is not possible, however, to separate redistribution from the structure of production. Where the supply of everyday consumer goods, especially foodstuffs, is inelastic, an increase in the demand from poor households could bring about a rise in prices and a reduction of the redistributive effect. An analysis covering several years would be needed the better to evaluate the incidence of public expenditure not only on the nominal income of those households but also on their standard of living.

There remains to be mentioned a point of view on the incidence of general expenditure (defence and other general services) which, though it may be a debatable one, is none the less original. Usually that expenditure is distributed either like the population assumption *(a)*—or like the incomes—assumption *(b)*. Gupta does not see the matter in these terms.[18] Instead of looking for the beneficiaries of the services provided, he regards as direct beneficiaries the personnel who are paid by the government to provide those services to the population. That point of view seems *a priori* to be at variance with the theory: the staff in question are not receiving subsidies while remaining inactive but are paid for their work; it is not possible to regard a wage or salary purely as a transfer of the kind discussed so far, even if it is paid by the government. Nevertheless, the money flow approach proposed by Gupta is of interest in two cases.

If some of the public servants do not put forth any real work or supply it for only a part of the time, it is not possible to allocate to the households a benefit equal to the total amount of the corresponding public expenditure. The real benefit is equivalent to only a fraction of that amount and the usual method overestimates the transfer. The total amount should be broken down, with allocation to the households of only the fraction that is transferred to them in the case of efficient administration and with allocation to the public servants, proportionately to their hours of inactivity while on duty, of the difference between the total amount and that fraction. In many developing countries where there is serious underemployment, governments may be under strong pressures to recruit a number of unskilled (or even qualified) public servants greatly exceeding the requirements of the work. A part of the salaries paid can then be regarded as a transfer to economically inactive persons.

Furthermore, even if those public servants do work full time, the salaries that they receive in the poorest countries that are hardest hit by unemployment and underemployment are much larger than those that they could earn in a business undertaking. In practice, most of them would be condemned to unemployment in urban areas or, in rural areas, to underemployment, working casually as agricultural labourers often for fewer than a hundred days a year. In these circumstances, the share of the wages of unskilled staff in public expenditure has to be taken into account in estimating the effect of government action on the distribution of incomes. That share depends especially on the structure of the budget and on the choices made by each government department within its allotted credits; the share increases if, for example, the budgeted expenditure on education is increased at the expense of military expenditure or if, within a given defence budget, the infantry is reduced and armoured forces are strengthened. Every change that leads to an increase of the share of the wages of unskilled staff in public expenditure increases the share of the first deciles in the national income. Gupta refers implicitly to that situation when he stresses in his introduction the extent of underemployment and of abject poverty in India.[19]

The share of the wages of unskilled labour in public expenditure is calculated from the share of wages and salaries as a whole in each category of expenditure. In the case of India Gupta estimates, for example, that wages and salaries account for about a third of total defence expenditure, and that 40 per cent of those wages and salaries accrue to unskilled labour, which constitutes 60 per cent of the civilian defence personnel. The share of the wages of unskilled labour in defence expenditure thus amounts to 13 per cent (0.33×0.40). The same method of calculation yields 3 per cent of the expenditure on general services (other than defence services), 9 per cent of expenditure on economic services, 7 per cent of expenditure on industry and mining, 8 per cent of expenditure on transport and communications and 8 per cent of expenditure on social and community services. The expenditure on education, health and agriculture, in as far as it consists of specific items of expenditure, is allocated in the usual way. It is clear that the share of the wages of unskilled labour in the foregoing items of expenditure would be very small, except in the case of agriculture. Thus unskilled labour benefits very little in the form of wages (8 per cent on the average) from public expenditure, most of which is devoted to the remuneration of skilled or highly skilled personnel or to the acquisition of capital goods incorporating very little unskilled national labour. Gupta's analysis leads to the following conclusion: that the "up-stream" effect of public expenditure on income distribution (as against the "down-stream" effect, that is, the advantage accruing to the users of public services) is very weak owing to the structure of government consumption and investment. A significant reduction of inequalities can be expected, therefore, only from the use of public services.

COMBINED INCIDENCE OF TAXATION AND PUBLIC EXPENDITURE

Table 39 indicates the distribution of incomes before and after government action (including the operation of the social security system) in Iran, the Philippines, Sri Lanka and Chile. (Owing to the lack of complete or sufficient figures for Hong Kong and for India, it is not possible to present a similar balance sheet for those two cases.) Those data, which summarise the overall effect of taxation and of expenditure in the public and semi-public sectors, are of considerable interest. General expenditure has been allocated on the basis of assumption *(b)* by distributing it according to the primary incomes.

Comparisons of the figures show the diversity of the situations prevailing among the developing countries. In Chile (1969), redistribution diminishes to a significant extent the inequality of incomes: the

Table 39. Distribution of incomes by income class and indicator of inequality before and after government action in Iran, the Philippines, Sri Lanka and Chile

A. Distribution

Country and income class	Per cent of population	Percentage of income	
		Primary income	Income after redistribution
Iran (1971)			
1	11.0	1.4	1.5
2	13.7	3.2	3.4
3	14.5	4.9	5.1
4	11.7	5.2	5.4
5	19.6	12.5	12.7
6	10.2	10.1	10.2
7	6.0	8.3	8.3
8	3.9	7.0	7.0
9	4.4	10.9	10.0
10	2.9	11.5	11.2
11	2.1	25.0	24.4

Table 39 *(cont.)*

Country and income class	Per cent of population	Percentage of income	
		Primary income	Income after redistribution
Philippines (1971)			
1	17.3	2.9	3.1
2	24.0	9.6	10.1
3	17.7	11.8	12.4
4	12.5	11.6	12.1
5	12.5	10.2	17.0
6	9.9	20.2	20.6
7	6.1	27.7	24.7
Sri Lanka (1973)[1]			
1	2.8	1.6	16.7
2	21.7	13.2	
3	49.5	40.7	43.1
4	21.4	28.6	27.8
5	2.1	4.8	4.3
6	2.5	11.1	8.1
Chile (1969)[2]			
1		2.4	2.5
2		2.6	3.5
3		3.5	5.0
4		5.5	6.0
5		6.0	7.0
6		7.0	8.0
7		9.0	9.0
8		11.5	12.0
9		17.5	16.0
10		35.0	31.0

B. Indicator of inequality

Country	Gini coefficient		
	Before redistribution	After redistribution	Difference
Iran	0.578	0.566	− 0.012
Philippines	0.479	0.457	− 0.022
Sri Lanka	0.234	0.179	− 0.055
Chile	0.449	0.389	− 0.060

[1] Only specific expenditure is taken into account.   [2] Distribution by deciles.

Sources: Iran: Mehran, *Taxes and incomes* (1975), and idem: *Distribution of benefits from public consumption expenditures among households in Iran* (1977), pp. 39–40 and Appendices A to H; Philippines: Tan, *Taxation, government spending and income distribution in the Philippines* (1975), pp. 29, 49–54; Sri Lanka: Alailima, *Fiscal incidence in Sri Lanka* (1978), pp. 34–36, 71–75; Chile: Foxley et al., *Redistributive effects of government programmes* (1978), pp. 43, 46; and idem, *Who benefits from government expenditures?* (1976).

Gini coefficient drops from 0.449 to 0.389. The share of the first three quintiles increases from 27 to 32 per cent while that of the last quintile diminishes from 52.5 to 47 per cent, whereas the share of the fourth quintile hardly changes. The reduction in the Gini coefficient (0.06) is close to the one in the United States (0.074) but is smaller than the reduction in the developed countries where there is a greater degree of redistribution such as the Scandinavian countries and the United Kingdom (minus 0.1). The drop is almost the same in Sri Lanka as in Chile: 0.055. The share of the poorest categories (income classes 1 and 2) rises from 14.8 to 16.7 per cent, while that of the richer classes (classes 5 and 6, or 4.6 per cent of the population) diminishes sharply from 15.9 to 12.4 per cent.

In Iran, on the other hand, the incidence of redistribution is almost nil. The Gini coefficient remains almost constant: 0.566 instead of 0.578. The share of the first four income classes (50.9 per cent of the population) increases very little from 14.7 to 15.4 per cent, while that of the last five classes (last quintile) diminishes by only 1 percentage point, from 62.7 to 61.7 per cent. The Philippines are in an intermediate situation but closer to Iran than to Chile: the drop in the Gini coefficient does not exceed 0.022; the share of income classes 6 and 7 (16 per cent of the population) diminishes from 47.9 to 45.3 per cent, that is, by 2.6 percentage points as compared with 5.5 percentage points in Chile and 1 percentage point in Iran (for the last quintile).

The same paradox appears in these countries as in the more developed countries: the greater the inequality of primary incomes the smaller the redistribution. The Gini coefficient falls by 0.012 in Iran and by 0.060 in Chile although at the start it is higher in Iran (0.578) than in Chile (0.449). Among the developed countries likewise, the rate of concentration of primary incomes is higher in Canada, in the United States and in France than in the Scandinavian countries and in the United Kingdom, but redistribution is weaker in the former countries than in the latter. Since the same information is available for three other developing countries or territories (Colombia, Panama, Puerto Rico), it is of interest to include them in the comparisons. In these cases, the general expenditure has also been distributed according to the primary incomes in accordance with assumption (b).

The results, as given in table 40, confirm those shown in table 39. In Puerto Rico, the redistribution goes as far as, if not further than, in Chile, with a fall of 0.081 in the Gini coefficient. The share of income classes 6 and 7 (16.2 per cent of the population) falls from 50.7 to 45.3 per cent, to the benefit of the first two income classes (46 per cent of the population). These changes, which are of the same order as those found in Chile, are due partly to the extent of social security in both these countries, making them exceptional in that respect among the developing countries. The

Table 40. Distribution of incomes by income class and indicator of inequality before and after government action in Colombia, Panama and Puerto Rico.

A. Distribution

Country, income class	Percentage of population	Percentage of income	
		Primary income	Income after redistribution
Colombia (1966)[1]			
1		0.9	1.2
2		1.9	2.2
3		2.7	3.0
4		3.5	3.8
5		4.5	4.7
6		5.5	5.5
7		7.5	7.6
8		10.0	10.0
9		15.5	15.7
10 ⎰ 5%		13.0	13.5
⎱ 5%		35.0	32.8
Panama (1970)			
1	30.0	3.5	5.4
2	16.5	6.5	7.4
3	16.4	10.9	11.5
4	12.5	11.8	12.3
5	7.5	9.1	9.3
6	8.2	13.5	13.2
7	5.3	14.2	13.8
8	2.4	10.6	10.0
9, 10, 11	1.2	19.9	17.1
Puerto Rico (1963)			
1	20.4	3.2	6.2
2	25.6	11.2	13.5
3	20.0	14.5	15.2
4	10.6	10.8	10.5
5	7.2	9.2	9.3
6	9.0	16.4	15.0
7	7.2	34.3	30.3

B. Indicator of inequality

Country	Gini coefficient		
	Before redistribution	After redistribution	Difference
Colombia	0.580	0.557	−0.023
Panama	0.590	0.540	−0.050
Puerto Rico	0.502	0.421	−0.081

[1] Distribution by deciles.

Sources: Colombia: Berry and Urrutia, *Income distribution in Colombia* (1976); Panama: Sahota, "The distribution of the benefits of public expenditure in Panama" (1977); Puerto Rico: Mann, "Net fiscal incidence in Puerto Rico" (1973).

Table 41. Combined incidence of revenue-raising and public expenditure as percentages of
I: Ascertained net incidence
II: Corrected net incidence[1]

Deciles	Chile 1969 I[2]	Chile 1969 I[3]	Chile 1969 II[3]	Deciles	Colombia 1966 I	Colombia 1966 II	Deciles	Panama 1970 I	Panama 1970 II	Deciles	Puerto Rico 1963 I	Puerto Rico 1963 II
1 ⎫ 2 ⎬ 3 ⎭	65.9	43.9	28	⎧ 1 ⎨ 2 ⎩ 3	47.9 21.2 3.5	42.9 16.2 8.5	1 ⎫ 2 ⎬ 3 ⎭	50.7	52.7	⎧ 1 ⎨ 2 ⎩ 3	102.7	99.0
4 ⎫ 5 ⎬ 6 ⎭	40.9	25.9	10	⎧ 4 ⎨ 5 ⎩ 6	14.1 8.8 5.7	9.1 3.8 0.7	4 ⎫ 5 ⎭	9.7	11.7	⎧ 3 ⎨ 4 ⎩ 5	28.7	24.7
7 ⎫ 8 ⎭	28.4	15.4	−0.5	⎧ 7 ⎩ 8	6.5 4.9	1.5 −0.1	6	5.2	7.2	6 ⎫ 7 ⎭	9.2	5.2
9	24.4	13.4	−2.5	9	6.5	1.5	7	1.7	3.7	8	−0.8	−4.8
10 ⎧ 5%	19.4	9.9	−6	.	9.1	4.1	8	0.2	2.2	9	−3.3	−7.3
10 ⎩ 5%	9.4	2.4	−13.5	.	−1.8	−6.8	9	−3.8	−1.8	.	−7.0	−11.0
							. ⎫ . ⎭	−8.3	−6.3			

[1] For which the sum of the transfers is nil. [2] Excluding economic expenditure. [3] Including social security. [4] Excluding social security. [5] The corrected expenditure is close to the ascertained expenditure.

political status of Puerto Rico partly explains the policy followed in matters of education and public health, a policy that has brought about relatively large transfers to the benefit of the poorest households. In Colombia, on the other hand, the redistribution is on a very modest scale: the effects are comparable to those that were noted in the cases of Iran and the Philippines, with a very small fall of 0.023 in the Gini coefficient and variations in the shares of the first three quintiles from 19 to 20.4 per cent and of the last quintile from 63.5 to 62 per cent. Lastly, in Panama the redistribution, leading to a fall by 0.05 in the Gini coefficient is positive up to and including income class 5 (for 82.9 per cent of the population), and then negative. Panama is thus situated between the countries where the redistribution is moderate or fairly pronounced (Chile, Puerto Rico and Sri Lanka) and those where the redistribution is only slight or almost negligible (Colombia, Iran and the Philippines).

These results confirm the paradox of inequality and redistribution: the redistribution is much smaller, for example, in Colombia, where the concentration of primary incomes is more pronounced, than in Puerto Rico. However, the paradox may be more apparent than real in so far as the redistribution and the distribution of primary incomes are both determined, at a given moment, by the same socio-political conditions.

The figures in tables 39 and 40 refer to population distribution by income classes varying widely with the country. It was desirable to present the results in a synthetic and uniform manner by estimating the overall primary household incomes, by deciles, in nine countries and territories

Hong Kong[4] 1971 I	II	Deciles	Iran 1971 I	II	Deciles	Philippines 1971 I	II	Deciles	Sri Lanka 1973 II[5]	Deciles	Canada 1969 I	II
27	20	1	19.5	10.2	1	4.0	7.7	1	13	1	201	198
20	10	2	14.8	5.5	2			2		2	91	88
20	10	3	11.9	2.6	3	0.0	3.7	3		3	44	41
20	10	4			4			4		4	22	19
17	8	5	10.5	1.2	5	0.5	4.2	5	6	5	10	7
17	8	6	10.4	1.1	6			6		6	1	−2
10	5	7			7	0.0	3.7	7		7		
7	3	8	8.8	−0.5	8	1.5	5.2	8		8	−8	−11
3	1	9	7.6	−1.7	9	−1.5	2.2	9	−3	9		
0	0	.	6.8	−2.5	.	−7.0	−3.3	.		.	−11	−14
−13.5	−13	.	5.3	−4.0	.	−16.0	−12.3	.	−19	.		

Sources: Tables 26 and 32. For Canada: Gillespie, *The redistribution of income in Canada* (1975), Appendix D.

effect of taxation and government expenditure by deciles. The incidence of taxation (table 31) and of specific expenditure (table 38) being known, it sufficed to calculate the algebraic sum of the two percentages and to add a constant percentage (11.4 for Chile, 8.3 for Colombia, 5.2 for Panama, 4.7 for Puerto Rico, 10.8 for Iran and 9 for the Philippines) for the general expenditure, since it is distributed, under assumption *(b)*, like the primary incomes. The product gives the overall incidence of the revenue-raising and expenditure of the public sector (and, where appropriate, semi-public sector) on the primary incomes. The figures are shown in table 41, which includes also Canada as a country in an intermediate situation between the United States and the United Kingdom. The figures make it possible to compare the redistributive effect at the same relative position in the scale of incomes; they are, however, approximations since they are estimated by extrapolation on the basis of data not by deciles but by income classes.

For the poorest households (first quintile), the incidence in the cases of fairly marked redistribution (Chile, Puerto Rico) is of the order of 80 to 100 per cent of the primary income, which is below the figures for Canada (201 and 91 per cent for deciles 1 and 2). In Iran and in the Philippines, on the other hand, the government's fiscal and budgetary measures appear to have a negligible effect on the standard of living of the poorest of the people; for the first quintile, there is a net incidence of 15 to 20 per cent of primary income in Iran and 4 per cent in the Philippines. Even in Sri

Lanka, the effect amounts to only 13 per cent. For the poor households of deciles 3 and 4, whose members obtain only a third or a half of the national income per head, the redistribution is significant in Chile and in Puerto Rico (about 30 per cent), whereas it falls to 12 per cent in Iran and to nil in the Philippines. For that second quintile, the extent of the redistribution is close to Canada's in Chile and in Puerto Rico. It is the broad scope of government action in favour of the poorest classes that generally distinguishes the developed countries from those developing countries in which there is a moderate redistribution, the developed countries being characterised by a policy of minimum income designed to ensure, for the underprivileged, the satisfaction of all their basic needs, a policy that gives a rate of 200 per cent for the first decile in Canada and an even higher rate in other developed countries.

The estimates of the incidence of redistribution in Iran reveal the somewhat artificial character of these international comparisons. For all the households, including the richest, the result is positive (5.3 per cent for the last twentieth). That result is due to the wide disparity between expenditure and revenue as allocated. The difference corresponds to about 9 per cent of the total primary income of the households and is financed by oil revenues which are not taken into account. There is a comparable situation for Chile, with a positive balance for all households, including the richest. In that case the disparity between allocated expenditure and taxation was financed mainly by inflation and to a small extent by revenue from copper. On the other hand, the amount of taxation distributed among households in the Philippines exceeds the allocated expenditure, some of which has not been taken into account (probably investment expenditure). It follows that the comparison of the estimated rates for these three countries makes little sense, especially for the tenth decile. Corrected estimates have accordingly been made. For the Philippines, the rates weighted by the share of each decile in the primary distribution show that the balance of all the expenditure and taxes thus distributed among the households represents -3.7 per cent of the primary income (sum of positive and negative transfers $= 0.037Y$, Y being the primary income of the households as a whole). It has been assumed that this balance corresponded to the omitted expenditure, and it has been distributed like the primary incomes, with the incidence for the first quintile then rising from 4 to 7.7 per cent. Where the balance is positive, as in Chile and in Iran, it has been assumed that it corresponded to omitted taxes and it has been distributed likewise according to the primary incomes; each household would have paid the same percentage of its primary income. A corrected estimate (estimate II in table 41) is thus obtained, for which the sum of the transfers is always nil.

The corrected results differ widely in many cases from the ascertained results, except for the first decile or the first quintile. They can be used in particular to compare the rates of redistribution for the rich households of the tenth decile. There are wide disparities between the countries; the deduction reaches its maximum in Canada (14 per cent); it is not much less in Chile and in Puerto Rico (about 11 per cent); in Sri Lanka it amounts to 19 per cent for the last twentieth. In Colombia and in Iran, on the other hand, the households in the tenth decile receive almost as much from the State as they pay in taxes, the balance amounting to − 3 to − 3.5 per cent.

The method chosen for correcting the ascertained incidence is open to criticism in some respects. For example, in the case of Iran it has been assumed that the revenues from oil, which is a national resource, were distributed like the primary incomes. These oil revenues, which are collected directly by the Government, balance the notional budget, a balanced budget being the necessary condition under which the algebraic sum of the transfers shall be nil. It could also be considered that oil is a natural resource belonging to the whole population. Taxes would then have to be distributed equally among all households on the assumption that every household has the same title to that resource, receives the same income from it and pays it back to the State. That would lead to a highly regressive situation, the balance of transfers ranging from − 27 and − 12 per cent for income classes 1 and 2 to + 4.6 per cent for income classes 9, 10 and 11. Thus in all the countries where revenues from natural resources (oil, minerals) account for an appreciable proportion of government revenue, the result of government fiscal and budgetary action depends closely, so far as the distribution of incomes is concerned, on the assumptions made with regard to the notional distribution of taxes on those resources among the country's nationals.

Lastly, where a budgetary deficit was financed by the issue of money, it would be necessary to evaluate how inflation distributed the amount of the deficit among the households. The share allocated to poor households could well be greater than their share in the distribution of primary incomes. In that case, the incidence of taxation and of public expenditure would be less redistributive than might appear from the estimates in table 41.

Notes

[1] Gillespie: "Effect of public expenditures on the distribution of income" (1965); Pechman and Okner: *Who bears the tax burden?* (1974); Dodge: "Impact of tax, transfer, the expenditure policies of government on the distribution of personal income in Canada" (1975); Reynolds and Smolensky: *Public expenditures, taxes and the distribution of income* (1977).

[2] Hsia and Chau: *Industrialisation, employment and income distribution* (1978), pp. 151 et seq.

[3] Gupta: *The rich, the poor and the taxes they pay in India* (1975).

[4] From 1960 to 1970, assessed incomes amounted constantly to the same fraction (6.7 per cent) of national income, which more than doubled in nominal value while there was an increase in the concentration of incomes. There is widespread fraud and evasion. ibid., pp. 42–44.

[5] Mehran: *Taxes and incomes* (1975).

[6] idem: *Income distribution in Iran* (1975).

[7] Tan: *Taxation, government spending and income distribution in the Philippines* (1975).

[8] Alailima: *Fiscal incidence in Sri Lanka* (1978).

[9] Foxley, Aninat and Arellano: *Redistributive effects of government programmes* (1978).

[10] Instead of referring to an adjusted income, the incidence of adjusted taxation could be estimated. The amount corresponding to consumption financed from public monetary transfers would have to be deducted from the indirect taxes. In most of the developing countries that adjustment would not diminish indirect taxation, nor, consequently, the ratio of direct and indirect taxes to primary income, whereas in the developed countries half or two-thirds of indirect taxation corresponds to publicly financed consumption.

[11] See Kende: "Le poids de la fiscalité en France" (1977).

[12] H. Aaron and M. McGuire ("Public goods and income distribution", 1970) propose a more consistent method based on the theory of utility. It can be considered under certain conditions that the value, in terms of income, accruing from these services to each household is inversely proportional to the marginal utility of income. From the assumption of a logarithmic utility function, one obtains, as is shown by the application of such a function in Iran by F. Mehran, almost the same results as from a distribution of expenditure according to the primary incomes. On the other hand from the assumption of a hyperbolic utility function one obtains a highly concentrated distribution to the advantage of high-income families. See also Mehran: *Distribution of benefits from public consumption expenditures among households in Iran* (1977), pp. 30 et seq.

[13] Hsia and Chau: *Industrialisation, employment and income distribution* (1978), pp. 161 et seq.

[14] Gupta: *Incidence of central government expenditures in India* (1975).

[15] Mehran: *Distribution of benefits from public consumption expenditures among households in Iran* (1977), pp. 5, 8 et seq.

[16] Foxley, Aninat and Arellano: *Redistributive effects of government programmes* (1978).

[17] Szal: *The regional distribution of government expenditures in Botswana* (1975); idem: *Income inequality and fiscal policies in Botswana* (1979).

[18] Gupta: *Incidence of central government expenditures in India* (1975), pp. 20 et seq.

[19] ibid., p. 15.

REDISTRIBUTION

6

ANALYSIS OF THE REDISTRIBUTIVE EFFECT
OF TAXATION AND PUBLIC EXPENDITURE

The incidence of taxation and of public expenditures having been noted, it is the results obtained that must now be explained. A first question is: why is the overall incidence redistributive in one country but has almost no effect on income inequality in another? Is it because the ratio of taxation or of public expenditure to the primary income of households varies with the country? Or is it because there are differences in the composition of revenue and expenditure? Or because the expenditure on the same service (for example, primary education or public health) is not distributed in the same way among households? An explanation of the results is not only of interest in order to understand them; it is essential for appraising redistribution policies and proposing measures for making them more effective. That will be the subject of the present chapter.

Method of analysis

In order to interpret the data on redistribution, there is a need for a method of analysis enabling the effect noted, such as a variation in the Gini coefficient brought about by a transfer (e.g. a tax or a subsidy), to be decomposed. Such a method was proposed in 1977 by N. C. Kakwani,[1] who differentiates between the progressivity of a transfer P and its intensity e.

The intensity e of a transfer corresponds to the percentage of total primary income that it represents, e being the average rate of deduction in the case of a negative transfer (taxation) and the average rate of the benefit in the case of a positive transfer (subsidies, community services).

The variation in the Gini coefficient brought about by a transfer is equal to—

$$G - G' = + \left(\frac{e}{1-e} \right) P \text{ for a negative transfer, and}$$

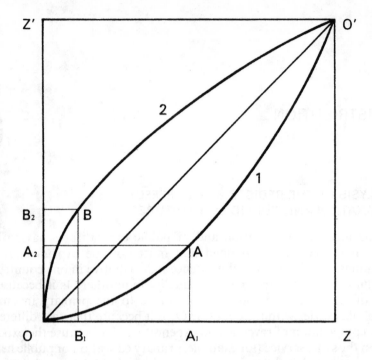

Figure 1.   Rate of concentration of transfer *c*

$$G - G' = -\left(\frac{e}{1+e}\right)P \text{ for a positive transfer,}$$

where G is the Gini coefficient for the distribution of primary income;
G' is the Gini coefficient for the distribution after transfer;
e is the intensity of the transfer;
P is the progressivity of the transfer.

Kakwani defines the progressivity P of a transfer as the difference between the rate of concentration of transfer c and the rate of concentration of the distribution of primary income G. In figure 1, the rate of concentration of transfer c corresponds to the ratio of the area comprised between the concentration curve and OO' to area $OO'Z$. The curve of concentration of a transfer is defined as the percentage of the total transfer paid or received by persons whose primary income is less than a certain amount. For example, in the figure point A on curve 1 indicates that 50 per cent of the households (the first five deciles of the distribution of primary incomes) pay or receive OA_2, that is, 25 per cent of the total transfer. The households are thus ranked according to their primary income along axis OZ, while the percentage of the transfer paid or received by those households is shown on OZ'. When the poorer households receive or pay a share of the transfer that is higher than their proportion of the total population, the curve of concentration is plotted in triangle $OO'Z'$, as is the case with curve 2. Thus point B on curve 2 indicates that 12 per cent of the households (the first twelve centiles of the distribution of primary incomes) receive 37 per cent of the transfer (for example, assistance to small and medium-scale farmers, which goes especially to low-income households). When the curve of concentration is situated in $OO'Z'$, the value of c is negative; it is positive when the curve falls in $OO'Z$.

Progressivity being the difference between c and G, the result is—

$$G - G' = + \frac{e}{1-e}(c - G) \text{ for a negative transfer, and}$$

$$G - G' = + \sum_i \frac{e_i}{1-e}(c_i - G) \text{ for several negative transfers.}$$

If the transfers are positive, the result is again—

$$G - G' = - \frac{e}{1+e}(c - G) \quad \text{or} \quad G - G' = - \sum_i \frac{e_i}{1+e}(c_i - G).$$

Lastly, for the over-all incidence of taxation and of public expenditure the result is—

$$G - G' = \sum_i^a \frac{e_i}{1-e}(c_i - G) - \sum_n^j \frac{e_j}{1+e}(c_j - G).$$

These equations make it possible to decompose the total variation in the Gini coefficient into indicators of intensity[2] $e_a \ldots e_n$ and indicators of progressivity $(c_a - G) \ldots (c_n - G)$.

Progressivity of transfers

Table 42 shows the results of our calculations of the progressivity of the transfers in nine developing countries or territories. The table also includes, for purposes of comparison, the corresponding data for Canada and the United States. The table is of interest, in particular, in showing a relative stability in the progressivity of each type of transfer for the various countries. This means that each type of transfer is marked by a certain concentration and, consequently, that the differences in intensity play an essential role in the variations of the Gini coefficient. Nevertheless, the

Table 42. Progressivity of taxation and of public expenditure[1] in 11 countries or territories

Item	Chile	Colombia	Panama	Puerto Rico	Hong Kong	Iran	Malaysia
Taxation							
Direct	+0.230	+0.147	...	+0.224	+0.528	+0.090	+0.068
Indirect	−0.059	+0.011	...	−0.043	−0.111[4]	−0.010	−0.030
Public expenditure							
Primary education	...	−0.548	−0.589	...	−0.509	−0.442	...
Public health	} −0.535	{ −1.093	...	} −0.710	{ −0.389	−0.641	...
Social welfare		...	...		...	...	...
Social security	−0.185	...	...	−0.405	...	...	...
Agricultural	−0.280	−0.658	−0.213	−0.446	...	−0.385	...
Housing	−0.211	...	...	...	−0.397	...	...
Secondary education	...	+0.008	−0.0426	...	−0.321	−0.273	...
Energy, industry, public works	...	−0.053	...	...	... }	+0.025	{ ...
Transport, communications	+0.007	...	−0.011	+0.133	... }	+0.025	{ ...
Higher education	...	+0.134	+0.354	...	−0.037	+0.346	...

[1] Difference between rate of concentration of transfers c and rate of concentration of distribution of primary income $G (c − G)$. [2] For Sri Lanka, the small value of the Gini coefficient (0.234) exercises an influence on the value of the progressivity and distorts to a certain extent the comparisons with the other countries (for example, if the rate of concentration of the transfer for primary education is equal to zero, the progressivity will be −0.234 instead of −0.4 or −0.5 elsewhere). [3] Calculated according to broad income adjusted (monetary and non-monetary incomes increased by positive transfers and diminished by taxation). [4] Excluding property tax. [5] For primary and secondary education.

differences in progressivity between the countries are not without interest, and are worth a detailed examination in the light of the taxation policy and public expenditure policy of each country.

Taxation

The rate of concentration of the transfer (c) is everywhere higher than the Gini coefficient for the distribution of primary income (G) in relation to direct taxation but is nearly everywhere lower in relation to indirect taxation. In most cases (excepting Canada and the United States), the difference ($c − G$), that is, the progressivity, varies for direct taxation between 0.1 and 0.3, the average being close to 0.2. For indirect taxation it is always lower than zero, except in Colombia and in Sri Lanka, with an average value of −0.05. In the case of Hong Kong, the property tax must be excluded from indirect taxation because it is in fact distributed as a direct tax on property.

In the case of direct taxation, the variations of progressivity are due both to the fiscal legislation and to tax evasion and fraud. The maximum

Philippines	Sri Lanka[2]	Canada	United States	Interval	Average	Item
						Taxation
+0.254	+0.361	+0.034 +0.106[3]	+0.027	+0.100/+0.300	+0.200	Direct
−0.136	+0.098	−0.129 −0.044[3]	−0.100	−0.050	−0.050	Indirect
						Public expenditure
	−0.228		−0.291[5]	−0.400/−0.600	−0.500	Primary education
} −0.294	{ −0.338 ⎫ ⎪ ... ⎬ ... ⎭	} −0.526	{ ... ⎫ ⎪ ... ⎬ −0.729 ⎭	−0.300/−0.700	−0.500	{ Public health { Social welfare { Social security
−0.282	−0.113	−0.112	−0.325	−0.300/−0.500	−0.400	Agricultural
...	...	...	...	} −2.00/−0.400	−0.300	{ Housing { Secondary { education
...	−0.057	...	...			
...	...	...	...	} 0	0	{ Energy, industry, { public works { Transport, { communications
−0.135	...	−0.150	...			
...	+0.096	...	+0.133	0/+0.400	+0.200	Higher education

Sources: Chile. Hong Kong. Iran. Philippines. Sri Lanka: see Chapter 5, tables 24 and 27 to 30; Colombia: Berry and Urrutia, *Income distribution in Colombia* (1976); Panama: Sahota, "The distribution of the benefits of public expenditure in Panama" (1977); Puerto Rico: Mann, "Net fiscal incidence in Puerto Rico" (1973); Malaysia: McLure, "Incidence of taxation in West Malaysia" (1972); Canada: Gillespie, *The redistribution of income in Canada* (1975); United States: Reynolds and Smolensky, *Public expenditures, taxes, and the distribution of income* (1977) Appendix, D–E, pp. 115–132.

value of the progressivity appears in Hong Kong (0.528), and the minimum in Iran and in Malaysia (0.09 and 0.068).

In Hong Kong the scale is very progressive, the rate varying in theory between 2.75 and 30 per cent though it is limited in fact to a maximum of 15 per cent. Deductions at source exempt 89 per cent of the households from income tax. As a result the distribution of direct taxes is highly concentrated: 77 per cent of them are paid by 1.6 per cent of the households.[3]

On the other hand the progressivity of direct taxation in Iran is very weak, for a number of reasons. The various constituents of a household's income are taxed separately, thereby reducing the effects of a progressive scale. The lump-sum deduction at source is used several times by persons having two or three incomes. Civil servants can benefit from large deductions. The taxation of persons who are self-employed in agriculture is very low: various deductions bring their taxable income down to some 10 to 45 per cent of the real income. A lump sum is levied on small traders. Although several scales of taxation are applicable to members of the professions, the total taxation of their incomes is small. At equal levels of income, self-employed persons are thus taxed much less than wage or salary earners. As for the tax on company profits, it produced very little in 1971 as a result of tax evasion and of allowances granted to companies to encourage them to invest or to export. In these circumstances and despite an apparently progressive scale of taxation with a rate rising from 15 per cent for low incomes to 60 per cent for large incomes, direct income tax amounted to a negligible proportion of the income: 0.7 and 1.3 per cent for wage and salary earners whose income placed them in the ninth and tenth deciles, and 0.3 and 0.6 per cent for self-employed persons in the same deciles.[4]

Chile and the Philippines are in an intermediate position, with a progressivity of 0.23 and 0.254 respectively. Although the majority of households in Chile may pay income tax, its progressivity is attenuated by several factors: statutory exemptions, erosion due to inflation, evasion and fraud. As a result the rate of taxation of the richest households (2 per cent of the households) is limited to 5.5 per cent; those households nevertheless contribute 40 per cent of the total amount of income tax. As for the tax on personal wealth, which was abolished in 1975, it provided for exemptions ranging from 15 to 120 times the minimum annual income; in addition, taxpayers benefited from a credit equal to 50 per cent of the amount of tax paid on total annual income. In the case of landed property, the main problem was not tax evasion but delays in the re-evaluations required to keep up with inflation.[5] In the Philippines, the amount of taxation remains at the moderate rate of 6–7 per cent even for the richest families (2.3 per cent of the population). Many transactions are not recorded, and the revenue authorities are short of staff. Allowing for the statutory exemptions, only 8 per cent of families have a taxable income. Tax evasion and fraud reduce appreciably the revenues from the direct tax to which those families are liable.[6]

With regard to indirect taxation, its progressivity, except in Colombia and in Sri Lanka, everywhere carries a negative sign, which means that such taxation increases the concentration of incomes.

The highest figures in absolute value are reached in the Philippines and in Hong Kong. In the Philippines that circumstance is the result of heavy duties on alcohol and on tobacco (the duties on tobacco reach a percentage of primary income 11 times higher for poor families than for the rich), as well as of import duties on consumer goods for the protection of national industries.[6] In Hong Kong duties on tobacco and on alcoholic beverages also account for a large proportion (48 per cent) of indirect taxation (not counting the tax on landed property) and their incidence diminishes as income increases (2–3 per cent for the poorer households and 0.5 per cent for those in the tenth decile).[3]

Indirect taxation in Iran is low. The greater part of the indirect taxes consists of taxes on imports (the main taxable items being vehicles, basic metals and machinery and equipment), excise duties on petroleum products and private cars, and stamp duties. The distribution of these taxes and duties is more concentrated than that of total household consumption: this counterbalances the incidence of taxes on other products and leads to a distribution of total indirect taxation that is almost as concentrated as that of primary incomes, the difference $c - G$ being equal to -0.01.[4]

Taken as a whole, indirect taxation is distributed approximately like consumption since the average value (-0.05) of the progressivity is equal to or a little less than the disparity between the rates of concentration of the distribution of primary incomes and those of consumption expenditure. The case of Sri Lanka is nevertheless instructive: it shows that indirect taxation at differential rates can have a progressive incidence.

In general, the progressivity of indirect taxation is much the same in the developing countries as in the developed countries. Thus in Canada there is a progressivity of -0.044 (instead of -0.129) after taking into account the positive transfers and the taxes (corrected income), and there would have to be a similar correction for the United States. The average value is thus close to -0.05.

Public expenditure

As table 42 shows, the progressivity of public expenditure is, in most cases, of the same order in the various countries and territories. There are four distinguishable groups of expenditure:

(1) Very progressive expenditure: primary education, health, and social welfare as well as social security where such a system exists. The rate of concentration (c) of this expenditure is under 0.2 or even negative, which means that the transfers received by the first deciles are greater in absolute value than those received by the other deciles.

(2) Progressive expenditure: agricultural, housing and, with less progressivity, secondary education. The rate of concentration is positive; it varies from 0 to 0.4.

(3) "Neutral" expenditure (i.e. neither progressive nor regressive): mining, energy, industry, public works, transport and communications, trade, tourism. The rate of concentration is very close to the Gini coefficient for the distribution of primary income (G).

(4) Regressive expenditure: higher education. The rate of concentration is higher than the Gini coefficient.

For the expenditure in group (1), the progressivity ($c - G$) has an average value of -0.53, which corresponds, for the rate of concentration of expenditure, to an average close to zero. For the expenditure in group (2), the progressivity tends to vary between -0.2 and -0.4. The expenditure in group (3) is distributed like the primary income; the progressivity is close to zero except for transport and communications in the Philippines and Puerto Rico. Lastly, higher education expenditure is regressive except in Hong Kong.

The distribution of public expenditure among households for these four groups of items calls for a series of remarks.

By its very nature, social welfare expenditure is more advantageous to poorer households than to the others. In Chile, for example, the households in the first six deciles received nearly 70 per cent of such expenditure;[7] in the Philippines the poorest households (17 per cent of the population) received 19.5 per cent.[8] Consideration must be given, however, to the composition of the expenditure in question. In Iran, for example, 87 per cent of it consisted of civil servants' pensions. Of the remainder, 4 per cent was for transfers to civil servants, 1 per cent for contributions to rural social security and 7 per cent for public assistance institutions. Thus only 8 per cent of the expenditure went mainly to poor families, most of it being paid to relatively well-to-do families since most of the civil servants are in the last quintile of income distribution.[9]

Where the children all go to school, primary education is as a rule of equal service to all the households except where there are differences in the composition of the households (the households in the first decile may have a smaller proportion of children owing to the presence of old and unmarried persons) or differences in the conditions of school attendance between one region or sector and another. Even if some of the children do not go to school the rate of concentration of expenditure may be low. Thus in Iran, where the children of poor rural families attend school less than others and where some of the children of rich families go to private schools, it is the medium-income families that benefit most from public primary education.[9] In Hong Kong, the rate of attendance at primary schools reached 86.5 per cent in 1971. Education was free in all public-sector schools and in most of the assisted schools; the children of low-income families are in any case exempted from the payment of school fees. Since the better-off families often send their children to private schools, poor families benefit more from public primary education than rich families. The share of expenditure allocated to the first four deciles reached 42 per cent, and the rate of concentration −0.07.[10]

The same applies to the expenditure on health. The existence of two sectors, the one public and the other private, may explain the low, if not negative, values of the rate of concentration, the richer families turning to the private sector. Such is the case in Hong Kong, where medical care is free in the public hospitals, which, however, are overcrowded. The number of medical practitioners is three times larger in the private sector than in the public, although 80 per cent of the patients are in the public hospitals. Since such services as prevention and health education affect all households equally, and since the public health care services are not much used by the rich families, the rate of concentration of health expenditure is low, with a progressivity of -0.389.[10] There is a similar situation in Chile. The poor households in the first three deciles benefit from one-third of the public expenditure on health, while the comfortably off and rich households in the fifth quintile benefit from only 15 per cent of them. On the other hand these richer families' share of private medical care exceeded 50 per cent while that of the poor households amounted to only 10 to 20 per cent.[7] In Iran, the financing of public hospitals accounts for 57 per cent of the expenditure on health; the remainder is devoted to such purposes as the eradication of malaria, vaccination, research and the programme of the Rural Health Corps, which concerns mainly the poorer households. According to a survey carried out in 1972, the poor households also benefited more from the services of the public hospitals because the richer households nearly always turn to the private sector; in absolute value, the benefit is ten times higher for the poorest households than for the rich. The rate of concentration of health expenditure is thus negative, with a progressivity of -0.641.[9]

These examples show that the rates of concentration (c) and of progressivity $(c - G)$ do not reflect the real inequalities in primary education and health services but only the differences in the utilisation of the education and health services that are free. The surveys carried out in Chile and in Hong Kong show that despite the values close to zero for the rate of concentration of expenditure, the rich families receive much better care than others, albeit at their own expense.

The progressivity, as a rule, of agricultural expenditure results from the composition of the first deciles, the majority of poor families being dependent on agriculture. The detailed analyses by country show that the effects are more or less progressive according to the kind of expenditure. Expenditure on land reform necessarily has a very progressive effect. In Chile and in the Philippines such expenditure is allocated to agricultural labourers, who belong to the poorest households. In Chile, two institutes gave assistance to farmers. One of them provided technical assistance to small farmers and encouraged the organisation of co-operatives, to which it granted loans on very favourable terms, the real rate, allowing for inflation, being about -20 per cent. The other institute lent to big and medium-scale farmers on less favourable terms at a real rate of about 7 per cent.[7] In the Philippines the expenditure for the promotion of animal husbandry and other farming represents a decreasing percentage of primary income as the latter increases (from 0.9 per cent for the first income bracket to 0.1 per cent for the last). On the other hand expenditure for the forest development is of benefit especially to the rich households.[8] In general the expenditure on irrigation is of benefit mainly to large landowners by reason of the distribution of irrigated lands. As a result of these facts the rate of concentration varies widely from one item of expenditure to another. The overall progressivity of the expenditure

(-0.28) is due to the large share of the expenditure on land reform and of assistance to small farmers. In other words, it is not assured *a priori* in every country.

In the case of housing only two examples are available, for Chile and for Hong Kong. The progressivity is more pronounced in Hong Kong, where housing is let at low rents to poor households, than in Chile, where the Government assisted households with housing loans and where the poorest families (first two deciles) benefited less than others from the assistance because they could neither save nor borrow.[10, 7]

The public expenditure on energy, mining, industry and transport and communications (including the necessary public works) has no effect on the inequality of incomes because it is distributed partly like total consumption (for example, the expenditure on energy) and partly like industrial profits, household expenditure on transport, and so forth. In the first case, the rate of concentration of the expenditure is a little lower than the rate of concentration of the distribution of primary incomes; in the second case, it exceeds it, the disparity becoming pronounced for transport by motor vehicle or aircraft with the rate of concentration then reaching 0.8 or more.

The expenditure on higher education is almost invariably regressive. The households in the first six or sometimes even first eight deciles derive no advantage from that expenditure, or only a little advantage where students can obtain grants. In Iran, that expenditure is insignificant for 88 per cent of the households, over 95 per cent of the expenditure benefiting 12 per cent of the households.[9] The situation is very different in Hong Kong. There the richest 8 per cent of households benefit from 45 per cent of the expenditure but the share of the households in the first six deciles reaches 35 per cent. In 1971 half of the students received grants for their fees and interest-free loans for their current expenses. These measures enabled all the students who, after a strict process of selection, had been admitted to the university to pursue their studies. That policy, which makes for a lower rate of concentration of expenditure than the rate of concentration of the distribution of primary incomes (the difference in Hong Kong is -0.037), appears to be a rarity in the developing countries.

Intensity of transfers

The analysis of the redistribution of income is carried further in tables 43 to 48 for five developing countries or territories (Hong Kong, Iran, the Philippines, Sri Lanka and Chile) as well as for Canada. The tables give the following data on the various categories of transfers, which are arranged so far as possible according to their degree of progressivity:

– intensity e_i of transfer i, proportion of primary income;
– concentration c_i (defined on pages 160–161);

– variation of Gini coefficient G (distribution of primary incomes) induced by the transfer, corresponding to the product

$\dfrac{e_i}{1 \pm e} (c_i - G)$; this variation is given in absolute value

and in percentage of the total variation;
– variation v induced by a hypothetical transfer, of constant intensity, of 9 per cent of the primary income for a negative transfer and of 11 per cent for a positive transfer (v/G).[11]

With regard to the intensity of the transfers, these data bring out wide variations between one country and another.

When the progressive transfers are considered (primary and secondary education, health, social welfare and security, housing, agriculture), very wide differences are found. From 23–24 per cent of primary income in Canada and from 25 per cent in Chile, the sum of those transfers falls to 3 per cent in Iran and 6 per cent in the Philippines. On the assumption that the progressivity of a category of transfers does not vary between one country and another, such differences would suffice to induce a re-distributive effect eight times greater in Canada or Chile than in Iran. These figures reveal the primary cause of the variations in the redistributive effect of public expenditure according to the country: the differences in intensity of that expenditure.

In that regard, Chile in 1969 may be compared with Iran in 1971. These countries are situated at the two extremes of the countries considered. As was seen in Chapter 5 (table 39), taxation and public expenditure entail a fall of the Gini coefficient by 0.06 in Chile and by 0.012 in Iran. Moreover, the rates of concentration for certain items of expenditure are very close in the two countries: 0.176 and 0.185 for agriculture; -0.079 and -0.071 for health. Since the Gini coefficient is higher in Iran (0.57 as against 0.456), the progressivity $(c - G)$ is higher in Iran for those two items than it is in Chile. The difference in redistributive effect between these two countries thus results from differences in the structure of the budget and in the ratio of public expenditure to household primary income, the product of which has already been noted (an intensity of 3 per cent in Iran and of 25 per cent in Chile for progressive expenditure).

The tax situation is more complex. In the developing countries under consideration, the share of indirect taxation is from two to three times larger than the share of direct taxation. Since the progressivity is close to 0.2 for direct taxation but amounts to -0.05 for indirect taxation, the redistributive effect is bound to be small. Such is the case in three countries where the fall in the Gini coefficient for the distribution of primary incomes is very small (0.008 in Chile), or almost nil (Iran, Philippines). In Hong Kong, taxation reduces the inequalities to a significant extent, with a drop in the Gini coefficient of 0.019, or about 5 per cent. That result is due not to differences of intensity relatively to the other countries but to a different distribution of the tax burden. The rate of concentration reaches 0.967 and 0.421 for direct and indirect taxation respectively. Thus it is the differences in progressivity, not in intensity, that distinguish Hong Kong from the three other countries with respect to taxation. The same applies to Sri Lanka, where the Gini coefficient falls by 0.032, or about 14 per cent. As in Hong Kong, that effect results from the progressivity both of indirect taxation, for which it amounts to about 0.1 instead of being negative, and of direct taxation.

While the differences of intensity are decisive with respect to expenditure, the differences in progressivity can also play an important role. Thus for social security expenditure the intensity reaches 0.115 in Chile, whereas in Canada it does not exceed 0.08 for the expenditure on social insurance and social security. Yet the redistributive effect is greater in Canada than in Chile (-0.0361 by comparison with -0.0159) owing to the differences in progressivity: -0.601 in one case and -0.185 in the other, the rates of concentration being -0.184 and 0.271 respectively.

Decomposition of the redistributive effect

Tables 43 to 48 make it possible to allocate its effect on redistribution to each category of taxation and of public expenditure.

Except in Hong Kong and Sri Lanka, the effect of taxation is the same in all cases: indirect taxation reduces and may even cancel out the redistributive effect of direct taxation: in the Philippines the two effects balance each other. In Chile and Iran direct taxation has a greater effect in absolute terms than indirect taxation: the figures are $+207$ and -107 per cent for Chile and $+124$ and -24 per cent for Iran. With neutral indirect taxation, the redistributive effect would have been appreciable in Chile (fall of 0.0172 in the Gini coefficient) and in the Philippines (fall of 0.0257). Indirect taxation leaves inequalities practically unchanged in Hong Kong, while in Sri Lanka indirect taxation contributes to a reduction of the Gini coefficient thanks to differentiation in rates on purchased goods and services.

At first sight, the incidence of taxation in Canada may seem paradoxical: the Gini coefficient increases by 0.03 because the regressive effect of indirect taxation, causing a rise by 0.0433, largely exceeds the progressive effect of direct taxation, causing a fall by 0.0133. As has already been explained, the effect of indirect taxation is due especially to the scale of monetary transfers to poor households. The results are very different if such transfers are excluded from the calculation of the effect of taxation: direct taxation then leads to a fall of 0.04 in the Gini coefficient

Table 43. Decomposition of the redistribution of income in Hong Kong, 1971

Item	Transfer intensity e_i: proportion of primary income	Rate of concentration c_i	Induced variation of Gini coefficient		Variation v induced by a transfer of constant intensity (v/G)
			Absolute value	% of total variation	
Taxation:					
Direct	0.034	0.967	0.0206	109	*0.120*
Indirect	0.099	0.421	−0.0018	−9	*0.005*
			0.0188	100	
Public expenditure:					
Primary and secondary education	0.037	−0.027	−0.0157	39.4	*−0.106*
Housing	0.038	0.046	−0.0136	34.2	*−0.090*
Health	0.029	0.054	−0.0102	25.7	*−0.088*
Higher education	0.008	0.406	−0.0003	0.7	*−0.008*
			−0.0398	100.0	

Gini coefficient	*a*	*b*
Distribution of primary income (G)	0.439	0.443
Variation induced by (a) taxation; (b) public expenditure	−0.019	−0.040
Distribution (G) after (a) taxation; (b) public expenditure	0.420	0.403

Source: Hsia and Chau: *Industrialisation, employment and income distribution* (1978), tables 6.1 and 6.2, pp. 154 and 165.

while indirect taxation leads to a rise of 0.015, the net incidence being a fall of 0.025.

In Chile and Hong Kong public expenditure appreciably reduces the concentration of incomes, by −0.052 and −0.04 respectively. The expenditure on education and on health plays a decisive role, accounting for 50 and 65 per cent respectively of the reduction in the Gini coefficient, although in the case of Chile the effect of expenditure on education is underestimated because higher education, which is probably regressive, is not differentiated from primary and secondary education. In Hong Kong a third important redistributive factor is expenditure on housing (34 per cent), while in Chile it is expenditure on social security (30 per cent). In Iran and in the Philippines, where the redistributive effect is very slight, it is mainly educational and health expenditure that determines the effect, 78 per cent of it in the Philippines and 104 per cent in Iran, where agricultural

Table 44. Decomposition of the redistribution of income in Iran, 1971

Item	Transfer intensity e_i: proportion of primary income	Rate of concentration c_i	Induced variation of Gini coefficient		Variation v induced by a transfer of constant intensity (v/G)
			Absolute value	% of total variation	
Taxation:					
Direct	0.032	0.644	0.0031	124	*0.016*
Indirect	0.051	0.544	−0.0006	−24	*−0.002*
			0.0025	100	
Public expenditure:					
Health	0.006	−0.071	−0.0036	36	*−0.112*
Primary education	0.018	0.180	−0.0067	68	*−0.068*
Agriculture	0.005	0.185	−0.0018	18	*−0.068*
Transport, communications, social welfare, etc.	0.020	0.603	0.0006	−6	*0.006*
Higher education	0.005	0.916	0.0016	−16	*0.061*
			−0.0099	100	

	a	b
Gini coefficient		
Distribution of primary income (G)	0.554	0.570
Variation induced by (a) taxation; (b) public expenditure	−0.002	−0.010
Distribution (G) after (a) taxation; (b) public expenditure	0.552[1]	0.560[1]

[1] Figures obtained by direct estimate for distribution after transfers: 0.553 and 0.559.

Sources: Mehran, *Taxes and incomes* (1975), and *Distribution of benefits from public consumption expenditures among households in Iran* (1977).

expenditure accounts for 18 per cent. This last category of expenditure also exercises an influence in Chile (10 per cent). In Sri Lanka, where the decline in the Gini coefficient caused by public expenditure is moderate (−0.024), it is likewise the expenditure on health and on education (primary) which, together with the subsidising of food products, accounts for 82 per cent of the decline.

It is of interest for purposes of international comparison to estimate the incidence of a hypothetical transfer representing a constant percentage of household primary income. That incidence has been calculated for a transfer of 9 per cent in the case of direct and indirect taxation and of 11

Table 45.   Decomposition of the redistribution of income in the Philippines, 1971

Item	Transfer intensity e_i, proportion of primary income	Rate of concentration c_i	Induced variation of Gini coefficient		Variation v induced by a transfer of constant intensity (v/G)
			Absolute value	% of total variation	
Taxation:					
Direct	0.078	0.750	0.0257		*0.051*
Indirect	0.147	0.360	−0.0258		*−0.027*
			−0.0001		
Public expenditure:					
Primary and secondary education	0.045	0.185	−0.0121	65.0	*−0.061*
Health	0.009	0.185	−0.0024	13.0	*−0.061*
Transport, communications	0.028	0.344	−0.0035	18.8	*−0.028*
Land reform, rural development	0.010	0.417	−0.0006	3.2	*−0.013*
			−0.0186	100.0	

Gini coefficient	*a*	*b*
Distribution of primary income (*G*)	0.496	0.479
Variation induced by (*a*) taxation; (*b*) public expenditure	0.000	−0.019
Distribution (*G*) after (*a*) taxation; (*b*) public expenditure	0.496[1]	0.460[1]

[1] Figures obtained by direct estimate for distribution after transfers: 0.494 and 0.461.

Source: Tan: *Taxation, government spending and income distribution in the Philippines* (1975).

per cent in the case of public expenditure.[11] The figures, which are shown in the last column of the tables, thus make it possible to compare the redistributive effectiveness of each type of transfer, that is, the relative induced variation of the Gini coefficient for the same intensity.

In the case of taxation, there are considerable differences according to the country. Thus direct taxation affecting 9 per cent of primary income would reduce the Gini coefficient by 15 per cent in Sri Lanka, 12 per cent in Hong Kong, only 5 per cent in Chile and in the Philippines and less than 2 per cent in Iran. With the same percentage, the effect would be no less variable in the case of indirect taxation: falls of less than 1 per cent in Hong

Table 46. Decomposition of the redistribution of income in Sri Lanka, 1973

Item	Transfer intensity e_i, proportion of primary income	Rate of concentration c_i	Induced variation of Gini coefficient		Variation v induced by a transfer of constant intensity (v/G)
			Absolute value	% of total variation	
Taxation:					
Direct	0.033	0.595	0.014	44	*0.154*
Indirect	0.150	0.332	0.018	56	*0.042*
			0.032	100	
Public expenditure:					
Social welfare, housing	0.004	−0.670	−0.0036	15	*−0.386*
Primary education, health, subsidisation of food products	0.094	−0.001	−0.0195	82	*−0.100*
Agriculture	0.014	0.121	−0.0014	6	*−0.048*
Secondary education	0.016	0.177	−0.0008	3	*−0.024*
Transport, higher education	0.011	0.389	0.0016	−6	*−0.066*
			−0.0237	100	

Gini coefficient		*a*	*b*
Distribution of primary income (G)		0.234	0.234
Variation induced by (a) taxation; (b) public expenditure		−0.032	−0.024
Distribution (G) after (a) taxation; (b) public expenditure		0.202	0.210

Source: Alailima, *Fiscal incidence in Sri Lanka* (1978), tables 2, 5 and 3.8, pp. 34–36 and 71–75.

Kong and 4 per cent in Sri Lanka and rises of 1 per cent in Chile and 3 per cent in the Philippines.

In the case of public expenditure, there is as a rule a maximum effectiveness of about −0.09 to −0.11, which means that expenditure representing 11 per cent of household primary income would cause a fall in the Gini coefficient by some 10 per cent. Such is the case for the expenditure on primary and secondary education, health and housing in Hong Kong; on health in Iran; on primary education, health, social welfare, housing and subsidisation of food products in Sri Lanka; on health and social welfare in Chile. (In Canada, certain expenditure has a

Table 47.   Decomposition of the redistribution of income in Chile, 1969

Item	Transfer intensity e_i, proportion of primary income	Rate of concentration c_i	Induced variation of Gini coefficient		Variation v induced by a transfer of constant intensity (v/G)
			Absolute value	% of total variation	
Taxation:					
Direct	0.061	0.686	0.0172	207	*0.050*
Indirect	0.123	0.397	−0.0089	−107	*−0.013*
			0.0083	100	
Public expenditure:					
Health, social welfare	0.039	−0.079	−0.0155	30.0	*−0.117*
Agriculture	0.024	0.176	−0.0050	10.0	*−0.061*
Education	0.061	0.232	−0.0107	20.6	*−0.049*
Housing	0.032	0.245	−0.0051	10.0	*−0.046*
Social security	0.115	0.271	−0.0159	30.0	*−0.041*
Energy, mining, industry, transport	0.073	0.463	0.0004	−0.6	*0.002*
			−0.0518	100.0	

Gini coefficient	*a*	*b*
Distribution of primary income (*G*)	0.456	0.456
Variation induced by (*a*) taxation; (*b*) public expenditure	−0.008	−0.052
Distribution (*G*) after (*a*) taxation; (*b*) public expenditure	0.448[1]	0.404[1]

[1] Figures obtained by direct estimate for distribution after transfers: 0.448 and 0.405.
Sources: Foxley et al., *Redistribution effects of government programmes* (1978).

higher redistributive effectiveness: the expenditure on social insurance and social security and on manpower programmes causes a fall by 0.144 and 0.134 respectively in the Gini coefficient.) The expenditure on the following purposes has an average effectiveness of − 0.04 to − 0.06 (4–6 per cent fall in the Gini coefficient): education (excluding higher education) and agriculture in Iran; education (excluding higher education) and health in the Philippines; agriculture in Sri Lanka; and education, social security, housing and agriculture in Chile. The other expenditure categories have a negligible and even regressive effect, such as expenditure on higher education in Iran, which causes a rise of 0.06 in the Gini coefficient.

Table 48.   Decomposition of the redistribution of income in Canada, 1969

Item	Transfer intensity e_i, proportion of primary income	Rate of concentration c_i	Induced variation of Gini coefficient		Variation v induced by a transfer of constant intensity (v/G)
			Absolute value	% of total variation	
Taxation:					
Direct	0.226	0.451	0.0133	−44	*0.005*
Indirect	0.194	0.288	−0.0433	144	*−0.031*
Public expenditure:					
Social insurance and social security	0.080	−0.184	−0.0361	42.1	*−0.144*
Manpower programmes	0.013	−0.143	−0.0056	6.5	*−0.134*
Health, housing	0.072	−0.025	−0.0239	27.8	*−0.106*
Education	0.088	0.211	−0.0136	15.8	*−0.049*
Agriculture, transport, etc.	0.076	0.300	−0.0067	7.8	*−0.028*
			−0.0859	100.0	

Gini coefficient		*a*	*b*
Distribution of primary income (G)		0.417	0.417
Variation induced by (a) taxation; (b) public expenditure		+0.030	−0.086
Distribution (G) after (a) taxation; (b) public expenditure		0.447[1]	0.331[1]

[1] Figures obtained by direct estimate for distribution after transfers: 0.446 and 0.331.
Source: Gillespie, *The redistribution of income in Canada* (1975), Appendix D.

These estimates are particularly useful for designing a policy of redistribution of incomes. They make it possible to calculate the effect on the Gini coefficient of a modification of taxation or of particular items of government expenditure by assuming a constant redistributive effectiveness of the transfer. They also make it possible, by means of international comparison, to determine the extent to which the effectiveness of a particular category of expenditure can be increased and to consider the means of increasing it.

REDISTRIBUTION POLICIES

Review of proposals

The studies that have been examined contain many proposals for increasing the redistribution of incomes. It will be desirable to consider the extent to which those proposals, if applied, would lead to an increase of the progressivity or intensivity of transfers. The analysis will prepare the way for a consideration of the theoretical and practical limitations to any policy of redistribution in developing countries arising out of their economic, social and political structures.

Direct taxation is an instrument that has always received much attention. For Chile, Foxley et al. have considered means of increasing the progressivity of taxation.[12] They show that the policy of granting tax exemptions for the purpose of promoting development was in most cases mistaken: owing to the monopolistic or oligopolistic structure of the markets, it was of benefit solely to the owners of capital. What was needed was a reduction in the number of exemptions and a policy of granting them for limited periods and only in cases that could be certain to have a favourable effect on the standard of living of a substantial proportion of the population. It seemed in any case preferable to grant a fixed amount of assistance to a particular sector or region. It was especially necessary to reduce tax evasion and fraud. Taxpayers who were not wage or salary earners benefited from numerous exemptions, from some gaps in the taxation system and from inflation, so that they could declare only a third of their real incomes. It was necessary to improve the tax legislation, to strengthen the revenue authorities, who had no means of making the necessary checks, and to impose heavy penalties for fraud. There was a need for an overhaul of the taxation of wealth. A main problem was that of galloping inflation in Chile; an annual re-evaluation of landed property was essential. It had been a mistake to abolish in 1975 the personal wealth tax, accounting in 1974 for 31.2 per cent of all revenue from the taxation of wealth. Lastly, death duties and taxes on gifts *inter vivos* were levied at such low rates that they produced only insignificant revenue.

There are similar findings in the other studies. In Iran, even without changing the scale of taxation the revenue from income tax could be increased considerably by checking the incomes of persons who were not wage or salary earners, by improving tax collection and by consolidating all the taxpayer's income from whatever source for taxation purposes. In the Philippines the best way to increase income tax revenue was to obtain more information on the incomes and to revise the exemptions. In India there was the paradox that 10 per cent of the families owned two-thirds of the wealth but that the taxes levied on them produced paltry revenue.[13]

All these proposals tell the same tale. In many countries it would be possible to increase the product of direct taxation and hence the intensity of the transfer by abolishing exemptions, by taxing together all the incomes of each person and by requiring non-salary-earners in the last twentieth of the distribution of incomes (about 2 to 3 per cent of economically active persons) to keep accounts to be checked by the revenue authorities or by chartered accountants. (These measures would not necessarily alter the progressivity of the tax on income because exemptions and tax evasion entail the same relative reduction of tax at the various levels of the distribution.) Furthermore, the concentration of wealth and the large proportion of investments in land and property in the wealth of the richest 5 per cent make it possible to institute a tax on wealth for a small number of households (under 2 per cent). The institution of such a tax would increase the progressivity of direct taxation since it would concern a smaller number of families than are concerned by the tax on income and they would be the families with the highest incomes.

In the case of indirect taxation, the first aim of a policy of redistribution is to change not the intensity but the progressivity of that taxation, the rate of concentration of indirect taxation being nearly always lower than that of the primary incomes and the progressivity being negative. This recommendation may seem surprising when one considers that the progressivity is, as a rule, likewise negative in developed countries. However, the structures of consumption are different. In the developing countries, production for own consumption still accounts for a large part of the consumption of poor households; there are also much more pronounced differentiations according to income, many durable goods being purchased only by households in the upper category. Various measures can ensure the neutrality of indirect taxation and even a slightly positive progressivity. In general it would be desirable to reduce duties on everyday consumer goods and to increase them on goods and services of interest especially to high-income households (petrol, motor cars, banking services). Duties could be extended also to the usually free services that are obtained from such public facilities as motorways and airports. The example of Sri Lanka, which has introduced a turnover tax and foreign exchange entitlement certificates, both of them highly progressive, shows the cogency of these proposals. The argument that technical difficulties stand in the way of instituting a neutral or progressive system of indirect taxation cannot be put forward in the case of countries with large inequalities of consumption where many durable goods and services are confined to a small minority, though there may be, of course, other obstacles, including, for example, political ones.

Turning now to public expenditure, the redistributive incidence of some items depends especially on its intensity. There is, for example, the expenditure that provides the whole population with free primary education or certain free medical services (vaccinations, annual medical examinations of children). Such expenditure is highly concentrated in favour of the poorer categories, with a progressivity of -0.4 to -0.6. In such cases the best way to increase the redistributive effect is to increase budgetary allocations in order to finance, for example, an additional year of compulsory schooling or a new medical service. (It may be noted here that the benefit provided, which is estimated here only according to its cost, is more certain for medical services than for education; a supplementary year of schooling may have no effect on the future incomes of the pupils if the teaching is ill-conceived, whereas any additional medical service must tend to have a favourable effect on the health of the population.) Since such services (primary education up to the age of 14, all the basic preventive and therapeutic services) are not generally provided free to the whole population in developing countries, it is clear that a start must be made by increasing the relevant expenditure to the extent needed to reach those objectives, thereby reducing the inequalities in the standard of living. If the expenditure on primary education and on medical services is equal to 7.5 per cent of household primary income, the Gini coefficient will fall by 7 per cent (by 10 per cent if they amount to 11 per cent of the income).

This reasoning presupposes an equal distribution of the services provided, without which the progressivity will not reach the values indicated. Unfortunately, and as many studies have shown, there are pronounced imbalances in many developing countries between urban and rural areas or between different regions. It is not enough to raise the expenditure on education or on health to a certain level: the whole population must be given access to schools, hospitals and clinics through properly planned provision of these facilities and of related public works.

For other items of expenditure the main factor is progressivity: in many cases measures intended to achieve redistribution have more or less missed their target and have been of benefit partly or mainly to medium-income and high-income households. Analyses of redistribution have given birth to many proposals aimed at modifying the distribution of transfers with a view to increasing their progressivity and to reducing the concentration of incomes without any appreciable increase in budgetary appropriations.

The most detailed study on the restructuring of public expenditure is one by Foxley, Aninat and Arellano.[14] It appeared that the expenditure on development had been of benefit especially to entrepreneurs in the modern sector. Half of that expenditure consisted of investment incentives, and most of them were for the modern sector in the form of purchases of equipment or the building up of the economic infrastructure. Only a small part of the assistance went to small entrepreneurs or to the self-employed, agriculture being the best-served sector by reason of programmes of help to small farmers.

In order to increase the progressivity of government action, it would have been necessary to abandon the policy of cheap credit for all undertakings, to make capital available only at its real price and to institute direct assistance to small entrepreneurs for the purchase of certain factors of production (such as fertilisers) or for the stabilisation of the prices of certain agricultural products. Any grants of cheap loans with public assistance would have to be confined solely to small producers and should be for limited periods. That new policy had to be applied also to public undertakings which benefited from various advantages such as loans at low rates of interest and exemptions from import duties.

Social expenditure also had to be reconsidered. Instead of offering everybody certain services free of charge (yet sometimes without ensuring that they effectively reached the poorest categories), low-income target groups should be identified and provided with those services free of charge while other households would be made to pay for them. Moreover, the government should not subsidise certain products for the benefit of all consumers and, in some cases, of producers and middlemen but should make that assistance more selective by giving it only to those consumers whose basic needs were not met. Where appropriate, a system of differential prices would make it possible to adapt that assistance to needs. Lastly, the schemes applied should be reviewed on the basis of detailed studies of the needs of the poor families for food, housing, medical care, etc., taking into account the attitudes and consumption habits of those families.

Gupta likewise draws attention to the many problems that have arisen in India with respect to social expenditure. In the case of housing and higher education, a comparison with Hong Kong is of interest. Whereas in Hong Kong housing assistance increased with the poverty of the household, in India medium-income and high-income households benefited much more than the others. Similarly, the system of student grants instituted in Hong Kong gave the children of poor families greater access to universities than the measures taken in India. Lastly, much expenditure in support of agriculture (especially for irrigation) which was used for capital equipment was of benefit mainly to the medium-scale and large landowners.[15]

These remarks confirm that the best way to increase the progressivity of public expenditure is to link assistance to the income of the beneficiaries instead of indiscriminately subsidising credit, the purchase of equipment, housing services and so forth. There is, for example, no good reason why the State should pay part of the price of irrigation equipment which the larger landowners can buy even if they have to borrow at market rates; on the other hand the State might reimburse 50 or 75 per cent of the purchase price to small farmers at once. Even expenditure on higher education can have a redistributive effect with a system of part payment and of grants enabling all proficient candidates to pursue their studies. The variations in the progressivity of public expenditure according to the country, as indicated in table 42, show that the progressivity could be increased in many cases by abandoning the principle of free services and of generalised assistance, by limiting assistance to the poor households and by making others pay at the ruling rates. Such a policy should cover all the goods and services in respect of which there is no equality of consumption. (There is necessarily equality in the case of services such as compulsory schooling for all children or vaccination of the whole population.)

An attempt to estimate the effect of these proposals is made in table 49 under asssumption 1. Under that assumption, the government increases the share of direct taxation in the revenue, raising it to 40 per cent. The government also increases the share of expenditure in category A for primary education, health, the subsidisation of basic food products, and social welfare (including social security); the total would amount to 10 per cent of household primary income. Moreover, the government would increase the progressivity of indirect taxation and of certain other items of public expenditure. Variable rates according to the product or service consumed give a concentration rate of 0.45 for indirect taxation, which is distinctly higher than the rate for the distribution of consumption among households. Expenditure for agriculture and housing is allocated in such a way as to benefit mainly small farmers and low-income households. In addition, a system of grants for secondary education guarantees access to it for all children of the requisite intellectual standard. This application of simultaneous government action on the intensity and progressivity of the transfers enables the Gini coefficient to be reduced under assumption 1 to 1.08 (0.025 for taxation and 0.055 for public expenditure), that is, by about 20 per cent. At present such a result is not achieved in many developing countries.

Assumption 2 shows, on the other hand, how the incidence of taxation and of public expenditure can be neutral. It suffices to assume that the share of direct taxation and of public expenditure in category A is halved (4 and 5 per cent of household primary income instead of 8 and 10 per cent), that indirect taxation represents a constant or decreasing proportion of expenditure whatever the level of household income and that public expenditure in categories B and C is distributed more unequally. For category B, the rate of concentration rises from 0.15 to 0.4. Thus assistance to agriculture benefits farmers proportionately to their income, while the opportunities of access to secondary education are not two or three times but seven or eight times higher for the children of households in the fifth quintile than for those of households in the first. Lastly, expenditure in category C is more concentrated than primary income, the effect of economic aid is nil and higher education has a distinctly regressive incidence.

A comparison of the effects obtained under the two assumptions shows how government action affecting either the intensity of direct taxation and of public expenditure in category A or the progressivity of indirect taxation and of expenditure in categories B and C can have an

Table 49. Redistributive effect of government action under two assumptions, in terms of variations in the Gini coefficient

I. Detailed data

Item	Rate of concentration c_i of the transfer	Progressivity $(c_i - G)$	Intensity e_i: proportion of primary income	Induced variation of Gini coefficient
Taxation				
Assumption 1				
Direct taxation	0.700	0.250	0.08	0.025
Indirect taxation	0.450	0.000	0.12	0.000
				0.025
Assumption 2				
Direct taxation	0.700	0.250	0.04	0.012
Indirect taxation	0.300	−0.150	0.16	−0.030
				−0.018
Public expenditure[1]				
Assumption 1				
Category A	0.000	−0.450	0.10	−0.038
Category B	0.150	−0.300	0.07	−0.017
Category C	0.450	0.000	0.03	0.000
				−0.055
Assumption 2				
Category A	0.000	−0.450	0.05	−0.019
Category B	0.400	−0.050	0.09	−0.004
Category C	0.500	0.050	0.06	0.003
				−0.020

II. Summary

Item	Gini coefficient			
	Assumption 1		Assumption 2	
	a	b	a	b
Distribution of primary income	0.450	0.450	0.450	0.450
Variation induced by—				
(a) taxation; and				
(b) public expenditure	−0.025	−0.055	+0.018	−0.020
Distribution after—				
(a) taxation; and				
(b) public expenditure	0.425	0.395	0.468	0.430

[1] Category A: Primary education, health, subsidisation of the sale of basic foodstuffs, and social welfare (including social security); category B: secondary education, assistance to agriculture, housing assistance; category C: higher education, assistance for industry and transport.

appreciable redistributive effect by ensuring the satisfaction of the basic needs of households in the first deciles or, on the other hand, may leave the inequalities in the distribution of primary incomes entirely unchanged.

Limits of redistribution policies

The foregoing conclusions must be qualified in so far as they may have been over-precise or over-optimistic. It must not be overlooked that the assumptions underlying the methods commonly employed for estimating redistribution, especially in the studies to which reference has been made, are liable to be easily upset. A first objection concerns the incidence of the transfers. Strictly speaking, it is not possible to calculate all the effects of a transfer without having recourse to a model of general equilibrium.[16] Is it correct, for example, to allocate the whole benefit of irrigation works to the large landowners who alone make use of them? In practice, such works will increase the demand for labour in rural areas, which, in view of the extent of underemployment, will have an incidence on the distribution of incomes to the advantage of the poorest categories of the population. Irrigation will bring about also an increase in the supply of agricultural produce; any change in the prices of that produce will have an effect on the distribution of real incomes since the share of foodstuffs in family budgets varies with income. Consider also the expenditure on public health. That expenditure can improve the productivity of the labour force; if there is an understanding between the employees, they can appropriate part of the benefit of that increase in productivity to increase the returns on their capital.

Nevertheless, there can generally be no question in budgetary policy of reconsidering all the previous expenditure, any more than it is possible to make entirely free choices in the budget as a whole. It is a question rather of increasing a particular item of expenditure or revenue and of launching a particular project, which are measures affecting only a small part of the budget. The consequences of particular measures of that kind on the distribution of incomes can be made the subject of detailed studies on both the direct and the indirect effects. Such studies clearly pertain to a second stage of research, after the over-all studies, which, because they are not made in the context of a model of general equilibrium, give only a rough view of redistribution, though they constitute an essential first stage.

There is also the problem of estimating the advantage obtained from public goods and services. To base that estimation on the costs of production of those goods and services is to bring in very questionable assumptions relating to, for example, the efficiency of the public sector and utility functions. It would be desirable in sectoral studies to reconsider that method of calculation and to try to arrive at a better estimate of the real value to households of the services made available to them.[17]

Even if one reasons on the basis of the usual assumptions, there remains the question, as raised by Harberger, of the inevitable limits to any policy of redistribution.[18] Harberger assumes that the scale of taxation is as progressive as it is in the United States. Direct taxation represents the same percentage of primary income for all the households belonging to the same centile of distribution, while indirect taxation amounts to the same constant percentage of 10 per cent whatever the level of income may be. Through the effect of taxation the Gini coefficient drops from 0.402 to 0.372 or, if the primary distribution is more concentrated, from 0.498 to 0.462, i.e. by 8 per cent. That reasoning tallies with the present authors' estimates. If direct taxation represents on the average 8 per cent of primary incomes, as Harberger assumes, and if indirect taxation amounts to 10 per cent, there will be a reduction of the Gini coefficient by 0.02 with a progressivity of 0.2 and by 0.03 with a progressivity of 0.3. As can be noted, Harberger's results correspond, so far as progressivity is concerned, to the second value, which is rarely reached in the developing countries. It can be concluded, therefore, that a reduction of the Gini coefficient by 7 or 8 per cent through taxation represents the maximum that is conceivable.

For analysing the incidence of public expenditure, Harberger assumes that the revenue from taxation is devoted to expenditure equally distributed among all households (concentration coefficient equal to zero). In that case the reduction in the Gini coefficient through public expenditure alone is by 0.024 (0.378 instead of 0.402) or, with a more unequal primary distribution, by 0.039 (0.459 instead of 0.498). Harberger regards the assumption of equal distribution as not very realistic in the case in which the share of public expenditure is a large one, that is, from 6.3 to 8.5 per cent. That point of view is at variance with the budgets of several developing countries. In Chile, for example, the expenditure on primary education, health and social welfare, for which the concentration rate was close to zero, amounted to about 7 per cent of the primary income of households. Reference could be made to other countries: in Kenya, Malaysia, Mauritius and Zambia, the expenditure on those items exceeds 9 per cent of the primary income, while in Mexico and in Tunisia it is close to 6 per cent.[19]

It is possible, therefore, to assume that the main items of social expenditure amount to 9 per cent of the primary income of households and, in addition, to take into account the less progressive expenditure on such items as agriculture and housing, which can amount to 4 per cent of the primary income (in fact 3 to 4 per cent in the case of the seven countries named above). These figures are plausible when a government wishes to carry out a policy of redistribution. In that case a significant reduction of the Gini coefficient by 0.046 is obtained when the coefficient amounts to 0.5 for the distribution of primary income and by 0.036 if it amounts to 0.4. In both cases there is thus a fall of 9 per cent, it being assumed that e amounted to 25 per cent of the primary income of households. That result has already been obtained in some countries. If certain programmes of international aid were specifically devoted to this type of expenditure it would be possible to obtain higher values of, for example, 12 and 6 per cent instead of 9 and 4 per cent of the primary income of households, provided that the governments did not relax their previous efforts. It would be possible then to reduce the Gini coefficient by 0.063 or by 0.049 according to whether the coefficient stood at 0.5 or 0.4 at the start.

The joint effect of progressive direct taxation, with a progressivity of 0.3, and of these choices for primary education, health, social welfare, agriculture and housing would be to reduce the Gini coefficient by 17 or 20 per cent with external aid. That would not be a negligible result. From 0.5 the Gini coefficient would drop to 0.415 or 0.4, which would correspond to an increase in the real income of the poorest households (first two quintiles) by 30 to 40 per cent depending on the assumptions and the various possible distributions of the expenditure among those households. That result would not suffice to bring about the disappearance of want among the groups with an average annual income of between US$100 and 300, but it would constitute an initial success by ensuring the partial satisfaction of basic needs with respect to health, education and housing.

Nevertheless, many economic, social, cultural and political obstacles stand in the way of the application of such a policy of redistribution. In the first place, it is difficult to reach the figure of 6 to 8.5 per cent of primary income for direct taxation. It is necessary to levy that taxation on households having an income a little above the average (ninth decile). A large part of the incomes of those households is derived, however, from the activities of individual undertakings, that is, from craftsmen, businessmen and farmers who do not keep accounts. In these circumstances it would seem to be impossible to avoid tax evasion and fraud. As for taxing households with lower incomes (for example those in the eighth decile), it is out of the question as long as individual income remains so low (under US$1,000 in most of the developing countries). The presence of paid foreign technical, supervisory and executive staff, as in African countries, can also make it difficult to establish a progressive scale of direct taxation; since an expatriation decision depends on the net salary, any increase in the tax burden would have to be balanced by an increase in the gross salary.

It is not certain that it would be possible to cover the whole of the target population equally by striving to place certain services such as health services and agricultural extension services at the disposal of the underprivileged. For example the poorest farmers, who live almost entirely on production for their own consumption, might also be those most opposed to progress. The ability to make use of certain services is partly related to income, so that inequalities may appear even if every precaution has been taken to make those services equally accessible to everybody. It is a mistake to suppose that supply automatically creates demand, whatever may be the cultural level, the habits or the standard of living of the people concerned.

Lastly, effective action will be hampered particularly by political obstacles, above all the opposition of high-income groups who would have to finance the redistribution and who, in many cases, have family or other links with the authorities, so that it is not possible to raise direct taxation and progressive expenditure up to the level required to reduce the concentration of incomes to an appreciable extent. Elsewhere and despite the weight of taxation and the amount of public expenditure, the objective of redistribution is not reached owing to another obstacle, namely the administrative machinery that is supposed to bring about the redistribution. A part of the public expenditure intended for poor households may be diverted to other ends. Gupta gives some examples of the questionable use sometimes made of public assistance to the benefit of certain officials. Foxley refers to the rigidity of the machinery of government in general, which finds it difficult to make the changes needed to increase the redistributive effect of expenditure. He regards it as the outcome of ingrained administrative routine and of pressure on the part of those who benefit from measures taken over the years and who do everything to protect their perquisites.[20] Thus the interests of possessors of large incomes stand in opposition to a policy of redistribution, especially in respect of the intensity of the transfers, while the administrative apparatus, in so far as it does not ensure an optimum utilisation of public resources, reduces the progressivity of government action.

INCOMES AND PRICES POLICIES

All the measures that have now been examined, whether they be tax deductions or the various services provided to households, exercise an indirect influence on distribution. A question that arises is whether they should be supplemented by direct measures applied to the distribution of primary incomes.

A fact that has to be stressed, however, is that the structure of real incomes and the structure of consumption derived therefrom are not independent of the organisation of production. A redistribution of incomes is liable to be quite ineffective if the new structure of demand which it generates runs into the rigidities of the system of production. An increase in low incomes would be an illusion if the supply of everyday consumer goods was inelastic; the most that it would do would be to raise prices and increase the volume of imports. Measures brought to bear directly on the distribution of incomes therefore, cannot be envisaged, independently of the pattern of production and of employment policy. An incomes policy constitutes an integral part of the general policy of development: it cannot be considered on its own.

The establishment of a minimum wage is one of the measures to which reference is most frequently made, perhaps in the light of the practice of industrialised countries. In the developing countries, where the majority of the population do not have the status of wage or salary earners and do not always benefit from stable employment, provision must be made for specific measures of support of the minimum wage policy, or even for an extension of that policy's range of application. In that way there can be substituted for the notion of a minimum wage the more general notion of minimum income. It would be possible also to bring pressure to bear, though with flexibility, on the prices of certain products and on the pattern of production.

Minimum wage

The justification for a minimum wage policy lies in the fact that since people earning low wages are usually in the lower income brackets, the establishment of a statutory minimum wage should improve their situation and at the same time reduce the size of the profits accruing to the rich. In practice, matters are not quite so simple owing to the secondary economic consequences of the measure, which can lead more or less quickly to a development contrary to the purpose in view: it is to be feared that a wage policy tending to transfer a part of profits to the workers may have unfavourable effects on the allocation of resources, on growth and on employment, and thus ultimately on the workers' real wages. Studies carried out under the World Employment Programme have accordingly dealt not only with the consequences and possible hazards attending such a policy but also on the methods of applying it and on the necessary supporting measures.[21]

General consequences

Economic theory has traditionally viewed the establishment of a statutory minimum wage with some reserve.[22] While that measure can improve the income of the lower-paid workers, it can also lead employers to reduce the volume of employment in order to meet the increase in the cost of labour. It is not easy to assess the importance of that reaction. If a rise in low wages causes the final demand of consumers to move in the direction of labour-intensive activities, the risk of unemployment may be appreciably lessened. If, moreover, unemployment is not too unequally distributed among households, it does not necessarily increase the degree of inequality in the community in question. Moreover, in the case of an imperfect employment market, the main effect of a rise in the minimum wage, provided it is a moderate one, may be to diminish wage disparities without adversely affecting employment.

It is always difficult to put these hypotheses to concrete tests owing to the large number of variables to be considered. Furthermore, the results of any attempt at an estimation depend upon the assumptions made with regard to the working of the different sectors of the employment market. The model designed by Bourguignon for Colombia envisages two cases, one in which the wage differentials are rigidly fixed and the other in which they are perfectly flexible.[23]

In the first case a general increase in wages such as would result from the establishment of a minimum higher by a certain percentage than the existing wage rates has disastrous effects on production and on employment. Those effects are not, however, strong enough to prevent a reduction in the inequality of distribution thanks to an improvement in the situation of the poorest households. The change in the structure of incomes causes final demand to shift towards agricultural produce. Agriculture thus escapes from the diminution of production and of employment which affects the non-agricultural sectors and urban activities.

These results tend to confirm the notion that there is an inverse relationship between economic efficiency and equality of incomes. In other words a vigorous minimum wage policy can promote equality, but at the cost of an appreciable loss of output and of employment, which is no doubt why it is not the best way of influencing the distribution of incomes.

There are, however, good reasons for thinking that the disparities of remuneration would not remain constant in the event of application of a minimum wage policy and of a consequential aggravation of the employment situation. The absence of any significant correlation between the minimum and the average wage suggests that the extension of unemployment or underemployment causes the range of wages to contract. In such circumstances the unfavourable effect of a rise in the minimum wage on production and employment is greatly attenuated, since the diminution in the disparities of remuneration partly compensates for the rise in the cost of labour.

There will be, of course, a diminution in the inequality of incomes, but an appreciably smaller cost in terms of production and employment. In the case of a rigid wage structure the diminution of inequality of distribution presupposes a transfer of profits towards wages, whereas in the case of a flexible structure the diminution results largely from a more equal redistribution of the total wages bill. The effect on the functional distribution of wages and profits is not the same in the two cases.

Methods of application

The existence of low wages in the comparatively undeveloped countries reflects a permanent excess in the supply of labour relatively to demand in the traditional sector. An increase in wages brought about by legislation would not necessarily have effects on employment and the allocation of resources comparable to those that it would have in a perfectly competitive employment market. The segmentation of the market generates disparities of remuneration that are not always economically justified; their disappearance would not, therefore, necessarily have adverse effects on development. The special usefulness of theoretical analyses is that they caution the authorities against any measure that might ultimately slow up growth, aggravate inequalities or reduce the real incomes of the most underprivileged categories through its unfavourable effects on production, employment and the price level.

From this angle, the first problem to be solved is that of the level at which the minimum wage should be fixed. The governing consideration is that of ensuring basic protection through the establishment of a floor to remuneration and not that of determining the general level of wages, although the measure cannot fail to have indirect effects on the general wage level and on the distribution of income between labour and capital. If the minimum wage exercises a significant influence on the average level of wages, it will be defeating its purpose, which is to protect the least well paid workers (and in the developing countries it is in fact the majority of workers who need such protection) in the event of imperfect working of the employment market or against abuses to which certain categories might be exposed. (It is not certain after all that the working of the employment market can always be blamed; thus a day-labourer can quite well offer his labour on a perfectly competitive market and have a very low marginal productivity.)

If the minimum wage becomes an instrument for the control of changes in the general level of wages and if the adjustments to which it is subjected reverberate on the whole pay structure, the disparities in wages, even those that are unjustified, will take firm root and the unfavourable effects described above may follow. The increase in the minimum wage then contributes to a spreading of rises in wages and prices throughout the economy and to placing the external balance at risk. This means specifically that the minimum must not be set too close to the average wage of unskilled labour and that the revisions that it undergoes must not anticipate a general rise in wages and in prices. As for as possible, the improvement of real wages should result from a stabilisation of prices and, in the long run, from a increase in the supply of everyday consumer goods rather than from a systematic increase in nominal wages. This question will be referred to again below.

Under this conception the minimum wage is not an instrument of macro-economic management but a means of protecting the worker and preventing undue disparities of wages.

Should several minimum rates be fixed? That is the second question to be considered. If the application of a minimum is called for in the modern urban sector, there are various arguments in favour of differentiation according to the particular circumstances of the various branches of activities and of the various regions and categories of workers. Local differences in the cost of living, particularly between town and country, are often mentioned in this connection. Since the objective is to arrive at a real wage that is more or less uniform throughout a territory, it is usual to fix a higher minimum for the urban areas that for rural areas. Under some systems, there are different minima by category, for example for agricultural labourers, domestic staff and public servants.

The systems of fixing minimum wages by branch of activity are somewhat complex from the administrative point of view. Their application in developing countries often gives rise to difficulties.[24] In itself the setting of different minimum wages rates is not without hazards: it seems to shed doubt on the very principle of a minimum wage. Once an appropriate basic rate that takes into account the economic constraints and the social requirements has been fixed, it is illogical, where the object is to ensure essential protection by establishing a floor for remuneration, to authorise reduced rates unless the reduction is balanced by advantages in kind or is justified because the cost of living has fallen; it is likewise illogical to provide for higher rates in certain comparatively prosperous branches of activity. That would deprive the legislation of its role of protection of unskilled workers and constitute a move towards a general regulation of wages. Differentiation can then have unfavourable effects on employment and on the allocation of resources, giving rise to cases of privileged status and generating new disparities among the workers.

The central point that emerges from these observations is that the establishment of a minimum wage must not serve as an instrument of general control of remuneration, especially where economic conditions hamper the strict application of the measures adopted in all sectors and all regions. Hence it may seem desirable to consider supplementary measures capable of promoting the success of the legislation and of attenuating possible negative effects.

Supporting measures

The particular conditions prevailing in the developing countries call for the adoption of measures to back up the application of a minimum wage policy.

In the rural sector, where the great majority of the population of developing countries live, a minimum wage policy can have only limited effectiveness. Wage employment is underdeveloped and in many cases represents only a marginal source of income for small farmers. The main problem is the general underutilisation of the labour force. The primary aim must therefore be to develop opportunities of employment and of earnings through public works projects, for example. A minimum wage policy can be effective only in combination with a policy of employment expansion.

That parallel policy of expansion of employment can be regarded, moreover, as necessary to the economy as a whole in order to avoid the unfavourable consequences of a rise in the lowest wage rates. Thus it is possible to envisage an increase in public expenditure that will favour the more labour-intensive sectors of economic activity. It is true that if such a programme is financed by the creation of money, it may lead to a rise in prices and wages without having had any influence on the level of activity. One is led, therefore, to advocate a simple redirection of public expenditure (to the detriment of investment) or to a supplementary tax deduction, thereby effecting a transfer from the taxpayers to those of the workers who are less well paid. Such measures in any case have an opportunity cost, as in the case of all the redistribution policies that have been considered.

If control of the volume and structure of final demand cannot suffice to correct the potential disadvantages of a minimum wage policy, subsidies can be introduced to balance the increase in the cost of labour resulting from the raising of low wages. That operation also involves a transfer of government revenue or the taxpayers' income to poorly paid persons. Such a system is not fundamentally different from a minimum income system, in that the transfer is conditional on paid work and does not remove incentives to effort, as can be the case with a straightforward assistance scheme.[25]

Minimum income

In most of the developing countries wage and salary earners account for less than half of the economically active population. In fact, taking into account the seasonal or casual nature of wage employment in agriculture and in the informal sector of the economy, persons holding a stable job and who are subject to the legislation on wages constitute little more than a third of the economically active population.

It is to be noted, furthermore, that it is possible to impose minimum rates of remuneration and to supervise their application only in undertakings of a certain size. In economies having a permanent excess supply of labour, many workers have to accept wages that are below the statutory minimum, especially in handicrafts and in employment provided mostly by small businesses. These circumstances limit considerably the equalising effect of the minimum wage, the institution of which may even be accompanied by a widening of wage disparities.

For these various reasons, a minimum wage policy cannot suffice by itself. The need to widen the scope of government action leads to a consideration of several possibilities. The emphasis can be placed on nominal incomes by passing on from the notion of minimum wage to that of minimum income; at the same time action can be taken on prices, especially those of products which form part of the everyday consumption of the most underprivileged groups; and, lastly, since the question is that of improving the real incomes of the poorest strata, action on prices can be supplemented by improving the supply of essential goods.

An extension of the notion of minimum income to the whole population leads to the institution of a guaranteed income for all households, both of wage earners and of non-wage earners. If households draw from the labour of their members or from their property an income falling below that minimum, the State pays them the difference, the system of allowances being financed by an increase in income tax. It is thus a policy of redistribution through taxation and transfers, the immediate consequence of which is a substantial reduction of the dispersion of incomes. To that should be added a change in the structure of final demand in the direction of labour-intensive activities, which would promote employment. The drawback to be expected is a weakening of the inducement to work, a slowing down of growth and a fall in the overall propensity to save.[26]

It is difficult to assess these various consequences and to measure the cost of equalisation of incomes in terms of production and, possibly, of employment. Two remarks can nevertheless be made.

The establishment of a guaranteed minimum income that will be equal in real value in rural and urban areas could have consequences similar to those of a general minimum wage policy, involving a considerable reduction of production and of employment irrespective of any weakening of the inducement to work; the equalisation of minima could reduce appreciably the flight from the land to the towns and impede the process of development. To avoid that possibility, there would have to be discrimination between urban and rural households, but it would be an arbitrary discrimination and there would be distinctly less reduction of inequality.

A policy of equalisation through transfers can be really effective only if it has no negative incidence on the volume of economic activity. The best way to secure that result is probably to act through the employment market rather than to control the levels of wages and incomes which it generates.[27] From that angle, the creation of jobs financed by an increase in income tax seems, in the last analysis, a better instrument of redistribution than a minimum income policy. It is the possibilities of earnings that must be multiplied: hence the primary importance of employment policy.

Price regulation

If it is accepted that any direct regulation of wages or nominal incomes will unavoidably entail a cost in terms of the allocation of resources, the growth of production and the volume of employment, an unfavourable repercussion on real incomes is to be expected sooner or later. For greater effectiveness it would therefore be desirable to influence prices at the same time as one sets an income floor. A stabilisation of the cost of living appears to be a means of immediately improving the real incomes of underprivileged groups. Such action would have the merit of affecting the population in general, since prices are the same for everybody, and it would contribute to a reduction of disparities in the level of living if it were concentrated on the essential goods accounting for most of the expenditure of the poor, beginning with the food products of agricultural origin.

From this angle it becomes important, in order to ensure a sufficient supply of products at reasonable prices, to provide fully in agricultural policy for a development of the cultivation of food produce.

With regard to the level of prices, experience shows that if they are set too low (with or without an obligation to deliver part of the harvest at those prices to a public body), sooner or later the consequence will be either the development of a black market with higher prices or a deterioration in quality and a diminution of supply at the prescribed prices.[28] The possibility given to producers to compensate for their forfeiture of earnings by setting high prices for products that are not consumed by the poor rarely provides sufficient compensation, and can further distort the structure of agricultural prices.

Instead of fixing prices officially, the proper course is, therefore, to make suitable adjustments in import and other duties or to grant subsidies to the producers. The underlying principle is the same as in relation to incomes: it is better to correct the effects of the price mechanism by means of measures of financial redistribution than to attempt to alter the working of the mechanism itself.

Furthermore, in order to ensure that the readjustments of prices shall be effective, it will be desirable to concentrate the measures on a small number of products that are essential to the bulk of the population.

Moreover, any dispersion of efforts can raise problems relating to the consistency of decisions.[29]

It is also important to reduce the price fluctuations associated with variations in the volume of harvests or with the situation on world markets. The aim here is twofold: to prevent price rises due to a temporary insufficiency of supply from affecting the whole structure of internal prices and from degenerating into a permanent inflation; and secondly to protect the income of the country's farmers in the event of a surplus of supply.

It would seem possible in most cases to regulate supply and to eliminate seasonal price fluctuations by means of buffer stocks representing a few weeks' consumption. Apart from those short-term measures, the only enduring solution of the problems that have been referred to here lies in the organisation of a system of production capable of improving the productivity of the country's agricultural sector.

Structure of production

As has already been stressed, a change in the structure of real incomes cannot fail to bring about a change in the structure of consumption. If the system of production cannot be adapted to that change, measures of redistribution and of equalisation of incomes are bound to fail. Hence it may become necessary to bring action to bear on the supply of goods.

The raising of low incomes tends to increase the consumption of the necessities of life, especially foodstuffs. It is therefore desirable to ensure that the production of food shall match the increase in consumption; otherwise the stability of prices would not be maintained, which would bring to naught the measures of regulation and equalisation of incomes.

In many developing countries the demand for foodstuffs constantly increases owing to the expansion of the population and urban concentration. Even in regions where the population has a sufficient ration of calories and where elasticity of demand relatively to income remains low, the food balance is constantly threatened by the rapidity of urbanisation and wide fluctuations in production. Agriculture must therefore produce surpluses if a growing resort to imports is to be avoided.

It is true that, in an open economy and depending on the economic situation, there can be imports of basic products in order to avoid an inflationary rise in prices in the event of a temporary shortage of supply. Such imports can even form part of a policy of price stabilisation. However, permanent recourse to imports of everyday consumer goods for the purpose of raising the standard of living of the poor can hardly be contemplated, even if such imports do not imperil the foreign trade balance. It is desirable to isolate the raising of the standard of living of the poor from the fluctuations of international markets and to secure national self-sufficiency in staple foodstuffs, if necessary within regional economic unions, as a prerequisite for a genuinely independent incomes policy.

The development of food cultivation can provide an opportunity for associating the rural sector more closely with economic expansion, for stabilising incomes at a higher level and for reducing the structural dualism that is a characteristic of underdevelopment.

In many cases, economic take-off presupposes a mobilisation of agricultural surpluses to finance investment in the modern urban sector. Taxation, the regulation of the prices of agricultural products and the operations of marketing bodies (especially for export crops) amount to a levy on the agricultural sector and a transfer of resources from that sector to non-agricultural sectors. That levy, which affects smaller farmers more than large and which, according to most research, is not balanced by public expenditure in support of agriculture, tends to increase the dualism of the economy and to aggravate the income disparities between the traditional and the modern sector.[30]

A reorientation of intersectoral transfers for the benefit of rural activities with a view to a development of food crops could make it possible both to raise the level of living of the poorer sections of the urban population and to increase the income of the traditional cultivators, thereby making the interests of inhabitants of town and country coincide instead of being in opposition.

Such a reorientation might no doubt cause a slowing down of the growth of the modern sector and a slight fall in the overall rate of growth, but the likelihood is that the new balance of development thus secured would tend to reduce inequalities and increase employment.

COMBINED APPROACH

As has been shown above, there are many and close inter-relationships between budgetary policy and measures concerning the distribution of primary incomes. It has been seen that there would be nothing much to be expected from the raising of low incomes if the supply of agricultural products were inelastic; an incomes policy would call for a whole series of measures in order to increase food supplies. Many other instances can be given of interdependence between the distribution of primary incomes and redistribution by government action. Among the major reforms that can be initiated in order to reduce the disparity of primary incomes there is land reform. This reform could not be brought to a successful issue if the government did not appropriate funds every year for the benefit of small and medium-scale farmers, without which the redistribution of land may lead to a fall in output and the innovation may be of benefit only to large landowners. In order to avoid these dangers rural credit must be provided, substantial funds must be appropriated for granting interest-free loans to small and medium-scale farmers, co-operatives must be set up and extension services must be developed. It is clear that such a policy implies that, each year and for a long time, there will be heavy expenditure for the benefit of small and medium-scale farmers and for agricultural labourers who acquire land. In view of the place which these beneficiaries occupy in the distribution of the national income, the expenditure would be very progressive and have a high redistributive incidence; a reduction in the Gini coefficient by about 0.03 for a transfer equal to 5 per cent of total primary income is to be expected.

A policy of agricultural development calls for a fundamental change in the utilisation of stabilisation funds, which should be invested in the rural sector, not in the urban sector. It should be accompanied also by the institution of subsidies for agricultural produce in everyday consumption. Such subsidies enable two objectives to be attained: to raise the level of living of low-income urban households and to increase the resources of farmers so that they can be induced to produce more. In Sri Lanka, for example, these subsidies amount to 4.7 per cent of household primary income, or about as much as all expenditure on education, and are highly progressive; they can thus have an important redistributive effect. Like the expenditure that must accompany the redistribution of land and agricultural innovation, they help to increase agricultural production capacity.

There must be government aid also to the industries producing goods in everyday consumption. Here too redistributive measures would be ineffective if the supply of manufactured goods was inelastic and if the increase in demand led to a rise in prices. As has been stressed, a redistribution of incomes cannot be considered independently of the structure of the system of production. Budgetary measures conducing to an increase in the cash income of poor households must be co-ordinated with a long-term policy of development of agricultural and industrial activities for the home market, without which the increase in the real incomes of those households may be much lower than the increase in their nominal incomes.

If the government wishes to benefit the small and medium-sized undertakings in industry and in agriculture it must grant them the necessary assistance through appropriate public works, and with regard to such matters as investment, technology, vocational training and marketing. In so far as the benefit accrues to the small and medium-sized undertakings, that policy affects the medium-income households, whereas assistance to large undertakings, the benefit of which can be imputed to the management and the shareholders, increases the incomes of the upper income groups. (In the case of large undertakings that are nationalised, government subsidies may correspond either to transfers for the benefit of the consumers of the goods produced by those undertakings or to transfers for the benefit of their employees; in the second case there is a net regressive effect if the taxes financing the subsidies are levied partly on low-income households.)

Among the measures for correcting the wide inequalities characterising the distribution of material assets, death duties constitute a flexible measure that can have an important effect in the long run if the rate of taxation increases rapidly with the value of the inherited estate. Tax policy in that field, the incidence of which enters into any estimate of redistribution, is linked to the fundamental choices relating to the ownership of the means of production. A moderate redistributive annual effect can correspond in the long run to an appreciable redistribution of those means of production among households.

There remains the distribution of "human" assets, beginning with health and education. The expenditure devoted to those two items, the incidence of which as consumption was evaluated in Chapter 5, clearly modifies that distribution, and consequently the distribution of primary incomes. In the case of health, any consumption of services corresponds to an investment; in the case of education, there frequently is such correspondence but not in all cases, especially where education imparts knowledge for which there never will be a demand on the labour market. Nevertheless, as has been shown, an improvement in health or in education does not always contribute to an increase in the individual's primary income. Between the distribution of the expenditure on health and education and the distribution of primary incomes, the relationships are complex, although in many cases they reflect the desired causal inter-relationship, the reduction of inequalities in the fields of health and education going hand in hand with the reduction of income inequalities. The analyses in Chapter 4 contain some useful indications for a restructuring of public expenditure on education. The measures proposed, which aim especially at reducing the private profitability of education for rich households and at increasing it for poor households by diminishing its cost and at applying special programmes for the agricultural sector, show that any redistributive policy calls for a new distribution of government expenditure on education.

Whether in the case of material assets or of human resources, budgetary decisions are one of the principal means of progressively securing the objectives of long-term policies with respect to the distribution of the factors of production, of employment and of income. It is clear, as has been shown, from the resistance to attainment of those objectives in various quarters that very progressive policies of redistribution will be even more effective if the State intervenes directly in the distribution of assets. Choices of economic structures, like the choices relating to taxation and to public expenditure, pertain to the same conflict or the same consensus among the groups that make up society as a whole.

Notes

[1] Kakwani: *Income inequality and poverty* (1980), Chapter 12.

[2] These indicators can be expressed in the form of a product:

$$\frac{\text{Public expenditure or revenue}}{\text{Household primary incomes}} \times \frac{\text{Amount of a transfer}}{\text{Public expenditure or revenue.}}$$

If the first ratio is constant from one country to another, the values of $e_a \ldots e_n$ will depend solely on the structure of the budget.

[3] Hsia and Chau: *Industrialisation, employment and income distribution* (1978), pp. 151 et seq.; table 6.1, p. 154.

[4] Mehran: *Taxes and incomes* (1975), pp. 17 et seq.; table 19, p. 60.

[5] Foxley et al.: *The incidence of taxation* (1977), pp. 19 et seq.; table A-1, p. 48.

[6] Tan: *Taxation, government spending and income distribution in the Philippines* (1975), pp. 23 et seq.; tables II.1 and 2, pp. 28–29.

[7] Foxley et al.: *Who benefits from government expenditures?*, (1976), especially table 22.

[8] Tan, op. cit., especially tables III.1 to 6, pp. 49–54.

[9] Mehran: *Distribution of benefits from public consumption expenditures among households in Iran* (1977), especially tables 15 and 16, pp. 39–40.

[10] Hsia and Chau, op. cit., pp. 161 et seq.; table 6.2, p. 165.

[11] A negative transfer of 9 per cent and a positive transfer of 11 per cent give respectively—

$$\frac{e}{1-e} = 0.1 \qquad \frac{e}{1+e} = 0.1$$

The relative variation induced by the transfer corresponds to—

$$\frac{G-G'}{G} = 0.1 \qquad \frac{(c-G)}{G}$$

[12] Foxley et al.: *Net incidence of government expenditures, taxation and social security* (1977) pp. 21 et seq.

[13] Mehran: *Taxes and incomes* op. cit., p. 64; Tan, *Taxation, government spending and income distribution in the Philippines*, op. cit., pp. 23–24; Gupta: *The rich, the poor and the taxes they pay in India* (1975) p. 45.

[14] Foxley et al., op. cit., pp. 14 et seq.

[15] Gupta: *Incidence of central government expenditures in India*, op. cit., pp. 34–36, 44, 46–48; Hsia and Chau, op. cit., pp. 162 et seq.

[16] See Paukert, Skolka and Maton: *Income distribution, structure of economy and employment* (1981); and Bourguignon: *General equilibrium analysis of the Colombian income distribution* (1978).

[17] On these various problems, see de Wulf: "The distribution of fiscal burdens and benefits" (1975).

[18] Harberger: *Fiscal policy and income redistribution* (1974).

[19] International Monetary Fund: *Surveys of African economies*, Vols. 2 (1969), 4 (1971), 7 (1977); United Nations: Statistical Yearbook, 1974 and 1975; *UNESCO Statistical Yearbook*, 1975.

[20] Gupta, op. cit., pp. 49–50; Foxley et al.: *Net incidence of government expenditures, taxation and social security* (1977), p. 21.

[21] On systems of minimum wages, see Starr: *Minimum wage fixing* (1981). The problems raised by a policy of minimum wages are also analysed in the report of the mission that went to the Philippines under the auspices of the ILO in 1973 for the purpose of preparing an employment development strategy; see ILO: *Sharing in development* (1974), pp. 344 et seq.

[22] Starr, op. cit., Chapter 8.

[23] Bourguignon, op. cit., pp. 50 et seq.

[24] Starr, op. cit., Chapter 2.

[25] Bourguignon, op. cit., pp. 65–70.

[26] ibid., pp. 70–78.

[27] ibid., p. 84.

[28] See for example Abdel-Fadil: *International terms of trade and transfer of resources from agriculture to non-agricultural activities* (1976), p. 12; ILO, op. cit., pp. 357–358.

[29] ILO, op. cit., pp. 359–361.

[30] See Lecaillon and Germidis: *Inégalité des revenus et développement économique* (1977), pp. 216–217; Abdel-Fadil, op. cit., pp. 18–22.

BIBLIOGRAPHY

The World Employment Programme research working papers that are among the works listed in this bibliography were originally mimeographed in a limited number of copies for restricted distribution only. However, those marked with an asterisk are now available to the general public in sets of microfiches.

Aaron, H., and McGuire, M. "Public goods and income distribution", in *Econometrica* (Evanston, Illinois, Econometric Society), Nov. 1970.

Abdel-Fadil, M. *Intersectoral terms of trade and transfer of resources from agriculture to non-agricultural activities: The case of Egypt*, Research Working Paper WEP 2-23/WP 39 (Geneva, ILO, 1976).*

Adelman, I., and Morris, C. T. *An anatomy of patterns of income distribution in developing countries*, Report prepared for the United States International Development Agency (Washington, DC, 1971, mimeographed).

—. *Economic growth and social equity in developing countries* (Stanford, California, Stanford University Press, 1973).

Ahluwalia, M. S. "Income distribution and development: Some stylized facts", in *American Economic Review* (Nashville, Tennessee, American Economic Association), May 1976, pp. 128–135.

—. "Income inequality: Some dimensions of the problem", in H. Chenery, M. S. Ahluwalia, C. L. G. Bell, J. H. Duloy and R. Jolly: *Redistribution with growth*, A joint study by the World Bank's Development Research Center and the Institute of Development Studies, University of Sussex (London, Oxford University Press, 1974), pp. 3–37.

—. "Inequality, poverty and development", in *Journal of Development Economics* (Amsterdam), Dec. 1976, pp. 307–342.

Alailima, P. J. *Fiscal incidence in Sri Lanka*, Research Working Paper WEP 2–23/WP 69 (Geneva, ILO, 1978).*

Anand, S. *The size distribution of income in Malaysia*, Report prepared for the Development Research Center of the World Bank (Washington, 1973).

Atkinson, A. B. *The economics of inequality* (Oxford, Clarendon Press, 1975).

Bacha, E. L. *The Kuznets curve and beyond: Growth and changes in inequality* (Harvard University, 1977; mimeographed).

Beckerman, W. "Some reflections on redistribution with growth", in *World Development* (Oxford), Aug. 1977, pp. 665–676.

Berry, A., and Urrutia, M. *Income distribution in Colombia* (New Haven, Connecticut, Yale University Press, 1976).

Blaug, M. *Education and the unemployment problem in developing countries* (Geneva, ILO, 1974).

Bourguignon, F. *General equilibrium analysis of the Colombian income distribution: Applications to rural development, wage and income policies*, Research Working Paper WEP 2–23/WP 68 (Geneva, ILO, 1978).*

—. "Oil and income distribution in Venezuela 1968–78", in J. de Bandt, P. Maudi and D. Seers (eds.): *European studies in development* (London, Macmillan, 1980), pp. 187–199.

—. *The role of education in the urban labour market during the process of development: The case of Colombia* (Paris, Ecole normale supérieure, Laboratoire d'économie politique, document No. 27, 1979).

Cairncross, A. K. *Factors in economic development* (London, Allen and Unwin, 1962).

Carnoy, M., in collaboration with Lobo, J., Toledo, A., and Velloso, J. *Can education policy equalise income distribution in Latin America?* A study prepared for the International Labour Office within the framework of the research programmes on income distribution and employment and on education and employment of the World Employment Programme (Farnborough, Hampshire, Saxon House, 1979).

Carter, C. O. "The genetic basis of inequality", with comments by J. E. Meade, and P. C. McMahon, in A. B. Atkinson (ed.): *The personal distribution of incomes* (London, Allen and Unwin, 1976), pp. 98–119.

Cline, W. R. "Distribution and development: A survey of literature", in *Journal of Development Economics*, Vol. I, pp. 359–400.

Cromwell, J. "The size distribution of income: An international comparison", in *Review of Income and Wealth* (New Haven, Connecticut, International Association for Research in Income and Wealth), Sept. 1977, pp. 291–308.

de Navarrete, I. "La distribución del ingreso en México: tendencias y perspectives", in *El perfil de México en 1980* (Mexico City, 3rd ed., 1971), Vol. I.

de Wulf, L. "The distribution of fiscal burdens and benefits: The quest for the Holy Grail", in *Tijdschrift voor Economie en Management*, 1975, Vol. XX, No. 2, pp. 177–184.

Dodge, D. A. "Impact of tax, transfer, and expenditure policies of government on the distribution of personal income in Canada", in *Review of Income and Wealth*, March 1975, pp. 1–52.

Ecevit, L., and Ozötün, E. *The changing structural distribution of income and employment in Turkey and Kuznets' hypothesis*, Research Working Paper WEP 2–23/WP 23 (Geneva, ILO, 1975).*

Encarnación, J. *Income distribution in the Philippines: The employed and the self-employed*, Research Working Paper WEP 2–23/WP 8 (Geneva, ILO, 1974).

Ewusi, K. *Employment performance of Ghanaian manufacturing industries*, Research Working Paper WEP 2–23/WP 49 (Geneva, ILO, 1977).

Fapohunda, O. J., Reijmerink, J., and van Gijk, M. P. *Urban development, income distribution and employment in Lagos*, Research Working Paper WEP 2–19/WP 13, WEP 2–23/WP 25 (Geneva, ILO, 1975).*

Farbman, M. *Sectoral employment and income distribution in rural India*, Research Working Paper WEP 2–23/WP 13 (Geneva, ILO, 1975).*

Felix, D. *Trickling down in Mexico and the debate over the long-term growth-equity relationship in LDCs* (St. Louis, Missouri, Washington University, 1974).

Foxley, A., Aninat, E., and Arellano, J. P. *Net incidence of government expenditures, taxation and social security*, Research Working Paper WEP 2–23/WP 53 (Geneva, ILO, 1977).

—. *Redistributive effects of government programmes: The Chilean case*, A study prepared for the International Labour Office within the framework of the World Employment Programme (Oxford, Pergamon Press, 1979).

Furtado, C. "The concept of external dependence in the study of under development", in C. K. Wilber (ed.): *The political economy of development and underdevelopment* (New York, Random House, 1973).

Gillespie, W. I. "Effect of public expenditures on the distribution of income", in R. A. Musgrave (ed.): *Essays in fiscal federalism*, Studies of government finance (Washington, Brookings Institution, 1965), pp. 122–186.

Gooneratne, W. *Land tenure, government policies and income distribution in Sri Lanka*, Research Working Paper WEP 2–23/WP 77 (Geneva, ILO, 1979).

Guest, J. F. *Income distribution, employment and economic growth: Issues in a development planning framework with application to the economy of Fiji* (unpublished doctoral thesis, University of Wollongong, New South Wales, 1979).

Gupta, A. P. *Incidence of central government expenditures in India*, Research Working Paper WEP 2–23/WP 19 (Geneva, ILO, 1975).

—. *Solving India's employment problem: Role of fiscal policy*, Research Working Paper WEP 2–23/WP 28 (Geneva, ILO, 1975).

—. *The rich, the poor and the taxes they pay in India*, A study of central government taxes and their impact on income distribution and patterns of consumption, Research Working Paper WEP 2–23/WP 12 (Geneva, ILO, 1975).

Harberger, A. C. *Fiscal policy and income redistribution*, Paper prepared for the Workshop on Income Distribution in Less Developed Countries, Princeton University, 12–13 June 1974 (mimeographed).

Harris, J., and Todaro, M. P. "Migration, unemployment and development: A two-sector analysis", in *American Economic Review*, March 1970, pp. 126–143.

Henry, R. M. *A note on income distribution and poverty in Trinidad and Tobago*, Research Working Paper WEP 2–23/WP 29 (Geneva, ILO, 1975).

Hirschman, A. O. "The changing tolerance for income inequality in the course of economic development", in *World Development*, December 1973, pp. 29–36.

Hsia, R., and Chau, L. *Industrialisation, employment and income distribution: A case study of Hong Kong*, A study prepared for the International Labour Office within the framework of the research programme on income distribution and employment of the World Employment Programme (London, Croom Helm, 1978).

ILO. *Household income and expenditure statistics*, No. 2: *1960–1972*, Part 1: *Africa, Latin America, Asia* (Geneva, 1974), and No. 3: *1968–1976* (Geneva, 1979).

—. *Sharing in development: A programme of employment, equity and growth for the Philippines*, Report of an inter-agency team financed by the United Nations Development Programme and organised by the International Labour Office (Geneva, 1974).

—. *World Employment Programme: Ninth progress report on income distribution and employment* (Geneva, 1981).

International Monetary Fund. *Surveys of African economies* (Washington, DC), Vols. 2 (1969), 4 (1971), 7 (1977).

Jain, S. *Size distribution of income*, A compilation of data (Washington, DC, World Bank, 1975).

Kakwani, N. C. *Income inequality and poverty, Methods of estimation and policy applications*, A World Bank Research Publication (New York, Oxford University Press, 1980).

Kende, P. "Le poids de la fiscalité en France", in *Annales économiques* (Clermont-Ferrand), 1977, pp. 5–22.

Knight, J. B. "Rural-urban income comparisons and migration in Ghana", in *Bulletin of the Oxford University Institute of Economics and Statistics*, 1972.

Kogut, E. L., and Langoni, C. G. "Population growth, income distribution and economic development", in *International Labour Review* (Geneva, ILO), April 1975, pp. 326–330.

Kravis, I. B. "International differences in the distribution of income", in *Review of Economics and Statistics* (Cambridge, Massachusetts, Harvard University), Nov. 1960, pp. 408–416.

Kuznets, S. "Demographic aspects of the size distribution of income: An exploratory essay", in *Economic Development and Cultural Change* (Research Center for Economic Development and Cultural Change, University of Chicago), Oct. 1976, pp. 1–44.

—. "Economic growth and income inequality", in *American Economic Review*, March 1955, pp. 1–28; reprinted in his *Economic growth and structure*, Selected essays (London, Heinemann Educational Books, 1966), pp. 257–287.

—. *Economic growth of nations: Total output and production structure* (Cambridge, Massachusetts, Belknap Press, 1971).

—. *Modern economic growth: Rate, structure and spread*, Studies in Comparative Economics, No. 7 (New Haven, Connecticut, Yale University Press, 1966).

—. "Quantitative aspects of the economic growth of nations: VIII. Distribution of income by size", in *Economic Development and Cultural Change*, Jan. 1963, Part II, pp. 1–80.

Lal, D. "Distribution and development: A review article", in *World Development*, Sept. 1976, pp. 725–738.

Langoni, C. "Income distribution and economic development in Brazil", in *Conjuntura Econômica* (Rio de Janeiro, Fundaçào Getulio Vargas, Instituto Brasileiro de Economia), 1975.

Lean, L. L. *Employment and income distribution in West Malaysia*, Research Working Paper WEP 2–23/WP 24 (Geneva, ILO, 1975).

— *The pattern of income distribution in West Malaysia, 1957–1970*, Research Working Paper WEP 2–23/WP 6 (Geneva, ILO, 1974).

Lecaillon, J., and Germidis, D. "Income differentials and the dynamics of development", in *International Labour Review*, July–August 1976, pp. 27–42.

—, with the assistance of Kerneis, J. P. *Inégalité des revenus et développement économique – Cameroun, Côte-d'Ivoire, Madagascar, Sénégal*, Etude réalisée pour le Programme mondial de l'emploi (Paris, Presses universitaires de France, 1977).

Lewis, W. A. "Economic development with unlimited supplies of labour", in *Manchester School of Economic and Social Studies* (University of Manchester, Department of Economics), May 1954, pp. 139–191.

Little, I. M. D. Bibliographical note on the works of Adelman and Morris: *Economic growth and social equity in developing countries*, op. cit., and of Chenery et al.: *Redistribution with growth*, in *Journal of Development Economics*, Mar. 1976, pp. 99–106.

Lydall, H. *Income distribution during the process of development*, Research Working Paper WEP 2–23/WP 52 (Geneva, ILO, 1977).

— *Unemployment in developing countries*, Research Working Paper WEP 2–23/WP 50 (Geneva, ILO, 1977).

McLure, C. E., Jr. "Incidence of taxation in West Malaysia", in *Malayan Economic Review* (Singapore), Oct. 1972, pp. 66–98.

Mach, E. P. "Selected issues on health and employment", in *International Labour Review*, Mar.–Apr. 1979, pp. 133–145.

Mangahas, M. *Income inequality in the Philippines*, A decomposition analysis, Research Working Paper WEP 2–21/WP 12 (Geneva, ILO, 1975).

Mann, A. "Net fiscal incidence in Puerto Rico", in *Caribbean Studies* (Rio Piedras, Institute of Caribbean Studies, University of Puerto Rico), 1973, No. 1, pp. 5–35.

Maton, J., and Garzuel, M. *Redistribution of income, patterns of consumption and employment: The case study for Malaysia*, Research Working Paper WEP 2–23/WP 71 (Geneva, ILO, 1978).*

Mehran, F. *Distribution of benefits from public consumption expenditures among households in Iran*, Research Working Paper WEP 2–23/WP 57 (Geneva, ILO, 1977).

—. *Income distribution in Iran: The statistics of inequality*, Research Working Paper WEP 2–23/WP 30 (Geneva, ILO, 1975).

—. *Taxes and incomes: Distribution of tax burdens in Iran*, Research Working Paper WEP 2–23/WP 33 (Geneva, ILO, 1975).

Miller, D. R. *Aspects of income distribution in Turkey*, Research Working Paper WEP 2–23/WP 34 (Geneva, ILO, 1975).*

—. *International migration of Turkish workers: A special case in the public policy of income distribution and employment*, Research Working Paper WEP 2–23/WP 41 (Geneva, ILO, 1976).*

—. *The dynamics of human resources development in Turkey and their implications for employment and income distribution*, Research Working Paper WEP 2–23/WP 35 (Geneva, ILO, 1975).*

Mizoguchi, T., Kim, D., and Chung, Y. "Over-time changes of the size distribution of household income in Korea, 1963–71" in *Developing Economies* (Tokyo, Institute of Developing Economies), Sept. 1976.

Morley, S. A. *Changes in employment and the distribution of income during the Brazilian "miracle"*, Research Working Paper WEP 2–23/WP 43 (Geneva, ILO, 1976).*

Oberai, A. S. *An analysis of migration to Greater Khartoum (Sudan)*, Research Working Paper WEP 2–21/WP 19 (Geneva, ILO, 1975).

Oshima, H. T. "The international comparison of size distribution of family incomes, with special reference to Asia", in *Review of Economics and Statistics*, Nov. 1962, pp. 439–445.

Paglin, M. "The measurement and trend of inequality: A basic revision", in *American Economic Review*, Sept. 1975, pp. 598–609.

Pang Eng Fong. "Growth, inequality, and race in Singapore", in *International Labour Review*, Jan. 1975, pp. 15–28.

Papanek, G. F. "Economic growth, income distribution and the political process in less developed countries", in Z. Griliches, W. Krelle, H. J. Krupp and O. Kyn (eds.): *Income distribution and economic inequality* (Frankfurt am Main, Campus Verlag; New York, Halsted Press; 1978), pp. 259–273.

Paukert, F. "Income distribution at different levels of development: A survey of evidence", in *International Labour Review*, Aug.–Sept. 1973, pp. 97–125.

—. Skolka, J., and Maton, J. "Income distribution by size, structure of the economy and employment: A comparative study of four Asian countries", in *Industry and Development* (Vienna, United Nations Industrial Development Organization), No. 5 (United Nations Sales No. E. 80.II.B.4), pp. 107–121.

—. *Income distribution, structure of economy and employment: The Philippines, Iran, the Republic of Korea and Malaysia*, A study prepared for the International Labour Office within the framework of the World Employment Programme (London, Croom Helm, 1981).

—. *Redistribution of income, patterns of consumption and employment: A case study for the Philippines*, Research Working Paper WEP 2–23/WP 3 (Geneva, ILO, 1974).

Pechman, J. A., and Okner, B. A. *Who bears the tax burden?* Studies of government finance (Washington, DC, Brookings Institution, 1974).

Pinto, A., and Di Filipo, A. "Notes on income distribution and redistribution strategy in Latin America", in A. Foxley (ed.): *Income distribution in Latin America* (Cambridge University Press, 1976).

Pyatt, G. "On international comparisons of inequality", in *American Economic Review*, Feb. 1977, pp. 71–75.

Reder, M. W. "A partial survey of the theory of income size distribution", in L. Soltow (ed.): *Six papers on the size distribution of wealth and income* (New York, National Bureau of Economic Research, Inc., 1969).

Reynolds, M., and Smolensky, E. *Public expenditures, taxes, and the distribution of income: The United States, 1950, 1961, 1970*, Institute for Research on Poverty Monograph Series (New York, Academic Press, 1977).

Richards, P. J. *Some distributional issues in planning for basic needs health care*, Research Working Paper WEP 2–23/WP 75 (Geneva, ILO, 1979).*

— *Underemployment and basic needs satisfaction*, Research Working Paper WEP 2–23/WP 48, (Geneva, ILO, 1977).*

—, and Leonor, M. *Education and income distribution in Asia*, A study prepared for the International Labour Office within the framework of the World Employment Programme (London, Croom Helm, 1981).

Sahota, G. S. "The distribution of the benefits of public expenditure in Panama", in *Finances publiques* (The Hague), 1977, pp. 203–227.

Sawyer, M. "Income distribution in OECD countries", *OECD Economic Outlook* Occasional Studies (Paris, Organisation for Economic Co-operation and Development), July 1976.

Sen, A. *Poverty and famines. An essay on entitlement and deprivation.* Study prepared for the International Labour Office within the framework of the World Employment Programme. Oxford, Clarendon Press, 1981.

Skolka, J., and Garzuel, M. *Changes in income distribution, employment and structure of the economy: A case study of Iran*, Research Working Paper WEP 2–23/WP 45 (Geneva, ILO, 1976).*

— *Income distribution by size, employment and the structure of the economy: A case study of the Republic of Korea*, Research Working Paper WEP 2–23/WP 67 (Geneva, ILO, 1978).*

Solís, L. *A monetary will-o'-the-wisp: Pursuit of equity through deficit spending*, Research Working Paper WEP 2–23/WP 55 and 56 (Geneva, ILO, 1977).

Starr, G. *Minimum wage fixing*, An international review of practices and problems (Geneva, ILO, 1981).

Stevens, C. M. *Health, employment and income distribution*, Research Working Paper WEP 2–23/WP 21 (Geneva, ILO, 1975).*

Szal, R. J. *Income inequality and fiscal policies in Botswana*, Research Working Paper WEP 2–23/WP 73 (Geneva, ILO, 1979).*

—. *The regional distribution of government expenditures in Botswana*, Research Working Paper WEP 2–23/WP 36 (Geneva, ILO, 1975).*

—, and van der Hoeven, R. *Inequality and basic needs in Swaziland*, Research Working Paper WEP 2–23/WP 46 (Geneva, ILO, 1976).*

Tan, E. A. *Taxation, government spending and income distribution in the Philippines*, Research Working Paper WEP 2–23/WP 26 (Geneva, ILO, 1975).

Theil, H. *Economics and information theory* (Amsterdam, North-Holland Publishing Co., 1967), Ch. 4: "The measurement of income inequality."

—. *Statistical decomposition analysis, with applications in the social and administrative sciences* (Amsterdam, North-Holland Publishing Co., 1972), Ch. 2, Section 2.6: "The measurement of income inequality".

Todaro, M. P. "Income expectations, rural-urban migration and employment in Africa", in *International Labour Review*, Nov. 1971, pp. 398–400.

— *Internal migration in developing countries*, A review of theory, evidence, methodology and research priorities (Geneva, ILO, 1976).

United Kingdom, Central Statistical Office: "Effects of taxes and benefits on household income, 1975", in *Economic Trends* (London), 1976, No. 278.

van der Hoeven, R. *Zambia's income distribution during the early seventies*, Research Working Paper WEP 2–23/WP 54 (Geneva, ILO, 1977).*

van Ginneken, W. *Rural and urban income inequalities in Indonesia, Mexico, Pakistan, Tanzania and Tunisia* (Geneva, ILO, 1976).

—. *Socio-economic groups and income distribution in Mexico* (London, Croom Helm, 1980).

—. *The regional and rural-urban income distribution in the Sudan*, Research Working Paper WEP 2–23/WP 14 (Geneva, ILO, 1975).*

Wada, R. O. *Changes in the size distribution of income in postwar Japan*, Research Working Paper WEP 2–23/WP 9 (Geneva, ILO, 1974).

—. *Impact of economic growth on the size distribution of income: The postwar experience of Japan*, Research Working Paper WEP 2–23/WP 37 (Geneva, ILO, 1975).

Webb, R. C. *Government policy and the distribution of income in Peru, 1963–73*, Research Programme in Economic Development, Discussion Paper No. 26 (Princeton, New Jersey, School of Public and International Affairs, Princeton University, 1972).

World Bank. *World Bank Atlas* (Washington, 1972).

SUBJECT INDEX

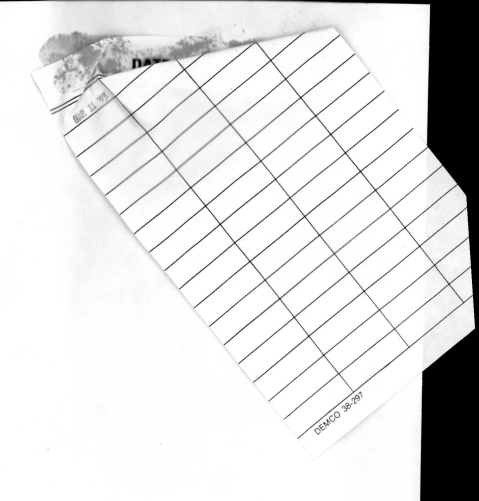